Cut it up! Yea! Yeehaa!

Congratulations
Matt

The Great Comedians

May 22nd, 1982

Matt,

Well Mateo, one of these milestones in your life has been achieved. From Orange Coast to Humboldt to Sacramento State, I'm glad I've been able to be close to you all the way. The Woodman has a saying that goes something like that comedy is not the hardest work to do, good work is the hardest thing to do, whatever it is. Hope your next journey through this great life of yours is filled with lots of friends, family, love and good work. Love

"I doubt if there is among us a more useful citizen
than the one who holds the secret of banishing gloom,
of making tears give way to laughter,
of supplanting desolation and despair
with hope and courage,
for hope and courage always go with a light heart."

FRANKLIN D. ROOSEVELT

The
Great
Comedians

LARRY WILDE

THE CITADEL PRESS
SECAUCUS, NEW JERSEY

Originally published as
The Great Comedians Talk About Comedy

ACKNOWLEDGMENTS

I wish to express my deepest appreciation to the
following people who contributed their time and great
effort to help make this book possible:
Joseph Viggiani, Ed Weinberger, Rona Jaffe, Charles
Joffe, Jack Rollins, Sam Carlton, Leonard Romm, Alan
Kalmus, Bill Faith, Jack Shea, Patricia Perry, Beverly
Kritchman, Jo Marie Metcalfe, Lou Alexander, Theresa
Murphy, Robert Romano, Rosanna Lopez, Merrill Jonas,
Madeline Kern, Jim Flood, Helen Whiteside, Lou Derman,
Tommy Leonetti, Dick Towers, James Thompson, Corrine
Carr, and Bert Scott.
L.W.

For Tony Noice

To Fred Allen, Fanny Brice, W. C. Fields,
Laurel and Hardy, Will Rogers, Bert Williams,
and all the other great comedians
who left the world just a little funnier

Contents

Preface

Laughter, the timeless wonder drug, is the tension-breaker medicine that permits man to cope with the stark reality of everyday tragedy. One hesitates to imagine how cold and colorless our lives would be without humor to give us what Moss Hart called "refreshment of the spirit."

Yet, for all its contribution to lightening the burden of living, there is less written about comedy technique—how laughter is produced—than any other subject of equal scope and significance.

At best, in discussing humor we are dealing with an intangible, elusive, and ephemeral product. It's not easy to put your finger on why one person laughs at a joke another thinks unfunny. Just as what one comedian* can coax an audience to react to, another, delivering the same quips, may not.

Educators, psychologists, and philosophers have tried to

---

* The origin of the word "comedian" goes back to ancient times. The Greeks had a festival of music and dancing called a "komos." The chief entertainer was called the "komoidos" and from this evolved our word comedian.

dissect comedy ever since Aristophanes, Aristotle, and Plato first put their analytical minds to it. Freud's *Jokes and Their Relation to the Unconscious;* Max Eastman's *Enjoyment of Laughter;* Henri Bergson's treatise on *Laughter;* George Meredith's *An Essay On Comedy* are just a few of the works purporting to provide definitive answers to comedic questions. However, Dr. Freud and his friends never had to stand up in front of a group of firemen at a New Year's Eve party and try to get laughs!

Making people laugh is not a science. It cannot be dissected or put under a microscope in a laboratory, then systematized and classified into neat truths. Being funny (for money) is a creative craft—an art, a skill practiced by persons gifted with extraordinary abilities and honed to supreme proficiency by trial, time, and tears.

I had been telling jokes from Milwaukee to Manhattan, from McKeesport to Miami—at weddings, confirmations, conventions, in golf clubs, night clubs, key clubs, hotels, at state fairs, and on television. After ten years, it occurred to me that I hadn't achieved the degree of recognition I dreamed of and that perhaps I needed help. But from whom?

My *agent*? Impossible! A theatrical agent's primary function is selling. His desk is cluttered with booking reports and availability lists. His hours are spent on the telephone, in conferences, and at appointments with buyers. He is busy with the work of getting you work. He cannot be expected to help you find your comedic character, instruct you on the importance of a comic attitude, or capture your sense of humor and develop it into a point of view.

Most *laymen* profess compassion for the mirthmaker's delicate task, but few have the least conception or comprehension of the jester's complex craft, let alone an understanding of the uncontrollable obstacles which are endemic to his profession. An ineffective microphone or sound system, improper lighting, limited visibility in the theatre or club, even the temperature may prevent the artist from appearing at his best. Work under these irksome conditions is exacting for any entertainer, but a vocalist may still sing, an actor emote, a ballerina dance, and a juggler perform without immediate audience response. None faces the horrendous plight of the comedian, for he must *communicate ideas* in order to evoke a reaction.

I've always maintained that nobody really understands a comedian better than another comedian. Not a manager or an agent or a wife, girl friend, relative or well-wisher— sometimes not even a comedy writer. I therefore decided to find out how my more successful colleagues functioned; to investigate the *modus operandi* of each of them. Just as the neophyte doctor or lawyer seeks advice from his betters, I naturally turned to the artists who were the masters of my trade. *Later, George Jessel confirmed my "comedians communication theory" when he said, "All comedians have the same kinship as women in childbirth."*

What began as extensive research and calculated inquiry, shortly led to invaluable information and priceless enlightenment. I soon learned there was much more to making people laugh than telling jokes. Maurice Chevalier explained that the comedian's rapport with the audience "depends on the *quality* of the laugh!" He indicated that a laugh coming out of a warm, human situation is more meaningful and longer lasting than the harsh, quick response that comes from embarrassment or shock. "You have fellows who make people laugh and at the same time, simply because they laugh, does not mean it is good."

Jack Benny pointed out that evoking laughter was not enough. "There has to be something more than just getting laughs. Laughs are *not* everything. People can scream at a comedian and yet can't remember anything afterwards to talk about. To become real successful, they must like you very much . . . they must have a feeling, like 'Gee, I wish he was a friend of mine. I wish he was a relative.' "

Milton Berle emphasized that "you gotta know *who* you are—before you know *what* you are—before you do what you do."

Woody Allen's view on achieving stardom is that "it isn't the jokes . . . it's the individual himself. It's the funny-character emergence that does it. The best material in the world in the hands of a guy who is a hack or doesn't know how to deliver jokes is not going to mean anything."

Danny Thomas put it another way: "For the younger people coming up . . . it's *what* you say and *how* you say it that gets you to where you become a *who* . . . and when you become a *who* your material doesn't have to be as good."

Then, as if summing it all up in one word, Jimmy Durante, when asked, "What is the greatest quality a comedian can have?" replied, "Heart! He's gotta have heart. Without *that* he's nuthin!"

It is truly a phenomenon that Mr. Durante and the other industry giants—Burns, Benny, Berle, Hope, Chevalier, Thomas, et al.—have maintained their popularity for so many years. Considering the frequency of change in automobile design, clothing fashions, decorating fads, and women's hair styles, their longevity is even more astounding. Yet, it is not so incomprehensible when one examines the character traits these men possess: intelligence, warmth, sincerity, and a genuine talent for getting along with people.

Although each comedian interviewed represents a different area of the comedy spectrum, I discovered they all shared certain basic common characteristics: tremendous *enthusiasm,* great *energy,* and enormous *self-awareness.* I got the feeling that George Burns could have told me the number of freckles on his face.

Since all are associated with the comic, you don't think of them in terms of good looks and yet most are extremely good looking. When Danny Thomas smiles, to me his face appears almost angelic, and Phyllis Diller, in spite of her comedic image, is an astonishingly handsome woman. As for "Schnozzola," perhaps glamour queen Tina Louise said it best, "Anybody who doesn't love Jimmy Durante just doesn't have an eye for real beauty." It is interesting to note that in America, a predominantly Protestant country, the great majority of nationally known comedians are of a minority religious faith—Catholic or Jewish. With the emergence of Negroes Bill Cosby, Nipsey Russell, Godfrey Cambridge, Scoey Mitchelll, Richard Pryor, Stu Gilliam, Flip Wilson, et al., it would now appear that persecution, poverty, and prejudice are still the breeding grounds for most of America's laugh-makers.

In assessing the success of the top-flight comedians, it is possible to pin down and analyze the qualities that made them big stars, but very soon you realize that there is in each man an intangible—an extra something—a magic which is the indefinable essence of that particular person's ability to communicate with masses of people.

Extracting laughter from an audience is the most specialized talent on earth. It matters not how successful or wealthy or secure a laugh provoker becomes—each time he faces an audience he has got to be funny. That agonizing, persistent pressure keeps the comedian honest—there is no let-up.

This book is an attempt to shed some light on the serious business of making people laugh; an effort to comprehend the inscrutable; an endeavor to gain some insight into the mechanics and craft of comedy.

Each comedian has his own method—his own approach to getting a laugh. Here, for the first time in their own words, is how the world's best known funnymen go about bringing laughter to countless millions.

LARRY WILDE

Woody Allen

Woody Allen was born in Brooklyn, New York, on December 1, 1935. At seventeen, while still in high school, he wrote comedy material for the radio and television shows of comedians Peter Lind Hayes and Herb Shriner.

After being expelled from New York University for an exceptionally poor academic record, he began turning out jokes for Sid Caesar, Art Carney, Garry Moore, Buddy Hackett, Kaye Ballard and Carol Channing.

He started his career as a stand-up comedian in 1962 at the Bitter End, a Greenwich Village coffeehouse. In a comparatively short time, Woody was headlining the nation's best night clubs and appearing on all the major television shows.

He has acted in the motion pictures *Casino Royale,* and *What's New, Pussycat?,* which he also wrote. Woody also supplied the dubbed-in dialogue for the Japanese-made film *What's Up, Tiger Lily?*

His two best-selling comedy record albums are distributed by Colpix.

Woody also wrote the long-running Broadway comedy *Don't Drink the Water.*

He is married to actress Louise Lasser, and they live in a six-room brownstone in Manhattan.

Excerpts from a Woody Allen monologue

I can take care of myself. In case of danger I have this cutlass that I carry around with me . . . and in case of a real emergency, I press the handle and it turns into a cane so I can get sympathy.

I keep having this birthday cake fantasy, where they wheel out a big cake with a girl in it and she pops out and hurts me and gets back in.

I went to N.Y.U. I got into the philosophy department and I took all the abstract philosophy courses, like Truth and Beauty, Introduction to God, Death 101 . . . and I was thrown out of college for cheating on my metaphysics final. Whereupon my mother—she is a very high-strung type—tried to kill herself with an overdose of Mah Jong tiles.

I'm afraid many members of my family are eccentric. You see this watch? This is an absolutely fantastic, very fine, elegant gold watch which speaks of breeding and was sold to me by my grandfather on his deathbed.

My grandfather had a wonderful funeral. It was a catered funeral with accordion players and a buffet table, and there was a replica of the deceased in potato salad.

After six years of marriage, my wife and I pondered whether to take a vacation or get a divorce . . . and we decided that a trip to Bermuda is over in two weeks but a divorce is something you always have.

My wife was an immature woman. I'd be in the bathroom taking a bath and she would walk right in and sink my boats.

JACK ROLLINS, Woody Allen's indefatigable manager, arranged this interview. The meeting took place in **Mr.** Rollins' inner office. Woody arrived wearing desert boots, brown corduroy pants, a black crew-neck sweater, tan corduroy jacket and three-quarter length car coat. He was courteous and cooperative and by the third question, we both relaxed and had good rapport.

WILDE: *Woody, what made you stop writing for other comedians and become one yourself?*

ALLEN: Writing for other comedians as a life-time pursuit is a blind alley. I never had any intention of continuing writing for other comedians before I started performing. At that time, I was just writing for them to earn a living. And I was interested in writing for the theatre, which I'm still interested in doing. But then I got interested in performing. It occurred to me it might be a good avenue of expression. So I decided to try it. But there is no future in being a TV writer. You can hack around from show to show and you're always worried—is the comedian you're writing for going to be dropped because of bad ratings? and if he is dropped you may find yourself moving three thousand miles to the other coast to write for a new comedian. It's a rough business.

WILDE: *When you began creating material for your act, did you first decide what your image was and then begin to write?*

ALLEN: No. There was never any sense of image. I still

don't have any sense of that at all. I just wrote what I thought was funny and wanted to perform it. I found after a year or two of performing some sort of image formed itself. The critics and the people would come away and agree on certain images they had of me . . . certain aspects . . . I think the worst thing I could do would be to believe the images of me I read in the newspapers.

WILDE: *Then you're simply doing what you feel is the right thing for you?*

ALLEN: Yeah, what ever I feel is funny, I do, no matter what it is, without any regard to the subject matter, and if an image emerges, fine!

WILDE: *Is it easier to write jokes for yourself than it was for the other comedians?*

ALLEN: It has different problems. Other comedians are much less selective. I would write jokes for ten other comedians and they would use eight out of ten, finally, in putting together their acts . . . and it would work. I find I'm much more cowardly. I use like one out of ten jokes. I'm much more selective with my own material. I pamper myself more.

WILDE: *You write ten jokes and only choose one. After a while what percentage of the jokes work for you?*

ALLEN: What finally remains in my act is really a very, very small percentage of what I come up with. When I write a piece of material . . . something occurs to me at some point, an idea, a notion that I think would be funny or something that actually happened to me and I try and develop a long story on it with as many laughs coming as close together as possible. I find after I'm finished I have a lot of jokes, a lot of remarks to make—comments—and as I look at them I find ninety percent of them don't meet the standards I would like to present publicly to an audience. Then I condense what was a twenty-minute thing to six minutes and I go out and do it, and I find my judgment was wrong on part of it. The audience is not laughing at some parts where I thought they would laugh. They're laughing at things I couldn't imagine they would laugh at, so I adjust it further and it comes down to four minutes, and gradually it's honed down. So in order to get a half hour act it takes me a long time, and I have to write a lot of material.

WILDE: *Do you write each piece to last a specific length of time?*

ALLEN: No. I have no regard to time. If it's fifteen minutes or fifteen seconds, it couldn't matter less.

WILDE: *Does each routine average six minutes in length?*

ALLEN: No, they vary completely. There have been times when all I could get out of what I thought might be a very funny idea for five or six minutes would be one good joke and nothing more—and that joke couldn't be put any place because it would be such an unusual joke it wouldn't fit in another routine. So I'd find I would just stop in the middle of talking about something else and do that one single joke and get a big laugh completely out of context and go on.

WILDE: *How many times do you need to perform one routine before it is perfected?*

ALLEN: I find the more I do it, up to the point of diminishing returns, it gets better. It's not the best the first night I do it. It gets better and better as the months go by and then it hits a point where it can fall off because it becomes too rote . . . too pat.

WILDE: *How do you go about writing a piece of material for yourself?*

ALLEN: There are two ways I have of working. One is spontaneously, where during my daily activities funny things occur to me. Ideas for jokes, premises. I write them down.

WILDE: *Excuse me, what do you mean by a "premise"?*

ALLEN: A premise would be like: If I was caught in an elevator during the blackout, trying to move a piano by myself. Now, that's not good for one joke. I found that that would lead me to a whole funny story of how I decided to move from one apartment to another in the same building . . . why I decided to move, what was wrong with the first apartment, how I looked for the second apartment, why I didn't have moving men do it because I wanted to do it myself, and finally the hard work of doing it. Trying to lift the piano and getting into a little elevator with it . . . trying to hold it up for the minute it takes to go up to the twentieth floor, and then the blackout comes and I'm stuck for six hours trying to hold the piano up. I find each step of the way should be told with as strong a joke as possible.

WILDE: *Then by "premise" you mean a story that has a beginning, a middle, and an end?*

ALLEN: Exactly. That idea which gives you a plot line to talk about for an extended length of time.

WILDE: *And allows you to hang jokes or laughs on.*

ALLEN: Right. As opposed to a single joke that would occur to me.

WILDE: *I didn't mean to interrupt you. Then what do you do?*

ALLEN: That's all right. So these premises or single jokes occur to me. I could be walking down the street or shaving, and I write them down on anything handy, like matchbooks or napkins, and I throw them in a drawer at home. Then when the time comes that I've got to get new material for appearances, I take them and lay them out in the room and I see which jokes are worth going for. I then combine those with the ones I write by mechanical process. That is, sitting down, without notes—just knowing that in three nights I'm going to appear on the Ed Sullivan Show and I've got to prefabricate a piece of material.

WILDE : *Since it takes a certain amount of time to break in jokes or lines, or a premise, would you take a chance on a major TV program with material you had just written two or three days before?*

ALLEN : I wouldn't want to and try to avoid it as much as possible. Sometimes it's unavoidable, and sometimes I have gone on television with things I have never edited or done anyplace before. I find it's not as good as things I've done before but that's because . . . say a routine I want to do consists of twenty laughs, and if I do it in a club, I find there's really only sixteen laughs and finally four laughs are knocked out because they consistently don't work. The bit becomes tight and has a lot of punch . . . but if I do that routine on television first and I discover there are four weak spots, it's been seen by everybody. It's too late, and those four weak spots considerably weaken the whole thing.

WILDE : *Do you try out new jokes on friends or anybody who will listen, as some comedians do?*

ALLEN : Not really, because I find it doesn't mean anything. It can only be discouraging.

WILDE : *You wait until you get in front of an audience?*

ALLEN : Yeah, that's really where it counts. And not

these late second-show spots where a lot of performers feel they should try out a new piece of material because if it doesn't go over they won't get hurt very much. The best thing to do is to come right out and lead with your best. Your Saturday night full-house show is the perfect opportunity, because the conditions are right and the new material stands a better chance. You're asking for trouble by breaking in material under any conditions that are not the best. If you tell it to friends, it's very depressing. They'll say, 'Yes, this joke is very funny, but that one doesn't thrill me too much.' There's no point hearing that from one or two people. It's better to do the joke before two hundred people. If someone says that joke isn't so great, I get very shaky and I might not try it on the floor.

WILDE: *How do you go about creating a joke? The actual process?*

ALLEN: That's very hard to answer. It depends on circumstances. When you do it, say when you're hired to write for Sid Caesar, there's a lot of different ways of doing it than you'd do it for yourself.

WILDE: *How about just for yourself?*

ALLEN: It's very, very intangible, really. Suppose I'm going to write the story about trying to move the piano. I try to take it right from the top. As far back as I can go. For instance, the first thought that occurs to you is getting stuck with the piano, and then I start retracing this backwards. Why am I moving myself? Because I don't want to spend the money on moving men. Why do I want to move? Because I don't like my apartment and I always have trouble with apartments. Why do I always have trouble with them? What other apartments have I lived in? What was my apartment in Brooklyn like? Why was it poor? Because my parents couldn't afford very much rent. What did my parents do for a living? I find this can go back and back forever. So I might start with the business about the piano by saying my mother married my father because he was a cab-driver and finally through a lot of stories of how she met him and how they moved to Brooklyn and how they got their apartment and by a lot of circuitous talk, a lot of jokes hopefully, I finally get up to the part of the piano.

WILDE: *Someone taking a course in journalism or creative writing or how to write a novel can learn certain basic methods and techniques. Are there also rules for creating jokes?*

ALLEN: I don't think you can learn to write jokes. Not good ones. You can learn certain mechanical things—to create variations of other jokes written, even good variations, but it's nothing you can learn. It's purely inborn.

WILDE: *Are there different kinds of jokes?*

ALLEN: I don't know what you mean by that.

WILDE: *Well, some jokes are two or three sentences, others last for five or six sentences. They have names.*

ALLEN: There are names that drift around, like a "one-liner" or an "ad-lib," but that's no advantage or help to you when you're writing material. I want to make one differentiation. There *is* a technique you can learn, if you are a person that has the ability to be funny or to write funny things. You can learn how to put them into different forms. Then the technique comes in. You can learn how to construct the monologue, how to construct a sketch, and ultimately how to use those jokes to construct a play. But you can't learn beyond that. You can't learn how to write funny things . . . how to write individual jokes.

WILDE: *Then it depends on the individual mind seeing a specific incident and seeing it humorously and expressing the humor he sees in words?*

ALLEN: Yes. That's what is so tricky about it. Given an absolutely straight sentence, with no punch line to it whatsoever, you can have twenty people read the sentence, and Jonathan Winters reads it or W. C. Fields—it's just going to be funny without changing a word, for some intangible, built-in thing that's beyond reason. You see, it's not the jokes. This is the part that traps people all the time. Not just with me, with anyone in the business. It's just a great, great fallacy that turns out so many mediocre comedians and causes so much trouble. It isn't the jokes that do it, and the comedian has nothing to do with the jokes. It's the individual himself. When I first started . . . the same jokes I did at that time that got nothing for me, now will get roars, and not because I am more known. It's the funny-character emergence that does it. You can take the worst material in the world and give it to W. C. Fields or Groucho Marx and there's just something that will come out funny. The best material in the world in the hands of a guy who is a hack or doesn't know how to deliver jokes is not going to mean anything. I'm not saying they won't get laughs. You watch the Ed Sullivan Show . . . you find a parade of comedians that get laughs, but the audience doesn't go away with anything. Then a Nichols and May will appear, and they'll get as many laughs as the hack comedians—or even less—but the audience goes away with something that has nothing to do with the material at all.

WILDE: *Is it a rapport that happened between the audience and that particular comedian? A love, an admiration, an affinity?*

ALLEN: It's hard to put into words why it is, but I guess you could use all those words because they are things that enter into it. You could watch Bob Hope or Jack Benny —Jackie Gleason is a good example. I didn't like his television show. I thought it was bad, a consistently bad show, and yet audiences would tune him in week after week. He could do one bad show after another and every one will love him and find him funny because there's something in him we respond to, and yet you take another comedian who will do brilliant work and the audience will laugh at him while he's there—and let him do one bad show and the public is finished with him. There's something built-in. . . .

WILDE: *I believe audiences identify with certain qualities or characteristics of the comedian. In Gleason's case, he's a heavy fellow who has a smiling Irish twinkly-eyed face, and he really is a loveable-type person. . . .*

ALLEN: He's a human being and we respond to him. I think, odd as it may seem, Ed Sullivan is a personality who has—he's not a polished performer or anything, and yet we welcome him every week for years because he's a real human being and you have a "live" feeling with him. He's not a slick, patent-leather kind of personality.

WILDE: *Is knowing grammar, or being able to speak English well, important in being able to create jokes or deliver them?*

ALLEN: Unimportant completely. It has no relevance at all. It has nothing to do with if you're funny or not. Jimmy Durante is irresistibly funny. It has nothing to do with any other qualities. As a writer, comedians came to me looking for a particular answer they never got. They thought the answer to their success would be in their clothing, or they thought to develop an attitude—that is, put on some sort of approach or point of view to things. Once one of them said to me, "Maybe just before I hit the stage, if I'd smile and try to get warm and gay when I walked out, it would infect the audience!" And he was very serious about it. These things never mean anything. A guy will come along who doesn't give any thought to those things whatsoever, just is a funny person, and he'll walk out on stage and there it is. You just do what you do and just pray the audience likes it.

WILDE: *That's not the general case. Most comedians work years to learn their craft and to enhance to develop their comedic character and attitude.*

ALLEN: Not the great ones. You see, once you have that intangible quality of funniness, then you can learn. I'm not saying that Bob Hope or Sid Caesar don't work hard. They do. They have to create an even greater work of art. But they are able to, because they had that thing in the beginning that some other comedian doesn't have. I mean a guy that will work consistently and get a lot of big laughs but will never really capture the public like Jack Benny has. A work of art is beyond him. He'll always make a good living, which will be nice, but then somebody will come along, like Jonathan Winters, who is capable of even greatness, and he'll come out and he'll be very funny and that's not to say that all he'll have to do is come out on the stage and just stand there. Then it becomes his obligation to work hard.

WILDE: *Is there a difference in reaction between a television audience and a night club group?*

ALLEN: The only difference I've found is that in a night club you've got all the time in the world to kill the audience, and you can kill ninety-nine per cent of them. If for any reason they are a very sluggish audience, after ten minutes you get them going and you've got them. Whereas on television you're on for six minutes, and if that night you happen to get a bad audience—they may be lovely people but just not for laughing—you do your bit and, sure you may get them at the last minute. It's pure luck. There are nights when everything I say, they are great—and other nights when I might do the same jokes or better ones, and the audience is nice and likeable, but they just don't let you hear it as much.

WILDE: *Why are some audiences more enthusiastic than others?*

ALLEN: The same phenomenon occurs if you're having a bad night—the audience is bad, they seem to be bad together. When the audience is good, they seem good. When they are bad, they seem very bad. I don't really know exactly why that is. I guess if you have group leaders in the audiences that lead group laughter, it's a big help. If I know three tables love me in a club, I can almost guarantee I can get the whole audience.

WILDE: *The laughter seems to spread.*

ALLEN: Yeah, it's like asking for an autograph. If you are sitting in a restaurant, fifty people may recognize you, but if nobody asks for that first autograph, you can eat your whole meal and no one will ask you. But if one person asks, guaranteed within the next half-hour everybody there will ask. Well, it's the same thing with laughter. If somebody starts laughing out loud, it begins to get around. It's a very cliché thing to say, because it's been said . . . but nobody really understands why all the bad ones are in one audience on the same night.

WILDE: *Aside from your being funny, why do people laugh at you?*

ALLEN: The only thing I can surmise is that there is something about me they are responding to, above and beyond the material—something in myself that I don't see. I don't believe the performer knows what's funny about himself, or can see it. They tell a joke, the audience laughs. That's all they hear. They can never stand outside themselves enough to know what it is. There's something about Groucho just standing there that's just comical, and he won't see it. He can't really appreciate himself as we can. I just go out and try to be as funny as I can.

WILDE: *How would you describe your humor?*

ALLEN: I come out and tell jokes. That's how I would actually describe it. I do the same thing that Henny Youngman does . . . Bob Hope. They come out and tell jokes and I come out and tell jokes. I may construct my stories a little differently. Henny Youngman's jokes may be less related to one another than mine, but we are all comedians doing jokes.

WILDE: *It used to take ten or twelve years for a comedian to become successful, and yet you did it in a shorter time. How do you account for it?*

ALLEN: It *does* take a comedian a period of time to grow. I'm not anywhere near my full strength, and I think it will take years to do that, but just by the nature of the business it takes time to develop your material and to get the experience. I don't see why it should necessarily take ten or fifteen years. It's perfectly conceivable someone will come along and in a couple of years emerge as a comedian. There's no reason why they shouldn't.

WILDE: *To emerge as a comedian and come out as a successful comedian are two different things.*

ALLEN: That's all luck. You can never go in there with that on your mind. It's pure luck that the public embraces you. You like to write jokes and you like to tell them, and you do it. After that, it's pure luck.

WILDE: *Is it possible for anyone to become a comedian?*

ALLEN: No, I think just the opposite is true. It's an inborn thing that some have. Like Jerry Lewis. I think he was born funny. I'm not saying he didn't and shouldn't continue to work hard to make the most of those gifts and do great things. But two babies lying side by side—one will never become a comedian no matter what he does. He may buy the greatest jokes in the world, he may get some bookings and then make a living at it, but it's like it was in the genes with Jerry Lewis.

WILDE: *What is the most difficult part about being a comedian?*

ALLEN: The pressure. It's very hard to constantly have to go before the public and get laughs. You have to appear on television and in clubs all over the country and constantly get laughs. A singer goes out, sings some songs, gets the applause and that's it . . . or a dramatic actor. I'm not saying that's not hard to do. It is. But a comedian has got to consistently get laughs. If they are not roaring, you're in trouble. You have to be great all the time. Your jokes have to be funny. You've got that pressure of facing an audience —get them laughing for forty minutes. You go to your dressing room, and in an hour you have to do it again for the second show that night or the third, and the next night you have to do it all over again, and this goes on year after year.

WILDE: *Does it require superhuman strength and ability, then, to sustain like Benny, Hope, Skelton, and the others?*

ALLEN: No, I think it's a combination of hard work and luck. Benny was born a comedian with a likeable, amusing personality, and he made use of it. Sustaining is a lucky thing.

WILDE: *Who are the comedians you respect most?*

ALLEN: Groucho Marx has always been for me the consummate artist. He looks funny, he sounds funny, he sings funny, he dances funny, he walks funny, the contents of what he says is funny, he operates within a framework that's funny. He has appeal to people who cannot read or write and is considered superbly funny by the most brilliant men in the world. For me, Hope is a close second to Groucho. Then W. C. Fields.

WILDE: *Did any of these men influence your work?*

ALLEN: It's hard to say. I think all the great ones have. I have been influenced by Groucho in certain ways—not to the point of coming out in a moustache and a cigar, but I do feel his influence heavily. Also W. C. Fields. And Mort Sahl. When he came on the scene, I think he had a tremendous impact on the business, and he was an original, a true original.

WILDE: *There's a theory that in order to be funny you have to come from a poverty-stricken background—having some insufficiency, either financial, emotional, or psychological. What do you think?*

ALLEN: I feel that poverty makes sense. But it's some

kind of privation or suffering not necessarily economic that turns someone into a comedian . . . that has squeezed your humor from the world or the world out of shape.

WILDE: *When you started performing, what problems did you have to overcome?*

ALLEN: Lack of confidence and the fear of getting up in front of an audience. Other comedians don't have that problem. They have something entirely different.

WILDE: *What counsel can you give to new comedians?*

ALLEN: There's not much to say. Just don't make the mistake of falling into the material trap. To the degree you are a funny person, that's how much you'll succeed . . . not what kind of material you have. When I first became a comedian, I thought, gee, I write funny material, I bet I could get up and just read this to people and they would laugh. I tried that. I took the sheets of paper out in the night club and it meant nothing to the audience. They wanted something else entirely. What they want is an intimacy with the person. They want to like the person and find the person funny as a human being. The biggest trap comedians fall into is trying to get by on the basis of their material. That's just hiding behind jokes. It's not getting out in front of an audience and opening themselves up. It's all so ephemeral. Such a thin line of luck and intangibles. There is no real advice anybody can give on what to do to become a comedian. The whole thing is such a rare combination of hereditary and environment and the audience that night and the temperature and the headlines in the papers and. . . .

WILDE: *You use the word "luck" a great deal. Is there anything you can do to push or influence your luck?*

ALLEN: Yes. If you are a person, like Jerry Lewis or Danny Kaye or Sid Caesar, who is just born gifted, then you can really discipline yourself. You'll get a comedian who has a great deal of talent and he doesn't discipline himself and he makes some contribution because his natural gifts help. But then you get the chap who really will discipline himself and develop.

WILDE: *Do you mean by doing specific . . .?*

ALLEN: I mean really hard work. Writing material for yourself, not believing your press notices whether they are good or bad, constantly doing new things, constantly moving into new areas—movies, Broadway—studying new projects, constantly risking everything without ever thinking about the money or how it will hurt or build your career. Just thinking about work.

WILDE: *You mean always being willing to take a risk and not caring if you fail?*

ALLEN: Right! Once you start to think about do the newspapers like me, or did the audience like me, or am I making enough money, or should I be doing this? The only important thoughts are: *Am I being as funny as possible in as many different ways.* Once you view the rewards too tantalizingly, you're dead. Then you start accepting and turning down jobs on the basis of how it affects your income tax. Then you might as well be working in Macy's, except that the money is better in this business.

Jack Benny

Jack Benny was born Benny Kubelsky on February 14, 1894, in Chicago, but he grew up in Waukegan, Illinois. He spent the early part of his career touring the vaudeville circuits, eventually doing Broadway musicals for Earl Carroll and the Shuberts. He entered the new medium of radio in 1932, and switched to television in 1950, where he proceeded to win eight "Emmy" awards for the excellence of his program.

His best-known movies were: *George Washington Slept Here, Buck Benny Rides Again, Man About Town, Charlie's Aunt,* and *To Be or Not to Be.*

Jack's latest enthusiasm is performing as violin soloist with the top symphony orchestras in America, with all proceeds going to charitable causes.

In 1932, as a guest on the Ed Sullivan radio show, his first words were "Hello, folks, this is Jack Benny. There will be a slight pause for everyone to say, 'Who cares?'" Today, Mr. Benny doesn't expect that question, for he has become an American institution.

Sample of Jack Benny's comedic point of view

Perhaps Jack Benny's most famous comedy moment has him walking down a dark street. Suddenly a hold-up man appears from out of the darkness and shoves a gun in his ribs, saying, "Your money or your life!"

Because he is notorious for penny-pinching, there is what seems like an interminable pause, during which the audience is convulsed with laughter. Then at the very last split-second, Jack says, "I'm thinking it over!"

*   *   *

As a guest on Fred Allen's radio program, on which the comedians carried on their hilarious "feud," to the delight of millions of listeners, Fred Allen got off a particularly funny ad-lib, which practically stopped the show. Jack Benny, not to be outdone, came back with: "Hmmm, you wouldn't say that if my writers were here!"

*   *   *

From a Jack Benny monologue:

Last week I woke up in the middle of the night with the most wonderful idea for a joke. I couldn't go back to sleep. I worked on it all night. The next day I came to the theatre and did four shows . . . and in between each show, I worked on that joke. That night, I stayed up all night trying to perfect the joke. And finally, the next day, I got it. I went out on the first show—and it was such a wonderful joke—I started to tell it and right in the middle of the joke . . . I fell asleep.

THIS MEETING took place in Mr. Benny's Beverly Hills office. Most of the five rooms contained filing cabinets of past radio and television scripts.* The walls of each room were decorated with plaques, pictures, awards, tributes, citations, copies of newspaper and magazine articles—even a photograph of Salisbury and Benny, his first act.

Fifteen minutes passed while Mr. Benny, worked on some material with his writer for an up-coming Lake Tahoe appearance. Suddenly, the door to his private office opened and Jack Benny, my idol, the man I admire and respect most in my profession—Jack Benny stood before me. A mortal. Wearing a gold sport shirt, tan slacks, a gold and black sport coat and smoking a cigar.

As we chatted, it became increasingly difficult for me to believe that the man sitting behind the desk was in his seventies. He looked fifty-five—sharp, alert, handsome. I sat enthralled and nervously began the questioning.

WILDE: *To kind of get started, Mr. Car . . . eh . . . Mr. Benny, I would. . . .*

BENNY: As long as you're gonna make a mistake with my name, call me Jack!

WILDE: *All right, Jack! How many years did you play the violin before you decided to become a comedian?*

---

* Mr. Benny recently donated 900 radio scripts and electrical transcriptions (1932–55) to UCLA. The gift included 296 TV scripts (1950–68), stills, clippings, and tapes of his life and career, business correspondence, personal letters and contracts. The business transactions and contracts will remain sealed until March 20, 1983.

BENNY: We-e-ell . . . when I was about fourteen, fifteen years old in Waukegan, I used to play with dance orchestras. We would play in stores on Saturdays and maybe get a dollar and a half for the day. Then I studied and I went into vaudeville as a violinist. There was a woman pianologist—or whatever they called them—who sang and did talking, comedy songs. Her name was Cora Salisbury. She took me with her on the road. We did a violin and piano act—Salisbury and Benny.

WILDE: *Did you do any comedy?*

BENNY: No, only a little bit of kidding with the violin, but I never talked.

WILDE: *What happened to make you give up being a musician and become a comedian?*

BENNY: Well, Cora's mother became very, very ill and she had to give up the stage. Sooooooh . . . I found another partner, a fellow by the name of Woods and I called the act Benny and Woods. That's how I have Benny as my last name —Benny is my right first name. We stayed together doing a violin and piano act until the First World War and then I joined the Navy.

WILDE: *Until then, you still had not done any comedy?*

BENNY: No comedy at all. Then in the Navy at Great Lakes, David Wolfe, who became a very dear friend of mine later, was the author of a couple of sailor shows for Navy Relief. And in this show I did my violin and piano act with Zez Confrey. But David Wolfe needed somebody to play the part of an admiral's orderly, who only had one or two comedy lines. He happened to see me and said, "Hey, young fella, come over here!" (I was a young fella then.) And I read a couple of lines and he liked it, because the next day he added lines for me and by the time the show opened in Chicago in the Auditorium, I had practically the comedy part of the show. Then I realized I could talk and get laughs. When I went into vaudeville again, I went back as a single act. But I always held the violin . . . did a lot of violin playing and just a little bit of talk. And then gradually I kept talking and less violin, until finally I dropped the violin entirely. If I wanted to have a finish for my act I borrowed a violin from the orchestra.

WILDE: *How many years did you continue to carry the violin on stage?*

BENNY: I carried it until one week I played the Palace Theatre in New York, which was the acme—you know, the highest—Jake Shubert came into to see me . . . but he felt because I held the violin it classified me as a violinist. So the next time I went to the Palace I dropped the violin—but I tried it in other towns first.

WILDE: *Even though you stopped playing the violin, why did you still hold it? For security?*

BENNY: Yes, for security. Also, it made all my jokes sound impromptu—when you hold an instrument, they always think you are ready to play.

WILDE: *How long was your spot?*

BENNY: Around fifteen minutes.

WILDE: *Where did you get the material you used?*

BENNY: I would get help occasionally from writers and I would pay them for that particular routine—thirty-five or fifty dollars—but I wrote a lot for myself. In those days I was able to write because I had to. The only trouble . . . I was always walking down the street staring and people would pass me and say hello and I would not even know who they were. I was always thinking of jokes.

WILDE: *Was your delivery basically the same as it is today—that is, leisurely, unhurried?*

BENNY: Basically the same, but I was always nervous, the first few years, when I talked. I wouldn't gesticulate enough . . . and though I work easy and smoothly now and I put something into it, in the old days I was afraid to. When I was a hit in those days, I was a big hit because I worked so easy and smooth, but if I flopped I was a big flop for the same reason. You see, there's such a thing as being too nonchalant on stage. It looked as though you were—

WILDE: *Too well rehearsed?*

BENNY: Yeah. It looked as though you were over-acting and under-acting at the same time. Trying too hard to be smooth and easy. I learned since then I have to have a little action. I learned that later in radio and television.

WILDE: *In the beginning of your career, did you sit with other comedians and discuss jokes and audiences and comedy in general?*

BENNY: Yes. Most comedians, strangely enough, are very good friends. It doesn't always happen in other branches of our business . . . for some reason or other, actors . . . although I do think in our business people are very very close, and even though there is competition and you have rivals or you try to reach a point where a friend of yours has already reached. Like Phil Baker never thought I would get any place. He thought I worked too blahh! But we were all pretty good friends. Maybe some of them in their hearts would not like to see others do well, but . . . comedy is not the easiest form of entertainment. That is, to reach a point in your career where you become a star or an institution or a household word—there are some great comedians now who won't make it, but they are great comedians—see, there has to be something more than just getting laughs. Laughs are *not* everything. People can scream at a comedian and yet can't remember anything afterward to talk about.

WILDE: *What qualities are required, other than being able to make people laugh?*

BENNY: In the first place, to become real successful they must like you very much on the stage. They must have a feeling like: "Gee, I like this fella"—"I wish he was a very good friend of mine"—"I wish he was a relative." You see, it's like a television show—if they like you, you may think sometimes you are doing a bad show and you're not at all. But if they don't like you, you cannot do a good show. Of course, we had great schools in those days—vaudeville and burlesque, which they haven't got today. That's why I give all the new comedians a lot of credit for making it as quickly as they do and actually getting big laughs. For instance, I can walk on stage and if I want to be secure I can open up with a stingy joke and everybody screams. Well, a lot of comedians who haven't got those characterizations have to actually make good as comedians, not as institutions —household words. Not that I'm bragging that I'm an institution, I'm just trying to explain. . . .

WILDE: *When you started, were there any comedians you admired or patterned yourself after? You said Phil Baker was your idol—*

BENNY: It was not so much that Phil Baker was a great comedian—he was a great personality. One of the handsomest fellas you have ever seen and people loved him. He would always have somebody working with him to get the laughs, like I do on television. I used to like Frank Fay very much. I was never a very good friend of his—there weren't too many people that were friends of his, but on the stage I admired him. Al Jolson was the world's greatest entertainer. I don't think there's been anybody since then that has his magnetism, and particularly when he was in blackface. He had a sympathetic quality. I have always thought Ed Wynn was the world's greatest comedian, and I still think there is nobody that has ever been as funny, or will be, in my time as he was in his heyday.

WILDE: *Most comedians work for a period of years before they "find" themselves; that is, before they discover the kind of material, attitude and delivery that's right for them. How long did it take you to acquire this self-awareness?*

BENNY: It took me a very short time when I was a monologist. It took quite a while to *perfect* it—to get to the point where I wasn't static. In those days everything had to be set. Every word had to be set. If we wanted to change something we had to go out of town and break it in, that's how nervous we'd be. George Burns talks about things like that. But . . . let me explain something . . . once I have the right wording and the jokes in the right place I try to keep 'em there, because I find that a certain joke is better second or third or fourth or fifth.

WILDE: *Do you get that by trial and error?*

BENNY: By experimenting and trying. I try to get from one subject to another gracefully so that the audience doesn't realize I have made the change—they think I'm on the same subject for twenty minutes. I don't tell a joke about my uncle and then the next one about a saxophone or something.

WILDE: *They kid Henny Youngman about that.*

BENNY: Yes, but then that's his style—and it's good.

WILDE: *Jack, has what people laughed at changed much through the years?*

BENNY: I don't think so. I think they laugh at the same things. Years ago you could do some corny things and be funny. I can look over what I used to do many, many years ago and pick out things to use now. The only thing is if you are working on characterizations, things that were funny thirty years ago have to be embellished—have to be smarter —wilder. Like, if I do stingy jokes I can't do an ordinary joke about leaving a guy a nickel tip—that's not funny anymore. Now you have to be more wild. Maybe the waiter leaves *me* a dime tip knowing how cheap I am. It would have to be that crazy, you see, in order for it to be funny. Today, it has to be actually funnier.

WILDE: *Many comedians earn an excellent living doing club dates, conventions—some as much as twenty-five thousand dollars a year or more—but the world will never hear of them. Some are very content with this anonymity while others are still striving to reach the top. Was it always your goal to become a star?*

BENNY: I would think so, and I think nearly every comedian wants to be . . . just like a politician would like to be President of the United States. And I don't care who the politician is—he might be the mayor of Carson City, but if he's in politics, he would like to end up being President. I think every dramatic actor, every singer, would like to be among the top few. Every concert musician would like to be considered among the top half-dozen. But when I say "would like to be the top" . . . you see, we didn't demand too much in those days. For instance, when I played the Palace in New York, which was the theatre every actor was nervous about, and I was a big hit . . . you had the feeling that everybody in the world knew about it and you didn't have to go any further. And the same with money. When I got to the point where I was getting four hundred and fifty dollars per week, I thought I was quite a rich man. I started to move in the first-class hotels . . . oh, my goodness, I thought, if I could ever make a thousand dollars a week, brother, then I'm ready to call it a day—this is it.

WILDE: *So you really didn't wake up one day and say, "I want to be a great comedian"? It was a step-by-step process?*

BENNY: Yeah, but I think everybody does feel that way, because if they don't, it's not good—it's better to feel that way. But mine has been, fortunately so, a step-by-step . . . not only in recognition, but in improvement in what I was doing. If you get up to the top step-by-step, you don't drop so fast. Some people are overnight sensations and then stop the same way.

WILDE: *Could you pinpoint the specific steps you've taken to remain a star all these years?*

BENNY: I think I have had, through my years of radio and television, almost always a very, very good show. I can't stand *bad* shows—I get embarrassed. I was the comedian, of course, but *I* think I was almost a better editor. Most comedians give me credit for being not the best comedian in show business, but the best editor—which is important— as important as being a comedian. It's not that I am such a particularly funny man. It's the things I do in routines. People will say to me, "Did you study the pauses in the tape?" This all comes as you go along, but there is nothing as important as editing.

WILDE: *Were you born with this talent for editing or do you feel it came about as a result of years of analyzing yourself and your material?*

BENNY: The latter—I don't think I was born with it. It was important to me never to have a superfluous moment in my act or in my radio or television shows.

WILDE: *How did all the Jack Benny trademarks come about? Thriftiness, bragging, playing straight to the people you work with, etc.?*

BENNY: All these things happened by accident . . . with one show. Now how I probably became a stingy character happened because on one show I did some jokes about my being stingy. . . .

WILDE: *This was in radio?*

BENNY: Yes. Then we did it again and again, until suddenly by accident it became one of my characterizations, and it's the easiest one to get laughs. My feud with Fred Allen was an accident. Fred said something one night, I answered him—he answered me—I answered him, and it went on and on. We never got together and said, "Let's have a feud." If we did, the feud would have flopped, because it would have been contrived. We would have worked so hard at it it would have been lousy.

WILDE: *Why was Fred Allen considered the comedian's comedian?*

BENNY: Because he was a great writer. Fred was a wonderful humorist. He wrote funny letters. He wrote funny books. He wrote great shows. I don't know whether he was altogether a great editor, because sometimes he would have sensational shows and sometimes they wouldn't be at all. They would be far from it. I always blame it on editing. Let's take you . . . you are preparing this book, you gotta edit it, right? They say a play is never written, it's rewritten. Well, the same goes for an article in the paper, or a monologue for a show—everything. My four writers and myself sit down and argue and discuss whether the word "but" helps or hurts a joke. That's how important editing is.

WILDE: *Your writers have worked for you many years. What does it take to have a successful relationship with the men who provide the comedian's material?*

BENNY: First of all, you should have faith in them. You should feel that one is just as good as the other. Never let any of your writers feel that one person is doing the big job and the others aren't. You usually find through the years that one week one fella has delivered the best and another week another fella has. I don't try to remember who gave me any particular joke. I don't remember if it was my idea or theirs. I don't care. I only care about the results. Some writers think fast—ad-lib fast. Others think first before they talk. Others are better for continuity. I can't tell you how many times I have felt some of the material they brought in would not make a good show, but it did, and I always wind up apologizing. I'd rather apologize than have a bad show. I learned something that was very, very important after being in television a few years: I must never be angry with writers. If you become angry it becomes difficult for them to work. I found out the happier we are as a combination, the more fun we have, the greater shows I have. My writers and I get along like four intimate friends who are having a good time and that's how we write scripts.

WILDE: *What percentage of your total performance is the writer's contribution?*

BENNY: Well, let's start with the ideas. In radio and television maybe thirty-three and a third per cent came from me—the theme of the shows—and two-thirds from them. I have always come up with ideas. Sometimes they were good and sometimes they weren't. Sometimes they were good ideas but my writers felt that they were one-joke ideas and they couldn't get enough out of it, so I would say, "Drop it." When it comes to actual jokes they would contribute ninety or ninety-five per cent. When I would see the script, I would add a line or two. Now when I give stage appearances or when I speak at a dinner . . . a lot of the jokes, I prepare. If it's weak, I give it to my writers.

WILDE: *How did the final scripts for your television shows come about—the step-by-step process?*

BENNY: Well, we never stopped. In radio we wrote right up to air time, because all we had to do was read it. Now on television we had to naturally do it before, so we could learn it. But it never stopped until the last minute of the time allotted to us to have it ready, because we were always changing, always editing—like I told you before.

WILDE: *When you got together for the TV show, getting back to that for a moment, let's say the idea for that particular show that week came from you. What was the next step?*

BENNY: We have a meeting with the writers. My writers had a wonderful way of working. They didn't just sit down and put stuff on the typewriter. They would go home and make notes about where can they go with this idea of mine and suddenly I would get a call and they'd say, "Jack, your idea is great, we're gonna have a wonderful show." Or "Jack, we're afraid that we are not going any place with it—it doesn't spread enough. It's a one-joke idea and is only good for a couple of minutes." So I would say, "Drop it! You figure which way you want to go!" Later they would call and say, "We got a great idea about so and so," and they would write it. Then they came in with the script and we would sit down and edit it and we would work on it.

WILDE: *How did "Love in Bloom" become your theme song?*

BENNY: Quite by accident. "Love in Bloom" is not a theme song I particularly like. It has no significance with a comedian. It happened that I was fooling with that number thirty years ago, and before I could do anything about it . . . it was an avalanche, and it became my theme song.

WILDE: *It's amazing how so many elements of your comedic character . . . the comic attitude . . . your theme song . . . have all come about without being planned.*

BENNY: That's why it was good. There's no reason for "Love in Bloom" being my theme song. I couldn't stop it.

WILDE: *Mr. Benny, eh, Jack . . . you are considered to have the best timing among comedians. What exactly is timing?*

BENNY: Sometimes I think I have been given more credit than I merit in that, because every good comedian has to have, right off the reel, good timing, otherwise he can't even appear anyplace. I think the reason other comedians [feel this way] and maybe the public, who are gradually getting to know about timing, they know the words now . . . because I talk very slowly and I talk like I am talking to you . . . I might hesitate . . . I might think. Everybody has a feeling, at home watching television or when they come to a theatre, that I am addressing him or her individually. They feel that I am doing it for them, and because I talk slowly . . . I make it a point to talk like I would in a room with fellows. So they think my timing is great for that reason. Other people have great timing but they talk very fast. It would be tough for them to talk slowly and it would be tough for me to talk fast.

WILDE: *Could you define timing?*

BENNY: It's tough to define.

WILDE: *Do words like "rhythm" . . . "pause" . . . help describe it?*

BENNY: Well, my pauses fortunately went over even in radio, when you couldn't see me. The audience *felt* the pauses, but pauses make an audience think you are thinking. Sometimes I might do a monologue three or four nights and not change a word and an audience sitting out front will think I am ad-libbing a lot of it because I hem and haw around. But how do you define timing? It's a necessity. It's something everybody has to have. A good joke without timing means nothing and a bad joke without good timing means nothing—except you can help a bad joke with timing where you can't help a good joke with bad timing . . . I don't know how to define it.

WILDE: *Is it a question of an easy flow . . .?*

BENNY: That's right—one word or one syllable too much can throw it off completely. I had an experience once . . . I was playing Las Vegas . . . wonderful audience every night and I knew that my very opening line would be a big laugh, and every night it *was* a big laugh, and I knew just how long that laugh would hold . . . and then I would continue.

One night I walked out and the laugh was good but not as long or as big . . . and that performance knocked me off my timing for about two minutes. I couldn't get back into the swing and rhythm.

WILDE: *Can anyone learn timing?*

BENNY: I think so, but innately he has to have something.

WILDE: *It has been said that instead of being a comedian you are the world's foremost comedy actor. Do you agree?*

BENNY: I don't agree on being the world's foremost comedy actor. I *could* be a very good actor, and I think I am. I think Jackie Gleason is a great actor. Red Skelton does pathos very, very well with his face and gestures . . . and his mimicry.

WILDE: *Is there a difference between a comedian and a comedy actor ?*

BENNY: Yes, you can be both, but you can also be a fine comedian and not be a good actor, and you can be an actor and not a comedian. I don't know if you ever noticed it, but I always get the greatest results in comedy with a dramatic actor. I had Ronald Colman [as a guest] for years and I asked him, "to read the lines that we have written for you as though you were reading a dramatic scene." Every good actor is a good comedian.

WILDE: *Aren't men like Cary Grant and Jack Lemmon comedy actors rather than comedians?*

BENNY: That's right, but they are great comedians. Cary Grant is one of the finest comedians we have ever had in motion pictures. He knows what to do with a comedy scene. Jimmy Stewart is great.

WILDE: *Jack, which medium—radio, television, movies, night clubs, or the stage—do you prefer to work in?*

BENNY: The stage—and my concerts. They're all charity, you know. I enjoy playing with the big symphony orchestras . . . Carnegie Hall. A concert is the finest background a comedian can have. I'm dressed in tails as though I were the world's greatest violinist. The musicians behind me are ninety or a hundred of the greatest musicians—Leonard Bernstein, George Szell, or William Steinberg, Alfred Wallenstein or Zubin Mehta are conducting for me like they would for Heifetz.

WILDE: *Do you find that the laughs come more easily when you are doing a monologue or when you are involved in a sketch?*

BENNY: They might be . . . they could be oftener in the monologue. However, there are certain jokes I like to tell that are very smart and very clever that do not get the laughs some of the others do, but they will be the kind of joke the audience will remember. There will be the kind of joke that will only call for a *nice* laugh, and you don't want to leave it off. You don't have to get a laugh every second.

WILDE: *Any average, intelligent person with practice and hard work can become a lawyer or a CPA. Is it possible for someone to put in the same amount of effort and become a comedian?*

BENNY: Only if he has something. Only if there is a spark that can develop into a flame. In the first place, he has to have a great sense of humor. Everybody should have a public and high school education. I never had a high school education and I never was good in public school, but the fellow who thinks he is going to be a comedian—be in show business—I think a college education can hurt him. He knows too much. He knows too many fine words. His vocabulary is too good. I have a fine vocabulary, but I never use it. He doesn't get down to earth. You look back and see who are some of the fine comedians, you will find usually that they are people without college educations. College does something to you. It makes you feel that you know a little bit too much and you do not then consider an audience your equal—while if you haven't had that college training you are very careful about what you say and how you say it.

WILDE: *A certain amount of capital is required to start in any business. How much would you say is needed to start as a comedian? And what would you use it for?*

BENNY: Well, I wouldn't know how much capital, because I never had any. But I would use it to buy material, buy jokes. If you don't know how to routine the jokes . . . if this doesn't come easily to you, maybe you have someone help you who knows how. I will go to a young comedian that I like, and I say, "You do a fine act but you open badly." They say, "What do you mean" I say, "You open like an act. If you would come out and say, 'Well, ladies and gentlemen, it's great to be here in Plainfield and you know, I haven't been in Plainfield in years' and you have a joke about it and *then* go into your routines. When you come out and start right off and say, 'I want to tell you, the way children are today . . .', they know it's a set act. They know immediately this is a routine you do every night. And even though they will laugh and everything, you have no rapport with an audience."

WILDE: *What advice would you give to a comedian just starting out?*

BENNY: This has been asked me, Larry, many, many

times. And it's the toughest question in the world to answer. You can't tell a fella where to go today. The minute he's any good he's thrown to the wolves, which means television. He hasn't had a chance to work out any background. It's a very difficult question to answer. More difficult than trying to explain timing. I never got advice and most of the fellas today never got advice . . . Joey Bishop . . . he's one of the funniest men I have ever seen. He's just naturally a funny man. Great ad-lib comedian . . . thinks fast. A lot of people think he worries too much . . . I think so too, but then this you can't stop . . . that's his style but he's great. What would you advise somebody to do? You see, in the old days there were schools . . . vaudeville . . . *then* I would say: Start out on small time, play Kokomo, Indiana. If you are a flop there, the only people that will know live in Kokomo. And then only the people in the theatre or who read the paper. By the time you get there next year you might have improved a lot. By the time you get to the Palace, Chicago, you have improved. Maybe it will take a couple of years. I played all the small little theatres.

WILDE: *Is there anything specific you have done to stay healthy and in good physical shape?*

BENNY: Everybody thinks I take such good care of myself. Actually I do not. I watch food because I want to look good at my age. If I intend to work, I intend to look good. I know I am at an age where a lot of people could look very old. I think it is better if I look young; otherwise my "thirty-nine years old" gag wouldn't be funny at all. It would be sad. If I actually looked my right age . . . people say to me all the time, "We know you are older than thirty-nine, but you certainly don't look your right age." So then I can have fun with the gag.

Milton Berle

Milton Berle was born on July 12, 1908, to Mr. and Mrs. Moe Berlinger on New York's West 118th Street.

The man who was to become "Mister Television" began his career at the age of five, under the guidance of his mother, Sandra, who brought him to the Biograph Studios in Fort Lee, New Jersey, where he made his silent screen debut in *Tillie's Punctured Romance* with Marie Dressler. Milton appeared in more than fifty silent films with such stars of yesteryear as Pearl White, Douglas Fairbanks, Sr., Mabel Normand and Marion Davies.

Milton's first stage role was in the Shuberts' revival of *Floradora,* which opened in Atlantic City in 1920. Shortly thereafter, he teamed up with ten-year-old Elizabeth Kennedy and played vaudeville theatres around the country in dramatic playlets.

In 1926, he created a different show business technique by injecting his comedy routines between other vaudeville acts—a device he used later with enormous success on television.

On June 8, 1948, Milton Berle on the "Texaco Star

Theatre" began to change the entertainment habits of the nation. "Uncle Miltie" was soon responsible for selling more TV sets than any other performer in the history of the newest medium.

Mr. Berle has won an Emmy nomination for his powerful performance as a straight dramatic actor on the "Dick Powell Theatre's" *Doyle Against the House.*

His recent movies include *Always Leave Them Laughing* and *It's a Mad, Mad, Mad, Mad World.*

He is married to the former Ruth Cosgrove. They have one son, Billy.

A Milton Berle monologue *

Good evening, ladies and gentlemen. (But why should I call you ladies and gentlemen? You know what you are).

But folks, on behalf of the Copacabana (and believe me, I'd like to be half of the Copacabana) . . .

I just want to [*slight belch*]—I don't remember eating that.

I just got back into town from Florida. I *flew* in. My arms are very tired.

Boy, they surely do gamble down there. You know that white flag above Hialeah race track. That's my shirt.

I had a wonderful compartment on the train on the way down. But the conductor kept locking me in at every station.

And now, folks, I'd like to bring out a wonderful little dancer. You've all heard masters of ceremonies say, "I now bring you a boy who needs no introduction." Well, folks, this kid needs plenty of introduction.

But first ladies and germs, I mean, gentlemen. Don't mind me, folks. It's all in fun. I'm just kidding. It all goes in one

---

* Reprinted with permission from Steve Allen's *The Funny Men* (Simon & Shuster, New York).

head and out the other. But I feel good tonight. I just came over from Lindy's. I always go over there for a cup of coffee and an overcoat. (I'll dig 'em up if you'll remember 'em).

But as I was saying—this boy needs no introduction. He just needs an act.

No, I'm only kidding. I want to bring him out here right now. Our worst act—I'm sorry, I mean our *first* act.

[*Woman laughs*] Say, are you laughing longer or am I telling 'em better? Say, lady, are you sitting on a feather?

[*More laughter*] Look, Madam, if you want to lay an egg don't do it here!

I just want you to know that I'm going to play piano with this first act and I want you to notice that at no time while I'm playing do any of my fingers leave my hands.

[*Frowns at audience*] All right, these are the jokes. What is this, an audience or an oil painting?

Looks like a staring contest out there.

And now folks, I'd like to prevent, I mean present, our first act. . . .

MILTON BERLE lives in a red tile roofed, Spanish style Beverly Hills mansion. It is tastefully furnished to match the period of the house. There are marble floors, wrought-iron banisters, and stucco walls.

Mr. Berle's male secretary escorted me to a small sitting room-library where I waited for Milton to conclude a business luncheon at the Beverly Hills Hotel. In a few minutes, Mr. Television arrived, collar open, breathing heavily, appearing totally exhausted.

He smiled warmly, settled on the couch, lit a cigar, and began questioning me about *my* career. His sincere interest startled me momentarily. Our discussion took on an intimacy right from the start, and when I left three hours later, I felt I had just met with the kindest, most infinitely thoughtful man in show business.

WILDE: *Mr. Berle, in . . .*

BERLE: Mendel.

WILDE: *Mendel . . . in recent years you have been doing a great many straight dramatic roles in movies and television. Is it easier to be serious than to make people laugh?*

BERLE: It *is* easier to be serious than to make people laugh. When you say dramatic roles, you are referring to acting. Actually, there is no such thing, Larry, as acting— it's reacting. Doing everything sincerely and playing it with believability. In the character you are playing you must be honest, you must be real, you must be believable.

WILDE: *But why is it easier than being funny?*

BERLE: In a straight role there's no going after laughs, no pauses or waiting—if this is supposed to be funny shall I take three beats? It is much more difficult to be funny and to get laughs, be it comic or comedian or a clown or a characterization of being a funny man or buffoon. There is no waiting for laughs in straight plays or straight acting, is the point I'm trying to make.

WILDE: *You draw more . . .*

BERLE: On the ability to be able to time, to know *what's* funny—if it *is, why* it is. You use more technique in trying to be funny and get laughs then in doing straight parts.

WILDE: *Is it just a coincidence that most good comedians are also fine actors?*

BERLE: No, it is not a coincidence. I'd say a comedian can make a better straight actor than a comic. I can take a straight actor and make him a comedian faster than I can take a comic and make a comedian out of him.

WILDE: *What is the difference between a comic and a comedian?*

BERLE: Let's go for some of the great comedians . . . Gleason, Phil Silvers, Sid Caesar, who is very ingenious, but if you have ever seen Sid try to do a stand-up spot he would *phump* and *phump,* and that goes for Gleason too—and Phil Silvers too—but I don't think it matters as long as they are comedians.

WILDE: *Could they be called "book" comedians?*

BERLE: That's a great joke. I was in the Copa once when Phil Silvers opened there to do his vaudeville act and before he got through we were all up on the floor, heckling him and clowning and Phil said, "Stop, please, I don't do that kind of one-line stuff, I'm a book comedian!" And a voice in the back, which was [Henny] Youngman, yelled: "Throw that man a book!" A comedian is a guy who is not afraid of silence . . . has the courage of waiting . . . of timing . . . of characterizations. Jack Benny, is one of the great comedians—if you look at a Benny script and you see it says, "BENNY: 'Well!' " "Well" on paper is not very funny, but when Mr. Benny says it, it's funny because of his attitude, his style, and his delivery. I think and I reiterate, Larry, it is more difficult for a comic to go straight than it is for a comedian.

WILDE: *Is it because he is so used to the rhythm of getting that laugh and getting into the next. . . .*

BERLE: It's called "crutch time." Now, Bob Hope is a dear friend of mine and I admire him tremendously. Bob is a joke man. Bob will buy the motion picture rights to *Critics' Choice* and then add quite a few dozen one-liners. I think it is a fear of not being able to wait—and not hearing your laugh a second. That is the difference in the comedian. Bob Hope could be a great comedian, but he unfortunately buries himself by spiking a play which has been established and putting in one-liners like, "That's a lovely suit, who shines it for you?" and then he goes into the plot. I think he is afraid to take the chance. This is *my* viewpoint.

WILDE: *You started your career as a child actor. Do you feel this foundation was responsible for your having developed into such a versatile performer?*

BERLE: Partly. I originally started as a straight actor. I'm not going back to when I was five years old, but when I was nineteen I did *Romeo and Juliet* in vaudeville. I did sketches—the courtroom scene from *Lightnin*. Besides in those days there was a Geary Society—you weren't allowed

to sing or dance under the age of sixteen, so all we had to
do was lend our talents to talking, never taking a lesson or
anything, but learning from experience . . . watching actors
. . . keeping my ears and my eyes open . . . being on the
bill in vaudeville with Victor Moore, who was one of the
world's greatest comedians—built only out of character.
Being in vaudeville with Lou Tellegen and great straight
actors, I learned something that gave me the background
for being a comedian. In my earlier days, watching comedians and funny men and clowns and buffoons gave me a
look at the different styles of each one.

WILDE: *You absorbed a great deal by osmosis as you were
growing up. . . .*

BERLE: Yes. I can be a stand-up comic, also play a sketch,
also black out my teeth, walk around and be funny funny,
low, hokum . . . that only comes from that training of being
legitimate when I was a young boy. When I was thirteen
or fourteen and I did a dramatic act, we had to make pauses,
we had to stop in direction, of waiting for beats so *that*
timing helped me develop timing my jokes. When I started
this sixteen-year-old stand-up by myself, I wasn't a comedian.

WILDE: *At that point, you were a headliner in vaudeville,
and when the cafés came into prominence, you were considered a top attraction in that field?*

BERLE: I wasn't always a headliner. When I got to the
age of fifteen, I got lanky, tall, skinny. I put on a long pair
of pants and started wisecracking—brash and flippant style.
But not until 1925 did I start as a single—fairly good, but
I wasn't my own style. I had copied my style from a great
comic, Ted Healy. I patterned myself after Healy, with the
hat turned up in front and the collegiate look. I was the

brash, flippant, wise guy, smart-ass type. I created *myself* just through guts and nerve—it would make Jerry Lewis look like a fag in those days—pushy . . . I created the thing of working throughout the whole show as Master of Ceremonies and working with the acts which is what I have been doing since 1925.

WILDE: *You did this in vaudeville?*

BERLE: Yes. I also did a fifteen or sixteen-minute spot, and I also worked with the acts . . . with the acrobats— stood on their feet.

WILDE: *What adjustments did you have to make in switching from the vaudeville stage to night clubs?*

BERLE: Well, in night clubs you had to be sharper because they were boozing. It didn't have to be dirty, but you did have to have a little sharper material. You had to have a different look. In vaudeville you could come out with the turned-up hat and raccoon coat, but in a night club you have to look like the person you are entertaining. That's the most important thing. Before an audience can laugh at you, they gotta like you . . . and they wait about a minute and a half and they look at you. If they have never seen you before, and if you are a newcomer, they say, "Gee, he has blue eyes, his shoes are shined or they are not shined, his suit is nice . . ." They have to look at you first before they laugh at you. Then they say. "I like his style, I like his personality. He's charming."

WILDE: *Are they doing this consciously?*

BERLE: Yes! If you are a newcomer. When you are established, you can come out and do it because you have them hooked already. When you are first starting—and this is for your young readers—just don't be afraid and don't be scared to take the time until the audience gets the feel and they can say, "Gee, he's a nice fella, he don't look like a comedian" or "He *does* look like a comedian." Bob Newhart is a good example, because he is playing to the guy that is him.

WILDE: *Instead of the raccoon coat and hat, did you wear a tuxedo in night clubs?*

BERLE: I never wore a tuxedo in a show when I was in night clubs or vaudeville—I might have worn it for a finale when we were all in opulent full-dress finish, but not throughout the show. A tuxedo is too formal for a comedian.

WILDE: *When you work night clubs are there any tricks or gimmicks you use to stimulate the audience if they are not responding as well as you think they should?*

BERLE: I don't call them "tricks"—nuances . . . technique. I have one technique that I use. I get the reservation list before each show from the maitre d' and I look down the names and I see who's in the audience. I also walk around unseen and see what kind of an audience they are—how they dress, what they look like. If it's an average audience, we might go into the "standards" and the "stocks." But I have what I call a test joke. If you want to call this a trick, there are three different levels to my jokes, to my material—three plateaus. One is the "in" jokes style that everyone doesn't understand, only a certain kind of audience . . . special. Then there is the other type of material which is a little easier to understand, and then there is the third plateau which is *very* easy to understand. So when I do my opening monologue I have two or three test jokes and if they laugh loud at one of these jokes, I know which way to go for the whole show. If they laugh at an "in" joke—for example, "This looks like an Arthur Murray lynching party," they have to know who Arthur Murray is. Or, "I've seen better crowds at group therapy." If they laugh loud at that, I can go a little more hip and wise for the rest of the show. If they don't, then I no doubt will say, "I'm so unlucky if they sawed a woman in half I would get the part that eats." Which is a "nose" joke . . . what we call a "platter" joke—you can't miss it—here it is folks—the *obvious* joke. Now if they laugh good and loud at that I will go *obvious* for the rest of the show. (*coughs*) Also buy some seals, I'm coughing.

WILDE: *There are theories that the temperature, world happenings, disaster, the weather—very hot or very cold—can effect the audience reaction.*

BERLE: I don't think the world trials and tribulations—front page, TV or radio—affect it as much as if the audience is not cool in temperature.

WILDE: *Room temperature?*

BERLE: Temperature of the room—the heat and warmth can make them very uncomfortable. I make it a point to let the actor sweat and the audience cool. If there is any air conditioning, it will be on for the audience. I don't particularly like air conditioning.

WILDE: *Some night club comedians do jokes that are considered to be in bad taste—religious, sick or death jokes—are these gags indicative of that particular comedian's personal taste or do they reflect what he believes the public wants?*

BERLE: Both—it might be his taste and it might be what he thinks the audience wants.

WILDE: *Is it necessary for a comedian working in clubs to do off-color material?*

BERLE: It isn't necessary to go way off-color—double-entendre, yes, but not dirty. Lenny Bruce is a big example.* Lenny Bruce is one of the most talented guys that we have today and proved it before he got into the four-letter words. But he don't need 'em because he's too smart, too clever, but this comes out of an illness in himself.

WILDE: *What is the difference between "blue," "risqué," and "double-entendre" material?*

BERLE: "Blue" is dirty. Risqué is . . . if you take a song or a parody I wrote, like:

> *He doesn't believe in making love*
> *He's the son of the rich*
> *And the pitch of his voice is high . . .*

. . . it might have a little fag idea to it, that's risqué. The Tom Lehrer or Dwight Fiske style. The Belle Barth style is on the nose of "blue" and "dirty"—of fuck, you know.

WILDE: *How about double-entendre?*

BERLE: You want the word "off-color," that's the word you are looking for. Double-entendre is practically risqué—dirt is shock—I call it shock-treatment jokes. Like, "We were going to open the show with a bang, but she didn't show up." Or, "Turn around and look at me!" And the fellow turns around and you say, "I'd rather look at your ass, it's better looking." It's the words that make it dirty.

WILDE: *What is meant by the comedian's "attitude"?*

BERLE: That's a style, a manner of working—his particular point of view of his own material and style of delivery. It can be a slow delivery, it can be a fast delivery, it can be a Texas drawl, it can be New Yorkese, if it is

---

* This interview was recorded prior to Bruce's death.

established indelibly and is characteristic of the comedian, which, by the way, will work longer for him than just being a non-sequitur comedian who talks and talks and has no attitude or style or label.

WILDE: *There is nothing specific about him you can pinpoint . . . ?*

BERLE: That's right. We have quite a few comics . . . they earn a good living and they will always earn a good living— I don't know if they will always earn a good living. But they will hear a joke in a parlor and they will go out and tell that same joke because it's funny, but it doesn't belong to their attitude—it's wrong for their act even though it's a laugh. There's a lot of comedians that do everything good and nothing great . . . referring to versatility . . . Jack Carter is an example. He does everything good but nothing great. Sammy Davis as an entertainer does everything good and nothing great. Because there is no Sammy Davis. Sammy is doing Mel Torme, Billy Eckstine, Billy Daniels, Sinatra. Jack Carter is doing Harry Ritz, Milton Berle (I have to put myself in there) and he got a mixture. *You gotta know who you are before you know what you are— before you do what you do.* There are three stages and it works just as well in comedy as it does in dramatics. *Who am I? What am I doing here?* And *why?* If you know who you are or what you are supposed to be, consisting of character and attitude, and have your own individuality—then you go a long way in show business.

WILDE: *What is meant by a rhythm joke?*

BERLE: A word can kill it, two words, let me think . . . it's a rhythmic sound which even if the joke has a point to it, it still helps the joke by the rhythm—the melody of it, the tempo of it. For example, a verse:

He's so cheap, he bought the cheapest groceries
He thought it didn't matter
His wife was so patient
Not a murmur did she utter
But she fed him tainted waffles
Till the effervescent batter
Was so bitter that he beat her
But he bought her better batter.

There's a joke there, it is an alliteration joke, but it's rhythmic and it's rhymed.

WILDE: *What's the difference between an "impressionist" and an "impersonator"?*

BERLE: An impressionist gives you a satirical viewpoint of the person he is doing the impression of. Frank Gorshin is an impersonator. An impressionist doesn't go full-fledged into the personality he is doing the imitation of. He is not honest and true. He's doing *his* point of view of Kirk Douglas.

WILDE: *Would Guy Marks fit into either of these categories?*

BERLE: Guy Marks is a big talent. He's an impressionist.

WILDE: *In your New York Times Magazine interview with Gilbert Milstein he explained that you felt "comics were men who depended on their material for laughs, while funny men were comics who could get a laugh before they even opened their mouths and who depended largely on what the trade calls 'sight gags' "* . . .

BERLE: Right.

WILDE: *Which category would you place yourself in?*

BERLE: Fortunately, I can do both, when the time comes for it. There is a different approach to each one. Like there is a different approach to motion pictures, there is a different approach to television, stage, and night clubs—they are all individual branches. If there is a hokey scene which is mostly visual there shouldn't be any jokes in it—the jokes come out of the visuality of it or the humor. If you are doing a verbal scene—a sketch like, "War Day at Macy's," which is tongue in cheek, or a satire or travesty on a sale, character is very important. When Gleason does "The Honeymooners," which is one of the great masterpieces of all times, he plays that guy he is playing.

WILDE: *Never comes out of character.*

BERLE: Right. Even though there is a lot of Gleason in it, he won't step down out of character to speak to the audience. He will not break up the sketch or the scene to do an ad-lib. Repeat that question.

WILDE: *Milstein wrote that you felt "comics depended on their material for laughs."*

BERLE: Yes, a comic is a guy who depends solely on the joke, and we have thousands of them. The comedian can get a laugh opening a door in the funny way that he does it and his attitude—that's a Comic versus a Comedian. Now a funnyman can get a laugh before he opens his mouth—looking funny. Lou Costello was one of your great funnymen. Harry Langdon, Larry Seaman; they were all funnymen—they looked funny. W. C. Fields was never a comedian. Slim Summerville was a comedian, yet looked funny. Now if you have both attributes, you are in good shape. There is a great line between the comic, the comedian the funnyman the buffoon and the clown. I don't maybe do everything well—but I know the difference.

WILDE: *You fall into more of those specific categories than any other funnyman in our time—being able to do so many different things.*

BERLE: Only because I made a research of it, like you're doing now. I have a file of four million jokes. I don't know if you know that. I have them cross-indexed. Whatever subject you want, I have a joke on it. They're in my vault—in my files. They're willed to the Library of Congress. I have sketches, scenes that have been done throughout the years from the *Vanities* and the *Scandals* and the *Follies* that go back to 1915—all the best of all the sketches and they all vary. One is satirical, one is right on the nose—what we call "funny-funny," one is all *verbal* one is all *low*, and I have made a study of all the characters and which direction they go—I can do it. I don't know if I can do them all well, but I can do them.

WILDE: *In that same article you stated there were certain basic premises of humor—insults, sight jokes, malaprops, puns or play on words, juxtaposition jokes or gags involving either mistaken identity or mistaken interpretation of something that is said. Are all jokes based on these formulas?*

BERLE: There are about eight or nine formulas. There's the Dumb Dora jokes like George Burns did with the late Gracie Allen. The phone rang and she says, "Oh, you are!" and hung up and George says, "Who was that?" and Gracie says, "That was a man and he said he was brown from the sun." Then the Maxie Rosenbloom type of joke, a malaprop. Saying, "This is a very auspicious occasion—some of my most ignorant friends are here." Misplacing words and putting words in the wrong places—that's malopropism. There is the one-liner, the block routines. . . .

WILDE: *By "Block" do you mean the comedy team of Block and Sully?*

BERLE: No, *block, chunks, segments,* like Abbott and Costello's "Who's on first base?" which is a play on words —mistaken identity, where one fella is talking about one subject and the other another. There's a sketch called "Selling a Car"—he wants to sell his car and the other guy thinks it's a girl he's got, so he says, "What about the bumpers?" The other guy says, "Oh, they're beautiful—you have to wash her every night." He's talking about the car. Another scene is packing a bag. It's an old burlesque routine called "This I Gotta See." Ben Blue did it for years. It's a split scene where the honeymoon couple check in and the guy's next door and his ear is against the wall and he thinks they are having an affair and they are just packing a bag. He says, "I can't get it in." She says, "Sit on it." "If you sit on it, I'll sit on you." "*You* sit on it and I'll sit on you." And the punch line, Ben Blue says, "This I gotta see!"

WILDE: *How do you decide if a joke is funny?*

BERLE: Just intuition, that's all.

WILDE: *Did you ever have a joke that got a big laugh for you consistently for a long time and then suddenly it stopped working for you?*

BERLE: No, never.

WILDE: *Is there such a thing as a "pure" ad-lib or are all so called ad-libs just joke plots that have been consciously or unconsciously remembered?*

BERLE: There are such things as ad-libs. I ad-lib a lot. I must say, what has become standard now as "savers" or "heckler squelchers" started as ad-libs. I used to have my secretaries or my brother or somebody write them down and I would say, "What did I say?" Last night I was at the opening of Nancy Ames—I introduced her—and at the end of her act I got up and applauded her, and one of the maitre d's came up and gave her a bouquet of flowers and I said (unconsciously in ad-lib) I said, "This is from Jerry Lewis' yacht."* Because it was topical, it was current, they laughed because of the fresh subject matter. The joke didn't have to be there—they knew it had to be an ad-lib. Knowing "stop" jokes (which has been said about me—I know a hundred and fifty thousand squelches—supposed ad-libs), the great line is, "His ad-libs aren't worth the paper they are written on." "Is that your nose or are you eating a banana?" . . . "Do you come in for entertainment or revenge?"—which are what we call "savers." Often, I intentionally put a weak joke in a monologue so I can do a saver.

WILDE: *Before you go out to perform, do you prepare yourself in any way—get into a mood or an attitude?*

BERLE: Oh, I'm clowning backstage or wherever I am so I can get myself . . . it's like working-out before a fight and shadow-boxing.

WILDE: *Is it necessary that a comedian be a totally different person onstage than he is offstage?*

BERLE: No. A comedian maybe yes, a comic no. That's another difference between a comic and comedian. A comic does a set, standard routine—monologue form—monologist style, which is pat: "I've got a girl and she's so thin that . . ." or a routine about a family and wife and the kids, the playpen, or "I'm breaking out of here"—whatever the rou-

---

* Jerry Lewis' yacht had sunk that day and it was headlined in all papers.

tines are about—they can recite this and they usually do when they are comics. The comedian usually has to get into it and think before he speaks and think before he goes on. The comedian is more of technician than the comic. There's a cliché . . . I was told this maybe thirty years ago: *If you don't believe yourself, believe in what you are saying on the stage, the audience won't believe it.* But the comic has forty minutes usually and he's gonna do them. I'm not bringing down comics, because I'm also a comic. The present-day comics who are very successful—we won't go into their names—are making ten to fifteen thousand dollars per week in cafés are complacent about their careers. They are making a mistake by not trying to enhance their careers by learning different traits and styles of the comedian.

WILDE: *Does that mean they can never make it really big?*

BERLE: Never! You see, they're hitting the big bracket and they think they have got it made. I don't know how long this lasts. They should develop a sense of timing without jokes. It was said that Ed Wynn could get a laugh by reading the telephone book or a newspaper.

WILDE: *Being funny requires the use of many sensory and physical and emotional attributes. Do comedians develop these characteristics to a finer degree than other performers?*

BERLE: Right.

WILDE: *Are the psychological motivating factors—the drive to become a successful comedian—the same as for singers and dancers and actors?*

BERLE: More. In the first place, it's much harder to get a laugh than to be a singer. It's much harder to get a laugh on the screen than to do straight drama. That's why I started off as an actor because it's easier to do dramatics than comedy. There's a thing called audience identification. You have to be *somebody* on the stage. I am brash, flippant, aggressive, smart-alecky. But unlike the present-day level comedians—the merchants of venom—I will throw a line at somebody in the audience . . . "Madam, will you pull down your dress?" and the audience will laugh. And I say, "Your legs, they look like Sonny Liston's." Then I will save it and save face with this woman *and* the audience by saying, "I'm only kidding." I will take the curse off by adding a little so-called humility. Years ago when I was a kid telling jokes, a guy wrote me up in Jersey City, He said, "Mr. Berle (even though I was eighteen) tells a joke like a kid eating an apple with an innocence." Now innocence is my audience identification. Smart-alecky, but innocent of it. Rather than on purpose, it comes out accidentally.

WILDE: *Is getting ahead in show business the same as becoming a success in any other profession?*

BERLE: You see, we are specialists—no matter what we do in our business. If you sing or you dance or you tell jokes, you are a specialist. If you are in the automotive industry—it's easy to sell cars. We are not running a factory. We have no one working for us but ourselves. We are our own workhouse. We are our own outlet and there are hundreds of thousands of us and there aren't hundreds of thousands of other people like us. It's a very special business.

WILDE: *How important is it for a comedian to have a good memory?*

BERLE: You mean to memorize? Well, I've always worked by the old saying, "Security is knowing your lines." Be it any branch of the profession. If you have to learn a song or a play, you gotta have a fairly retentive memory.

WILDE: *You did for television what Al Jolson did for talking pictures. As a pioneer in TV, what problem did you encounter trying to sustain the quality of a new show each week?*

BERLE: It was murder. It was a rat race. The writers used to come in after the show Tuesday night at nine and start kissing on the lips. "You did it again!" "Wonderful!" or "It wasn't wonderful—it was good!." I said, "Thank you, boys, what are we going to do next week?" In those early TV days, it was very, very difficult getting new material every week. The first year I was on, '48 and '49, I didn't even have a writer. I just remembered what I did for the last twenty years 'cause we couldn't afford a writer—there wasn't any money. So it was a pretty difficult thing and the facilities were difficult.

WILDE: *With the advent of motion pictures new devices and new ways to make people laugh were created—things that were not possible on the stage—like chase scenes and hanging from flagpoles, falling off trains. A whole new world of comedy opened up. What new horizons in comedy were made possible by television?*

BERLE: Well, I don't know. I don't think anything is new. Nothing is old, let's say, unless you have seen and heard it before. I don't think motion pictures lent anything to TV. It's a different technique altogether. I think TV lent a lot of things to motion pictures—such as the "three-camera" shows, like Dick Van Dyke and Danny Thomas. They save time with motion pictures after they saw the technique.

WILDE: *Three cameras shooting at one time?*

BERLE: One time. The wide shot, the close-up, and the medium. On the motion picture set they have a monitor now and they know how it's going to turn out before it's made into the rushes. That's the reverse of what you are asking.

WILDE: *What suggestions can you make to someone wanting to become a comedian?*

BERLE: The suggestion that was made to me before we had TV or even night club style shows: Keep your ears open, keep your eyes open, watch and study. The young girl or fellow who has the aspiration to be a comedian or a comedienne in their teens, or young people who feel they have a funnybone—the quickest way I think which has been proven—is to make an album. The kids today, be it Desi and Schwartz, or Paul Revere and His Riders, Clyde and Clydes, or Gomer and his Four Pyles, they make a home record and it may turn out to be a very big hit. They have this new machine called the Sony, which is this instant tape machine. Make a screen test of yourself . . . see how you look . . . see what not to do. Go and make this tape. Get in front of it. Make funny faces, do a routine, and play it back. Don't rush. I think the quickest way today is to go out and make a funny album—get it played and you might get lucky. The other way is to get yourself under the umbrella of somebody big, even if you have to be a third or second banana, and work your way up. Bill Dana was my page boy at NBC getting six dollars or something and now he's the producer of my show, getting seventy-five hundred a week. But he took his time. He became a writer. Many good writers turn into comics and comedians and vice-versa. If you think you are funny—if you think funny—put it down on paper. There's not only a world of being a comedian or comic, there's just as much money and success in being a writer or producer, if you are stuck on show business.

WILDE: *What would you advise a young comedian to do to get material?*

BERLE: I think experience is very important. There are so many summer theatres, where they can carry a spear, where they can see a stock comedian. Watch 'em. Get that experience of what's not supposed to be done . . . what's supposed to be done. How he walks, how he talks. One of the most important things is what I did until I found myself as Berle, and that is pattern yourself after someone you admire, even if you have to imitate them. Now I gave Alan King advice eighteen years ago. Alan had no money to buy material. He didn't have a style or an image. He patterned himself after me, and he did *schtick*,* one-liners. He did a lot of my stuff, which I didn't mind because it wasn't all mine anyway—but my style. One night at the Latin Quarter at a benefit (my mother was the president), he got up and he got mad that he couldn't get over there on time because of the cabs. He started to knock the cabs and he got laughs and he was pretty funny, and after it was over I said, "Allan, you hit it. That's it. You found yourself." He said, "I don't know what you mean." "What you said on the floor, that's your character. Get mad, put down everything, dig everything." Now he's doing routines on "insurance," "airplanes"—which is Alan. He stuck with a character. It does take time to develop a characterization and be a great comedian. You have got to have an image. So a youngster should look up to somebody they admire—their style—pattern themselves after them, and then after a while when they get security and self-assurance, start to branch out and find their own niche.

* Piece of business.

Shelley Berman

Shelley Berman was born in Chicago on February 3, 1926. He spent ten years as an actor playing summer stock and television while supplementing his meager income with jobs as a cab driver, social director, drug store manager, and ballroom dancing instructor.

In 1955, Shelley joined the Compass Players in Chicago, a group of talented actors who did comic improvisations in a cabaret on the North Side. (Barbara Harris, Mike Nichols, and Elaine May were also members at that time.)

He soon developed his own act and rapidly gained recognition in the country's top night clubs and best television shows.

His first three comedy albums for Verve Records made show business history. "Inside Shelley Berman," "Outside Shelley Berman," and "The Edge of Shelley Berman" were the first non-musical records ever to gross over a million dollars each.

Mr. Berman has appeared in the films *The Best Man* and *Divorce American Style,* with Dick Van Dyke and Debbie

Reynolds. He is the author of *Shelley Berman's Cleans and Dirty's*, published by Price, Stern and Sloan.

Shelley and his wife Sarah were married in 1947 and live in Beverly Hills with their adopted children, Joshua Getzel and Rachel, five French poodles, an XKE Jaguar and a 1952 Army Jeep.

A Shelley Berman monologue

Hello, desk clerk . . . ah, desk clerk, no, I want the desk clerk. Desk clerk, oh, Berman, seven oh two. Ah, just checked in. No, everything is all right. I just wanted to tell you about one thing—I don't seem to, ah, to have a window. No, I looked. No, I looked over there, too. I don't have a window I'm pretty sure about that. No, there's nothing specific I want to see. I'd like a window if I can get hold of one. No, I don't know why . . . I really feel a man should have a window wherever he goes. I didn't think to request a window when I booked the room. I thought for sure I had one. Well, I have everything else, wallpaper, Utrillo prints, the Gideon Bible. I have everything, I just don't have a window.

No, there's plenty of hot water—from both taps. I wanted to ask you about that in case I get thirsty during the night. You know the dresser, four drawers . . . three of them are painted on. Now why is that? Getting, getting back to that window. What do you think we can do about getting one installed or finding the one we have. Where do you think I'd find it? Near which door? Well, now, that's, that's the other thing I wanted to ask you about, sir. I can't find my door, sir, I don't know where it is. I'm not denying I have a door, there must be. I didn't materialize in here, but I cannot find the damned door. That's all I'm saying, where can I find it? Near which window? I don't have a window.

Wouldn't that be an odd place to put a door next to a window? I mean, if you walk through, you'd fall out of the building, wouldn't you, sir? I have one door over here, but that's the door to my closet. Oh, I thought I had one. Well, then, uh, well, then, maybe that's the door to my bathroom. You're kidding. Well, where is it? I don't need a pencil. Just tell me how to find it will you please. Yeah . . . yeah . . . yeah, just a minute, I'll get a pencil. I'll be right with you. Will you talk a little slower—it's difficult for me to write. Well, it's dark in here. I would, if I could find the switch. There is no light switch between the window and the door, sir. I'm not admitting I have a window and a door, sir, all I'm saying is if there was a window and a door, there wouldn't be a light switch there. [*Pause*] Well, I know because the first thing I did when I came in was feel all the walls and there was no light switch. Will ya do me a favor and send me up a bellhop with some candles? Well, where are they? Well, what time do you reopen? Is this place closed at night? Well, how about your other guests, how do they feel about this? I am? Goodbye!

AUTHOR Rona Jaffe, a mutual friend, arranged this meeting. Mr. Berman was a most gracious host. We talked in his exquisitely furnished den, fortified with refreshment served by his wife, Sarah.

Shelley greeted me barefoot, wearing tattered Levi's rolled up to the calf, a worn white sweatshirt and a straw hat which he maneuvered into various shapes throughout the afternoon. Though his dress was casual and relaxed, he was quite nervous and chain-smoked Kents during our talk.

Later, Shelley proudly showed me around his twenty-room Spanish style home, complete with swimming pool and garden overlooking Los Angeles.

We continued to chat long after the official interview was over. Soon his lovely secretary, Patricia Perry, entered with the revised version of the first act of Shelley's new play, which he proceeded to read.

If just one act can be a criterion, it appears Mr. Berman will yet have another medal of success to wear on his chest.

WILDE: *Your comedy evolves from situations rather than from jokes. What made you choose this particular approach to making an audience laugh?*

BERMAN: I don't think you *choose* an approach. I think the word that you used—"evolve"—is the important word. I didn't choose. It simply was the way that I performed. What I thought would sound funny and what struck me funny. It isn't something you decide upon. You just do it.

WILDE: *What is the difference between a routine consist-ing of jokes and one where the laughter comes from a situation?*

BERMAN: Well, even when the laughter comes from a situation it comes out of what I think may be defined as a joke. First of all, we may begin by splitting hairs about the definition and the semantics involved with the word "joke." I think whatever really makes you laugh can be called a joke. The form and the execution of the joke is what will determine its difference, but I know what you're saying. You're saying a funny moment that arises out of a performed or articulated or related situation as opposed to a funny moment which arises on say a pun, a play on words, or a statement—a "one-liner" in which the result is a mom-ent of laughter. I don't think that one is more valuable than the other. Anything that makes you laugh is of some value.

WILDE: *What are the problems in developing situation pieces as opposed to the formula gag construction? The step-by-step process?*

BERMAN: The way I work is I do an action which is really Aristotelean in its process. I don't know if I adhere, neces-sarily, to the poetics or the unities, but I do know a play or a playlet is an action. It requires a conflict. It requires some-body who wants to do something and a problem in the way of doing it—not necessarily an obstacle, but *you* want some-thing and somebody doesn't want you to have it—a conflict. Or you say something and somebody disagrees with you— you have a conflict. I must get in that door. Somebody doesn't want me in that door. We have a conflict. You also have a structure of obstacles within the framework of the conflict. The reason I can't get in the door is the bell is broken—or the person inside can't hear me, so that the main action is: Entry. Let's say the main action is entry. The obstacles are those things which keep you from entering, from going into that room.

WILDE: *Could you be more specific . . . use one of your routines?*

BERMAN: All right, let's trace it from the beginning in my favorite piece—the one I feel is of most value, at least to *me*. I play the part of my father and I am supposed to be at the other end of the phone asking for a hundred dollars to go to acting school. That is the "action."

WILDE: *Is that particular piece most indicative of your point of view?*

BERMAN: No, it doesn't typify my work—it's a very specific routine. But it's the best way to describe what I'm trying to say. In this one, I am portraying my father. I don't want my son to go to acting school. There is our initial conflict. The obstacles which arise out of that conflict or are a result of that conflict or which are demonstrated during that conflict . . . the fact that I am on a completely different cultural level than the boy that is requesting a hundred dollars. I can't conceive of anybody wanting to go to acting school. I also don't believe there can be any good result from this. I dislike actors. I dislike show business. I dislike everything about this. There's another obstacle . . . I speak with a foreign accent—an enormous cultural gulf. The idea that my son will be going away to New York rather than staying in Chicago is another barrier.

WILDE: *While you were creating this routine did you put all these components down on paper?*

BERMAN: No. I improvise my pieces when I begin—even

when I write material or when I write a play (as I am doing now) I play the parts here alone in my studio. I play various roles. I improvise. Eventually they become *set* . . . after repeating the routine about three or four times you know pretty well what lines you want to lay in and the lines you want to keep—how you want to edit. It becomes a set routine after awhile, then it can be written. In this particular case, we are talking about the development of a *situation* routine—playing the action provides me with sufficient humor because I can somehow draw on whatever ability I have to recall. I can imagine certain words being said or I can recall subconsciously conversations that I have heard, or lines I have heard, or words I have heard, and bring them all out into this context. So starting with and playing only the "action," I have learned that I am able to create a piece of comedy.

WILDE: *What was the very first routine you did professionally?*

BERMAN: A piece called "The Morning After the Night Before," which was an improvisation in Chicago when I was with the Compass Players. The suggestion was made for somebody to do the morning after the night before and on that night I couldn't find a partner to work with, so I simply used the telephone as the device. That's how the telephone began.

WILDE: *What exactly were the Compass Players? How did they come about? And was that the beginning of your entry into comedy?*

BERMAN: Yes. It was organized by a University of Chicago student, Dave Shepard. We were a group of improvisationists. We worked on the very same basis as the commedia dell'arte—we performed in cabarets, saloons, making about fifty-five or sixty bucks a week. We simply improvised plays, one-acts, sketches, blackouts. We did a variety of improvisations.

WILDE: *Up to this point you had never done any comedy?*

BERMAN: I had been funny at parties, which is a colossal bore, but that's what I was—the lampshade man. But I was moderately humorous—nothing memorable. I was funny much more than witty. I never was a Disraeli or Voltaire.

WILDE: *What is the difference between "improvisation" and "ad-lib"?*

BERMAN: There's really not much difference, because an ad-lib is an improvisation—it's a matter of length, a matter of degree. If you do ten minutes of ad-libbing, you have done an improvisation. If you ad-lib a single line, you have an ad-libitum, which really means a spontaneous moment of wit. I don't think it is necessarily equated with humor— you can ad-lib a speech.

WILDE: *Having developed several comedy routines with the Compass Players, you then had enough material with which to go out and work?*

BERMAN: Yes, there are a lot of people who are very gifted comedicly, but can't somehow fall upon that routine or fall upon that amount of material essential to get one started. You can have a great talent for comedy yet not have a *comedy act*. Now Dick Van Dyke is a very good example of this. He never was a comedy *act*—tried to be, but he wasn't a good one. Jackie Gleason was a pretty bad comedy *act*—

WILDE: *—But a fine comedy actor.*

BERMAN: Yes. Now in both cases these men had *enormous* talent, but they were without a comedy act. It is a matter of coincidence that I found a place in which to develop a comedy act. If I couldn't, I'd still be looking for work today.

WILDE: *What difficulties did you encounter after you made the decision to become a professional?*

BERMAN: The biggest problem was the hurdle of introducing a new comedy form in our time. It was not a new comedy form for *all* time—there have been monologists before, and that's what I was essentially, a monologist. When I began, I only had beginnings, middles, and ends of routines. I had nothing between them. I came out and said, "We will now do a phone call about," or "Have you ever been in a situation which?" and then I did the routine, finished that, took a bow, then started the next routine. So I was not, in the strict sense of the word, a comedian. I was unable at the very first to cope with the kind of atmosphere in a night club. Now in the days of vaudeville a man came onto the stage—he had a proscenium, he had distance from the audience, and he also had all the chairs facing him, and people weren't drinking booze. He was able to do a quiet, gentle, more subtle, full monologue. Now when vaudeville disappeared and the night club arose with a *different* set of circumstances all together, the monologist languished. He was unable to cope with the problems presented. Then the *new* comedian was born—the one-liner, the "tumler" (which means noise, the noise-maker)—the man who is strong, quick with the ad-libs, and able to handle the drunks —with the turned-up brim and fast talk. The pioneers, of course: Jack E. Leonard, Milton Berle, Jackie Miles . . . I can't even think of the number of great ones who really made a new form of comedy happen—that was night club comedy.*

---

* Comedians Morey Amsterdam, Joey Adams, Jerry and Buddy Lester, Phil Foster, Jan Murray, and Gene Baylos were also a part of and contributed greatly to this era.

WILDE: *How long does it take you to write one piece of comedy material—from the moment you get the idea until it is polished to meet your standards for a set piece?*

BERMAN: It all depends on what you are doing. There are pieces that you can write very quickly—I mean write in the way that I told you. I improvise them very quickly. Sometimes you put a certain piece down in writing, depends on the kind of thing you are doing, but I can't really give you a time because there are too many different forms. That "airline" routine, which seems to have stuck with me for years and I haven't done that piece since 1960—that was a matter of one joke, a joke I added to, on one end and on the other end in ensuing performances. So it took me about six months before that piece became a routine. The father and son piece I talked about took me about a year to finish because I kept trying it and trying it. I performed it many, many times and I took it back to the drawing board and re-did it and performed it again, then dropped it for a few months and then performed it again.

WILDE: *Does each piece run a specific number of minutes?*

BERMAN: Generally, a good piece runs about seven. Many of my pieces run much longer, but a good piece runs short because sometimes you want to use it on television. That's one reason the newer comedians are cleaner in night clubs. They are doing their material with an eye toward performing them eventually on television, so you have less smut, less risqué humor, in your night clubs.

WILDE: *Are you able to perform each line the same way every time you do it?*

BERMAN: You can't perform it the same way each time. It's impossible. Just get rid of that idea right away. When you get into a room before an audience where there is some disturbance or some lack of attention which means you push a little harder or you may do quite the opposite—you may find an audience is enjoying a specific form of delivery which affects the way you handle your sketches, your routines. You must retain spontaneity, but you can't deliver your routines in the same way each night. You can't. You simply can't. Each night presents you with an entirely different atmosphere.

WILDE: *Do you have a technique you use to help you?*

BERMAN: I use the actor's technique. An actor who performs a role in a play for a period of years can't approach it the same each night's performance. He can't *imitate himself*. Frequently, we fall into the trap of imitating ourselves, but that certainly isn't a virtue. You try as hard as you can to approach it as a *fresh* performance.

WILDE: *Did you ever have a single joke or entire piece of material that got big laughs for a long time and then suddenly, for no explicable reason, it doesn't get the same reaction?*

BERMAN: Yes! Yes!

WILDE: *Why is that?*

BERMAN: Don't ask *me*. Yes . . . you have a line that has been working for you and working for you and suddenly ceases working for you. I have tried to analyze it on more than one occasion. There are too many reasons, and it would take a long time to tell them to you. The easiest is to say that you have done something with that specific line . . . you are doing something different . . . doing it a little differently. In my analysis of these occasions it is not the specific line which is no longer getting a laugh, it is something you are doing *before* it. You have started to play the routine in a little different way.

WILDE: *You begin to lose the psychological illusion of the first time?*

BERMAN: Nope, you are talking about the same line. We are not talking about the line that doesn't get the laugh anymore. We are talking about the line in the context of the act, of the routine, the routine has changed somewhat. To try to pin *that* down is almost impossible. Actors have it in plays all the time. The line which has always gotten a laugh suddenly stops getting a laugh. That line is beyond help unless you return to something *prior* to it and the exact atmosphere in which that line had been spoken on all previous occasions.

WILDE: *How did your sitting on the stool come about?*

BERMAN: When I began, all I had were telephone calls, and I can't imagine anyone doing a ten-minute phone call standing up, so I wanted to sit down. In night clubs the stage was too low—if I sat in a chair, I couldn't be seen, so I borrowed a bar stool. That's exactly what happened. From that came a kind of attitude, something that set me apart. All I did was the little one-act type things—primarily with the phone. Then I was almost the vehicle for my material. The transformation comes when you use the material as vehicle for yourself and you begin to perform outside of the routine. You do other things. You begin to play with your audience more, in night clubs and concerts. You break away from your script, you begin to relax a little bit and find moments of spontaneous humor which are there for the picking.

WILDE: *The vocabulary and the references in your rou-*

*tines are in many cases highly intellectual. Do you require
a better educated audience to fully appreciate your humor?*

BERMAN: If I had to have a better educated audience, I
couldn't have drawn crowds and sold those records. I don't
equate a polysyllabic word with intellect at all. Just because
I use a few esoteric references and occasionally use a big
word, it doesn't mean anything. You can't play to a specific
audience. You have to play to everybody—that's bread and
butter. When you play as many times as I have on television
. . . you don't get invited back again if you are only appealing to a certain group. I don't assume that the majority is
uneducated. I assume that the majority is educated and I
also assume that if they are not educated, at least they have
sense enough to know what I am talking about. Maybe not
catch on to a certain word or reference, but that doesn't
make them uneducated, nor does it make them stupid.

WILDE: *There is an economic and cultural distinction
between the people who frequent the off-beat, so called chi-
chi rooms like the Hungry I (San Francisco), Mr. Kelly's
(Chicago), and the Blue Angel (New York), than those who
go to the Copacabana (New York), the Americana Hotel
(New York), or the Fontainebleau Hotel (Miami Beach). Is
there any difference in the reaction in the audience when
you play these rooms?*

BERMAN: No difference. Not at all. Either you make them
laugh or you don't.

WILDE: *Did you change your material for the "commercial" clubs?*

BERMAN: No. No! Listen those chi-chi rooms are just as
commercial as any room. That's a lot of nonsense. There's
no such thing as a chi-chi room. A night club is a night club.

Just because it is small, they call it a chi-chi room, or because they bring in certain oddball forms of entertainment.

WILDE: *Certainly a business executive or a secretary in a large firm has a better education or is a little more sophisticated than a woman say in the foothills of Pennsylvania.*

BERMAN: That's a bunch of crap. That's pure hokum—junk. That's nonsense!

WILDE: *Then what they will laugh at in a club in Pennsylvania, they should laugh at in a chi-chi room and vice-versa?*

BERMAN: They do—they *will,* not *should.* This snobbish attitude is absurd, it makes no sense at all. A comedian who can only make a certain group laugh just better get with it or he ain't gonna be there very long. You've got to make a lot of people laugh, and I suspect that the woman who lives in the foothills is . . . can see a moment of humor just as easily as anybody else. She just may see it better than anybody else cause she isn't clouded.

WILDE: *In certain instances you mention Kafka. You make many esoteric references that this average woman is not familiar with.*

BERMAN: Yes, I sure do. It was okay at the beginning, but after awhile you sort of grow out of that. A lot of people may not have read André Gide. I'm fed up to the chin with this so-called intelligentsia. It's a lot of nonsense. Suppose they have read André Gide but haven't read Gertrude Stein. They may not have read Camus or Kierkegaard. So, all right, an occasional reference, for that little in-group that wants its own little chuckle occasionally, but they're no more bright or more informed than—maybe they are more informed, but we're talking about comedy, not information. We're talking about what makes people laugh.

WILDE: *The point is that on some of your earlier records—*

BERMAN: *Earlier. Earlier* is the key. When I began, I was a darling of a certain select cult or . . .

WILDE: *Then you do admit that as the years have gone by—*

BERMAN: Admit? I brag about improving my comedy area. I've improved and enlarged my comedy devices. I'll trip over my feet, I'll do *hokum,* I'll do *farce.* I'll do anything to make people laugh, as long as I think it's funny.

WILDE: *Do you have certain lines or jokes you use as a barometer when you first come out, to tell if the audience will be receptive?*

BERMAN: No. You don't use them as a barometer. However they become a barometer. Youl don't really employ them that way. You go out and tell those jokes, but you know from the first few minutes a little bit more about the audience you are going to play to. You can tell, but the joke itself is not a barometer. You get an attitude, but that doesn't help things, it doesn't change things. It will determine the way in which you will execute some of your work but it doesn't determine the words you'll use or the language.

WILDE: *How about which pieces of material to use?*

BERMAN: No, it may cut it. If you find a room full of heckling drunks, which is not that frequent, but if you *do* find hecklers or tired people, you may decide that certain pieces won't fit this show. It's more a matter of what you cut than what you replace it with.

WILDE: *Why do audiences react differently to the same piece of material on different nights?*

BERMAN: I wish you could tell *me*. I don't know. But I do know that they do react differently. I can face an audience and have an entire show which is "down"—but it's down only in your own terms. It's down relatively. You remember your best show or you remember the loudest laughing audience. The audience that is before you now, on this particular occasion, if they're not laughing loud, you say they are not receiving you or not accepting you, and it may be that they *are* receiving you and accepting you, but they don't know what happened last night. They don't know what's being missed. There are times, of course, when it is a bad show, when you're not working well, when the audience does not come to you with a willing suspension of disbelief—when they have not come too "ready."

WILDE: *What are the reasons they may not be "ready" to receive you?*

BERMAN: I don't know. I really don't know that. There might be a great variety of reasons. I know that on *Sunday* nights it is very tough, on Saturady night it is very easy.

WILDE: *When the audience does not react as well as you think they should, what do you do?*

BERMAN: There isn't much you can do except do your best show. Sometimes, in the vernacular of the business, you "go out and get 'em." There are ways of doing that, there are devices. You may leave the planned show and try to perk up your audience by ad-libbing with them—joking with them to get to them. The comedian who makes the mistake of developing a hostility towards his audience—which is a common thing, we all do that on occasion. You have to fight the desire to become hostile. The comedian who says, "These are the jokes, folks" is making a mistake, but we are all prone to make an error of this kind.

WILDE: *Is it easier to make an audience laugh in a television studio or concert hall than in a night club?*

BERMAN: Not necessarily easier. On television it is very difficult because you don't have time to warm up your audience, and in a night club performance if eight minutes doesn't work, you have more time to make up for it. You can joke about it and do some other stuff. On TV you shoot the wad in six or eight minutes, and you either made them laugh or you didn't and there's thirty-five million people watching you at that time . . . and you could really bomb in that few minutes. But you get a large sum of money to take that chance.

WILDE: *Is it a matter of luck?*

BERMAN: It's not luck. Maybe the bit isn't funny that night. You got a bit that's always worked for you and you get in the studio and there are three hundred people in the studio audience and they're busy looking at the cameraman. What are you gonna do? There's nothing you can do about that. On the concert stage you generally have a better chance because the people are there only for one reason, that is, to see you and to enjoy you.

WILDE: *Do you believe there were certain childhood traumas or experiences that motivated you to become a comedian?*

BERMAN: Oh, well, I don't know about that. I don't know what makes me a comedian. I don't know what makes anybody funny or un-funny. I don't know about traumas or my subconscious or that my parents didn't love me. I don't know what *makes* a comedian a comedian. I don't know what makes a man complain in a certain way, and generally a comedian has a complaint—a peculiar oblique complaint which he disguises in a specific way.

WILDE: *Is it important for a comedian to be educated?*

BERMAN: Yes ... my God, yes! He must be educated, but I don't know how you define *education*.

WILDE: *I wasn't thinking necessarily of* formal *education—most comedians are self-educated men.*

BERMAN: That's all—and self-educated in what *way?* Maybe they were educated in ways that you never dreamt. Maybe they had never read a book. There are comedians today who don't bother with such things. But there is another form of education. There is a guy who has a fantastic ear, who listens well, and he is able to take what he hears and translate it into a lovely moment of humor. He has educated himself, but maybe he is educated about a very specific item—the dialogue of longshoremen, the dialogue of truck drivers or farmers or golfers.

WILDE: *Do you read a lot?*

BERMAN: I read, yes, but I don't know if that's essential. I read for the pleasure of reading—to satisfy my curiosity, not to become educated. Education is the least important of man's achievements. Being born with a curiosity is the most important gift that God can bestow upon any individual. What he will do with what he learns by virtue of his curiosity—that's exciting, that's wonderful. But who the hell cares about some knowledgeable man—some guy who knows all about everything and doesn't function with it?

WILDE: *What advice would you give to someone now who decided to become a comedian?*

BERMAN: Frankly, speaking, the most important piece of advice I can give is not to take anybody's advice. Somehow, some way, that individual will find himself. He'll see it, he'll learn it . . . he'll do it if he has a capacity for it. Not only the talent but the capacity to take the disappointments, the heartbreak. (That's involved in any business.)

Joey Bishop

Joey Bishop was born Joseph Abraham Gottlieb on February 3, 1918, in the Bronx, New York. He began his show business career as part of a group called the Bishop Brothers Trio.

After World War II, Joey went out on his own and was soon playing the top hotels and night clubs throughout America. Introduced to television audiences by virtue of his many appearances with Jack Paar, Mr. Bishop became a nationally known comedian.

For three years Joey did a situation comedy series on TV and he is presently the host of a late night show for the ABC network. His motion picture credits include: *Oceans 11, Texas Across the River, Guide for the Married Man,* and *Who's Minding the Mint?*

Mr. Bishop is married to the former Sylvia Ruzga and they have one son, Larry.

Excerpts from a Joey Bishop monologue

This is a nice family crowd—so many middle-aged men with their daughters.

I'd like to work one club—just one club—where they have a Jewish orchestra and Spanish people dancing.

I was in *The Naked and the Dead*. I played both parts.

In my new movie, I play the part of a psychoneurotic Robin Hood. I steal from the rich, but I keep it.

"Momma," I said to her in 1942, "I'm going into the Army." She told me, "All right, but don't come home late!"

My doctor is wonderful. Once, in 1955, when I couldn't afford an operation, he touched up the X-rays.

I like working in Hollywood as opposed to New York. You get paid three hours earlier.

I put Dean Martin on my show one night, and wherever he went the next day people recognized him.

If Senta Berger married Corbett Monica—today, she would be Senta Monica.

When asked how I hurt my back I told them, "I fell off a series!"

The series was cancelled in spite of excellent ratings. One week we beat out "Let Us Pray!"

SITTING ON THE living room sofa of his Beverly Hills home, wearing a brown Paisley bathrobe, face unshaven, hair uncombed, Joey Bishop is the same man audiences throughout America have enjoyed for over thirty years. Serious, pensive, disarming, he chatted with the same charm (despite his costume) and assurance he projects on the television tube.

Bishop spoke authoritatively, completely secure in his views on comedy, as well as in his philosophy of life. He continually removed Kents from a nearby glass cigarette box and smoked while listening to the question being framed. His long-time friend and former partner, Mel, contributed to the relaxed atmosphere by serving coffee throughout the meeting.

WILDE: *While you were with the Bishop Brothers, did you have any idea or plan to one day do an act by yourself?*

BISHOP: No . . . no. But then the war came . . .

WILDE: *You worked with the trio prior to World War II?*

BISHOP: Oh, yeah. 1938 until '41.

WILDE: *And then you went into the service?*

BISHOP: I went in in '42. Mel went in before me and Rummy went in after me.

WILDE: *Did you get your own bookings?*

BISHOP: More or less. In those times, there were local agents, like Pete Iodice in Detroit . . . Al Norton, in Rochester. They used to put you in with a revue. Like, they had the Bishop Brothers and the Eight Cocktail Girls. We would augment the revue.

WILDE: *What did the act consist of?*

BISHOP: A lot of shit. No, it consisted of satires on radio programs. *Lights Out, We the People, Gangbusters.* Rummy did all the commentator impressions—Boake Carter, Westbrook Van Vorhis, the *March of Time* voice. Mel sung and I did all the comedy and dramatic impressions. Actually, it only stayed together about three years, until I went into the service. When I came out, Mel stayed in—he was an officer. Rummy didn't come out until about ten months after. I got discharged at Brook General Hospital, Fort Sam Houston, Texas, but I couldn't leave town because my wife was ill. So I went to work in a place called the Mountain Top Dinner Club—for Captain and Mrs. Talmadge. I stayed there twelve weeks, until my wife was well.

WILDE: *Doing an act?*

BISHOP: Doing a single, yeah. In the meantime, Bob Lee, an orchestra leader who was working the St. Anthony Hotel in San Antone, went up to the Mountain Top Club and he called the Morris Office about me, said, "I saw a kid that would be very good." So, they sent me a wire and said, "When you leave San Antone, let us know" and they booked me in the Greenwich Village Inn. I worked there with Joan Barry, who had just overcome the Charlie Chaplin incident. Then Barry Gray came in for four weeks.

WILDE: *He did a radio show there?*

BISHOP: No, he did a show as a comic.

WILDE: *Barry Gray has always been a successful radio personality. I never knew he did an act.*

BISHOP: Yeah. As a matter of fact, he had all the jokes written and he read them and as each one bombed, he threw it on the floor. When I followed him, I picked them up and said, "You should read the other side," and I pretended to read jokes from there.

WILDE: *Then that was the beginning of an act for you?*

BISHOP: Right. Well, I could always do the impressions. I did Cantor, Jolson, Robinson, Cagney, Fred Allen. . . . I used them as a crutch for my comedy. I originated lines like, "Cagney—five thousand a week and he can't afford a belt."

WILDE: *Did you write your own material?*

BISHOP: I *never* write my stuff. I do what I call "thought humor." If the thought went through my mind, I'd go out and do it without writing it.

WILDE: *And if it worked it became a part of your act.*

BISHOP: Right.

WILDE: *If it didn't you eliminated it.*

BISHOP: It rarely didn't work because if it didn't work I would do something on top of it to salvage it. In other words, if it bombed, it would afford me the opportunity of getting funny about its bombing.

WILDE: *Many people in show business point to you as the classic example of the performer who took twenty years to become a star overnight. As you look back now, why do you feel it took so long to become recognized?*

BISHOP: There are many reasons why someone doesn't become recognized. A new style—until people get used to it —can take a certain amount of time. No exposure, not being known, can take you a long time. In those days there was no

television, so consequently I had to . . . "Okay, he did good
in New York, let's see how he does in Chicago, let's see how
he does in Detroit, let's see how he does in Buffalo." And
three or four or five years could go by. I don't think it really
took me that long. I started working in '46, and in '49 I was
the comic with Tony Martin at the Chez Paree—twelve
weeks. In '49 I headlined the Latin Quarter in New York
for fourteen weeks.

WILDE: *In his autobiography,* Groucho and Me, *Groucho
Marx wrote that "all comedians arrive by trial and error."
During those years were you consciously experimenting to
find your comedic attitude?*

BISHOP: No. No. I don't think you experiment with a
comedic attitude. You experiment with a routine. Now,
there is a difference. A routine can be terribly funny and
still have no attitude about it. On the other hand, you can
do no routine and still have a certain attitude and be terribly funny.

WILDE: *What is the comedic attitude, then?*

BISHOP: It is not a comedic attitude. It is rather an attitude of life that produces the comedic end of it.

WILDE: *The end result?*

BISHOP: Right. I'm sure you know many friends who are
not comedians, who are terribly funny because of an attitude they have toward life. Not because of an attitude they
have toward comedy. My attitude was always one of being
overheard rather than *heard.* The audience thought only
they individually heard me. The others did not hear me. So
you'd hear people say, "Did you hear what he said?" Of
course, if *you* heard, naturally *he* heard. That's why people
sometimes were kind of shocked when I said something

clever. You know, terribly brilliant. They were shocked because I didn't say it loud, I said it softly and people would say, "What a chance he took. You got something that clever to say, why don't you say it loud?"

WILDE: *Then, in essence, this was a part of your personality you were simply bringing on stage?*

BISHOP: Yes. Well, not so much of a personality but attitude toward life. I don't like loud people who want to be heard. Speak softly and carry a big stick. And the big stick in my case was a clever line.

WILDE: *Is there any luck involved in getting ahead in show business, or do you have to make your own breaks?*

BISHOP: I don't know what you mean by luck. We're dealing now with semantics. What does the word luck mean? Luck cannot sustain you. Only talent can sustain you. Luck can be working in a lounge somewhere and having a big director come in, who has a few drinks and thinks you're a riot that night, and under the influence of alcohol signs you to a picture—that's luck. But if you have talent, you will then sustain it. And if you don't have talent and it was only luck, then it's all over.

WILDE: *What about making your own breaks? Taking advantage of opportunities?*

BISHOP: That's not my way of life, so I don't know. But that doesn't mean that that's not right. It's just not my way of life. I don't like to start a day fighting. I don't like to start a day organizing that day. I feel *que sera, sera.* If you become that ambitious, you plan every day, even if you attain the goal, look how much of life you've lost in the attainment thereof.

WILDE: *To what degree were Jack Paar and Frank Sinatra responsible for your success?*

BISHOP: Well, Frank Sinatra using you as a comic was kind of a stamp of approval, which made it very good, 'cause in show business the one thing you strive for is acceptance. You would rather walk out and be acknowledged than have to work eight minutes for that recognition.

WILDE: *To prove yourself before they do accept you?*

BISHOP: Right, right. When Frank Sinatra takes you on the show, they say, "He must be good, otherwise Frank wouldn't have him on." So there is a point of acceptance, a stamp of approval, immediately. What Jack Paar did was make it national for me. Remember, in those days, if Jack Paar had you back three or four times, you were a hit.

WILDE: *If you could put a label or name on it, how would you describe the type of comedy you do?*

BISHOP: It's a camouflage. Whatever success I've had in comedy is based on the fact that I don't look like I'm gonna say something that's terribly clever. I think I was the first night club comic to use the word "folks" to hip audiences. "Now, come on, folks, be fair."

WILDE: *This was disarming . . .*

BISHOP: Of course, of course.

WILDE: *They didn't expect this, especially in a night club atmosphere where they had been used to the brash, hit 'em on the head, forcing them to laugh, type of comedian. And you came on the complete opposite.*

BISHOP: Exactly. Right. "Folks, I don't want to be a hit, just let me finish!" Then when I worked with Frank, I said,

"Look at this crowd. Wait till his following shows up." But
. I did it *believing it*, rather than a joke, see? Again we get
back to attitude—the attitude with which I did it, not so
much that which I said.

WILDE: *Then would you call it "underplaying" comedy?*

BISHOP: Yeah, yeah. But it has to be done with a kind of
a twinkle.

WILDE: *Is this how you gained recognition as a "deadpan"
comedian?*

BISHOP: Well, I think the "deadpan comedian" came from
the complaining type of comedy that we all used to do and
naturally when you're complaining you can't be full of
smiles or laughter. So everybody says, "He works deadpan."
But if you're complaining, you can't do it from a happy
frame of mind.

WILDE: *In a* New York Times Magazine *article by Gilbert
Milstein, you said, "I always use a couple of jokes that don't
come off." Did you mean you did that on purpose?*

BISHOP: No. I think what Gilbert was saying was . . .
catching the audience off-guard. What the audience thought
was the punch-line was not. They thought that was the
finish of the joke, and that I purposely put in a joke that
didn't get a laugh. But that was not true. It sounded like the
end and then I would build to the punch-line, looking like I
was *saving* that particular joke—but I wasn't.

WILDE: *Could you give me an example?*

BISHOP: "We were very poor when I was a kid. I remember one winter, it snowed and I didn't have a sled." Now
that kinda gets a laugh, but it sounds like the end of a joke,
but not a good joke, 'cause the next line is: "I used to slide

down the hill on my cousin." "And she wasn't bad." They're thinking of it as three jokes and they're not. It's one joke.

WILDE: *"Sliding down the hill on my cousin" is the joke.*

BISHOP: It's not. The joke is "She wasn't bad."

WILDE: *Isn't that the "topper?"*

BISHOP: But that's what a joke is—it is a finish, the final punch of the joke. It's not a topper. That's the line I'm going for, so consequently that's the end of the joke. If the end of the joke is the topper, that's the topper.

WILDE: *In that same article, you said, "An audience always feels inferior. When you make them feel equal, you are actually making them feel superior." Would you explain that?*

BISHOP: Yeah. Too many guys put down audiences. Sometimes there are some who have a right to, but they have to have shortcomings themselves. Jack E. Leonard has his obesity. Don Rickles with his anger. You can't go out there, a nice-looking fellow, and put down the audience, because the audience wants to know what the hell are you complaining about. Unless you complain about some shortcoming in your life. But you cannot *blame them.* A handsome comedian has no right to go out there and be angry or complain, because the audience will say, "You're a good-looking guy, you dress well, you make a good living, what the hell are you complaining about?" The only way you can balance it is letting the audience know that everything isn't rosy with you in spite of the fact that you're wearing a three-hundred-dollar tuxedo and you're making thousands of dollars.

WILDE: *Are you saying that when you make them feel on the same level with you, actually they become superior because . . .*

BISHOP: Not superior. If an audience feels superior to you, then you are in trouble. I did not say superior. No. *They* don't feel superior . . . if you can *pretend* they are superior. There's a difference there. If an audience feels superior to you, they can be rude. They won't even turn around to watch you. If they feel equal to you, then you're in good shape.

WILDE: *What makes a supper club audience react differently each night to the same joke or piece of material?*

BISHOP: The attitude of the performer.

WILDE: *It's his fault?*

BISHOP: Absolutely. Sometimes a guy will take something that works for him, and instead of working *for* it, like he did in the beginning, he now says it mechanically and the audience senses it, so they kind of turn off.

WILDE: *Some comedians believe that weather conditions can affect an audience's reaction. Has this ever been your experience?*

BISHOP: That would seem like a very poor excuse, simply because you can take adversity and speak about it. Let's suppose I'm working in Chicago and there's thirty-seven people there because there's fourteen inches of snow, right? If I can convey to them I had a tougher time getting here than they did—if I say, I *have* to be here but *you!"*—you can break down the barrier that quickly, so I cannot see where weather conditions would have any influence at all.

WILDE: *Joe E. Brown, in his autobiography,* Laughter Is a Wonderful Thing,* *said, "No comedian ever got a big enough reaction to suit him." After a performance are you ever dissatisfied with the audience's reception?*

* Barnes & Co.

BISHOP: I don't think so, because it is so spontaneous that whatever reward you are getting, you are getting sincerely.

WILDE: *Even though some nights the response may be bigger than other nights?*

BISHOP: There are many extenuating circumstances. You can sometimes get a group of seventy people who have never been to a club who are a great audience, and the next night you can get a whole room full of couples, so . . . what makes the difference?

WILDE: *Then the rule is: Never compare tonight's reaction—loudness of the laugh—to last night's because this is a completely different group.*

BISHOP: When you start to do that, there is a form of deterioration taking place right away. Because then you don't believe in yourself. If an audience's reaction is all you base your performance on, then you are in a lot of trouble.

WILDE: *Why do you feel that way?*

BISHOP: Because you are saying that *they* are judging which is funny and as a comedian *you* must judge which is funny. I would rather do what I think is funny and not go over than do that which in my heart I don't think funny and go over.

WILDE: *What about the nights you have to change your material and your attitude to please that particular audience?*

BISHOP: You can't do that. Sammy Davis once had a sign in his dressing room. It said, "I don't know the meaning of success but I do know the meaning of failure—trying to please everybody."

WILDE: *What happens when you play to a specific audience—like in the Catskills—you often have to do material to fit that ethnic group?*

BISHOP: If you do that, you'll never be big in show business.

WILDE: *You have to decide which audience you want to please?*

BISHOP: No, you have to decide that which *you* want to do . . . not which audiences you want to please. Based on what you are saying, if we moved from comedy and went to music, everybody would still be playing "Should Old Acquaintance Be Forgot" because it pleases everybody—or "God Bless America." That's why you have guys who will divorce themselves from commercialism and strike out on their own. That's why you have an Elvis Presley. That's why you have the Beatles. Now I'm sure in the beginning they did not meet with success, but if you believe it firmly enough—Dean Martin is your best example. It was like the kiss of death when he broke up with Jerry Lewis. Now he could have tried to please audiences, but he decided to remain Dean Martin . . . and he even carried it over into television, where they wanted to rehearse a whole week, and he said, "That's not me. I'll rehearse one day."

WILDE: *It's doing what you believe is right—win, lose, or draw.*

BISHOP: If you really believe it. Some of us have only a façade, some of us pretend to believe in it. Don Rickles must have endured an awful lot of punishment, but he believed in it. The Smothers Brothers believe in it. Jonathan Winters believes in it. You can pretend you believe in it, but you

really have to believe in it. I'm sure great artists many centuries ago felt the same way. Van Gogh was scoffed and
laughed at, but he really believed in it.

WILDE: *Do you have a strategy or a device to control an
audience?*

BISHOP: Yeah, complete honesty. That's my strategy.
Don't bullshit an audience. You can never be a star until
you can take an audience by the hand. That's very important
to remember. An audience must trust you implicitly. They
know in five minutes whether you are just doing what you
are doing to go over that night or whether you are doing it
to entertain them.

WILDE: *Does that hold true for all audiences—no matter
what intellectual or social level. . . ?*

BISHOP: Yes. It also depends on whether you are known
or unknown. If you are unknown, then you are in a lot of
trouble. If you are known, they come in knowing what to
expect. As the unknown, you've got to make a compromise
and the compromise is in the first few minutes—to get
their attention. You are just a salesman then. Once you've
got their attention, you can then do that which you think is
your type of comedy.

WILDE: *Must you also establish a laugh climate?*

BISHOP: Not even that. A respect and recognition. You've
seen people where they would mumble after they have seen
an unknown comic, "Hey, he's pretty good." That's what I
mean.

WILDE: *Many psychologists feel that most comedians are
shy, introverted people who clown and joke primarily to
cover up their own insecurity. What is your—?*

BISHOP: To cover up their *own* insecurity? Then what makes them different from all other people from all walks of life? Who in life doesn't pretend if he's going to the dentist that he's not frightened? What layman doesn't joke about going to the hospital with an operation—even a feeble joke. So he too looks to cover up his own shortcomings. What guy jilted in love doesn't pretend for the first day or two "Who needs her?" So what makes him different from the comedian?

WILDE: *Are all comedians, when they are not on stage, basically serious?*

BISHOP: That depends upon your company. I'm not going to be "on" if I'm with Lyndon B. Johnson and Vice President Humphrey. What I think most psychologists overlook is that there is a certain amount of natural intelligence with comedians. When they hear them talking about subjects other than comedy, they think they are trying to be serious.

WILDE: *They're merely expressing themselves.*

BISHOP: That's all.

WILDE: *I think perhaps the public has an image of the comedian—*

BISHOP: No, it depends upon the comedian. If he is a "tumult" comedian they expect him to tumult. If he's what I call the "verbal" comedian, they expect him, once in awhile, to drop a little bomb during the conversation. Naturally, we're serious people. I know of no one who devotes himself more to charity than do comedians. That's a form of seriousness. Danny Thomas with his St. Jude Hospital, Bob Hope entertaining the troops in Vietnam, me with Cystic Fibrosis, Jack Benny with the philharmonics of every city—trying to help the orchestras—Jerry Lewis with Muscular Distrophy. When we meet to decide how to raise money for these charities, it's not in the form of a joke. Is that serious? Then we're serious! If one of our children is having trouble in school, or if he's been hurt in a bicycle fall, yeah, we're serious then too. If we lose a parent, no one expects us to do humor instead of saying *Kaddish.**

WILDE: *The Greek philosopher Aristotle said, "Melancholy men are the most witty." Why is that?*

BISHOP: It's an outlook on life, They take that which is adversity and juxtapose it. But that's not only true of comedians. You go to any battlefront, and if there is a near-hit, somebody there will inevitably do some joke to relieve the tension. He doesn't have to be a comedian.

WILDE: *Does it have to be someone with a sense of humor?*

BISHOP: How do we define sense of humor? You could have a sense of humor if you receive good fortune, and not have a sense of humor any other time. Is that a sense of humor? You can be a miserable guy who apparently has no sense of humor and say some of the funniest things in the world. And yet you're not funny . . . you have no apparent sense of humor. Again, you get back to a way of life.

WILDE: *And the individual's approach to it?*

BISHOP: Absolutely. Comedy is a form of religion.

WILDE: *Why do you say that?*

BISHOP: Because it's how you live a life.

WILDE: *And your approach to it is total and complete*

---

* Jewish prayer for the dead.

honesty—toward the audience, toward your work. It is an
honest approach toward your religion.

BISHOP: Right. Years ago you could fool an audience,
'cause you were in that town for one week and you may not
come back for two years. With the advent of television, you
can't fool an audience anymore. Because they see you week
after week. Now, if they see you five nights a week, you are
going to run the gamut of your emotions. They're gonna see
you angry, they're gonna see you happy. They are gonna
see you melancholy one night, supercharged the next. So
unless you have the ingredient of honesty, unless you let
them know that there is nothing wrong with your being
angry. . . .

WILDE: *That's a human emotion.*

BISHOP: Right.

WILDE: *It appears that many comedians come from poor*
families or had unhappy childhoods. Do you think these
emotional and psychological scars were the reasons they be-
came comedians?

BISHOP: Again, comedy is merely a way . . . humor is a
way of overcoming adversity. I think some of the funniest
things to come out of the Israeli-Arab conflict were things
that Moishe Dayan may have said. It is comedy that gets
you out of adversity.

WILDE: *Do loneliness and being a comedian generally go*
hand in hand?

BISHOP: I think preoccupation and being a comedian go
hand in hand. Not loneliness. Preoccupation is misconstrued
as loneliness. I can be sitting here, preoccupied, with some
thought I may be going to use and people will say, "He's sit-

ting there all by himself, he's not talking to anybody, he wants to be alone." During my show rehearsal from six-thirty to seven-thirty, I sit there and . . . the script girl, when she first started, would talk to me, and I said to her, "Don't get the impression because I'm doing nothing, that I'm not doing anything." She thought that I'm just sitting at the desk. It's not loneliness when you are involved with something—it's preoccupation. Last night, for example, I had to dance with Jose Greco and I had to make a change. During the course of the show, I was looking for minutes where I could make that change and I found those minutes when Don Ho sang a song . . . and then his "discovery" sang . . . and then they did a song together . . . which ran four minutes, which was all the time I needed to change.

WILDE: *Can the discipline and training of a comedian be compared to any other professional?*

BISHOP: Well, I am an *un*disciplined comedian. Only because I work better that way. See, a disciplined comedian would get a thought, write it down, rehearse it, work it over and make it a routine. I am an undisciplined man—get a thought, will go out on the floor and do it . . . only because I have no fear. I say, "What's the worse that can happen? If it bombs, I tell the audience, 'Folks, it's the last time I get a thought like this and not work it out.' " See, I can overcome it with honesty.

WILDE: *A doctor has to put in at least ten years before he learns his trade and can hang out the shingle—is it possible to compare his training to that of a comedian?*

BISHOP: I don't think so. I think we are dealing now with *a)* a God-given talent and *b)* an academic talent.

WILDE: *The doctor learned his skill by formal education and—*

BISHOP: Right! Right! That is where we get great doctors from. That's where you get great comedians—you have the dedication and the desire. We've often sat and talked— "What ever happened to so-and-so, he was great." He didn't have the dedication. He was at the track or he boozed it up a lot. . . .

WILDE: *Lost along the way.*

BISHOP: Right.

WILDE: *Are the requirements to become a recognized comedian the same as they would be in any other business?*

BISHOP: No. No, because there are so many different forms of what makes people laugh. You can be the greatest comedian, and there are still some people who think you are not funny. But if you are the greatest doctor, everybody accepts you as the greatest doctor. Unless it's another colleague, who thinks he's greater.

WILDE: *Because we are dealing with individual opinion, personal taste. . . .*

BISHOP: You are dealing with many things. I never saw anybody if you said, "He's a professor," dislike him personally.

WILDE: *He's got the respect.*

BISHOP: Right. But I've heard people say, "He's a great comedian—I still don't like him. He couldn't make *me* laugh." Naturally, you couldn't make someone laugh if he didn't want to . . . and the audience must trust you and you have to be able to lead them by the hand. Once you can lead them by the hand, you can take them through any avenue of comedy. You can take them on a very serious subject and they will go with you. All of a sudden you hit them with a block-busting punch line . . . but they must trust you. There are some comedians that don't have that trust. I've seen in Vegas, sometimes a guy wants to do a community-sing number with the audience, and the audience will not sing with him, for fear that he is going to embarrass them. So they don't trust him. Now an audience trusts Dean Martin implicitly.

WILDE: *What are the necessary requirements to become a comedian?*

BISHOP: *Curiosity* is the primary requisite. That's the only way to get material. There is no other way to develop thought waves. If your wife buys a gift for the house, and if you look at the gift and you dismiss it, you may be blowing a six-minute routine. But if you are curious about it, if you say, "My wife came home with a gadget and I defy anyone to tell me what the gadget is. You put it in a socket, you turn on a switch, and nothing happens." You've started a routine. You look at all good comedians . . . they will walk into a house and pick up articles and look at them. It's curiosity. It's curiosity about the news, about science, it's curiosity about anything that develops material. Unless you have a curious mind, you cannot be a comedian.

WILDE: *What else?*

BISHOP: I would say *honesty*. The biggest opening thing I ever did was . . . I worked a neighborhood spot in Chicago for forty-nine weeks . . . and for the first time in the history of the Chez Paree, someone went from a neighborhood spot to the Chez. Even Danny Thomas, as successful as he was, had to leave the 5100 Club and go to the Martinique [New York] and then come back to the Chez. It was a policy they had. I was the only—now I'll show you the ingredients. First, I became curious as to how I would open, 'cause I had just come from a neighborhood spot and now I'm going to the Chez Paree, so curiosity started my wheels going. Then

I dealt with honesty. And the routine I came up with was: "Ladies and Gentlemen, I am here through the generosity of you people. For forty-nine weeks I worked at the Vine Gardens and every night one of you nice people would come and say, 'What are you doing here—why aren't you at the Chez Paree?' I feel after tonight's appearance, a lot of you are going to say, 'What are you doing here—why aren't you at the Vine Gardens?' " A thought went through my mind, see? But it had those ingredients . . . it had honesty, it had humility, it had humor. . . .

WILDE: *It was also spontaneous.*

BISHOP: It appeared spontaneous. The thought went through my mind, you see, not the night I opened.

WILDE: *You worked on it before you opened?*

BISHOP: Right. Just the thought.

WILDE: *It seems that many comedians who become successful have been fortunate enough to have worked in one spot for longer than the two- or four-week booking that is available today. Danny Thomas spent three years at the 5100 Club, George Gobel. . . .*

BISHOP: At the Helsings' Vaudeville Lounge [Chicago]. . . .

WILDE: *For a long time. Bob Hope spent something like six months at a theatre in. . . .*

BISHOP: Even Don Rickles' fame only came to the front from working the Sahara Lounge. Shecky Greene, from being in one place . . .

WILDE: *Working that one place, does that allow you to develop confidence and to relax and—*

BISHOP: No. What it allows you is the thought pattern

that I'm discussing. When you're a hit in a place, you can go out and do something that you thought about this morning.

WILDE: *And not be afraid?*

BISHOP: Exactly. Exactly.

WILDE: *Then it does build confidence.*

BISHOP: Well, then you go back to attitude again. Those people are now waiting for you to perform. So, instead of going out and trying to overcome them, or overwhelm them, you take your time, 'cause they are waiting to hear what you've got to say. This is the secret of great comedy. If you can put the audience in a position to wait to hear what you've got to say—and nobody does it better then Benny. They are *waiting* to hear what he's got to say. You can defeat yourself by doing so much comedy that they accept it and don't wait to hear what you've got to say.

WILDE: *Then the mistake the inexperienced comedian makes, in his anxiety and his desire to—.*

BISHOP: Not the *inexperienced* comedian, the *compromising* comedian. There is a difference. See, even the inexperienced comedian, if he's not compromising, will come off well. The guy who wants to be a hit *that* show, that's the compromising comedian.

WILDE: *Instead of looking for career.*

BISHOP: Longevity. I once said to a comedian, "Why are you developing such a terribly funny, dirty story. You will never use it anywhere else. Why spend years developing a story you can't use on television?" He can't use it at the White House. Where *is* he going to use it? That's why I say the [Catskill] mountains are a fallacy. You spend years there, killing the people, but what have you developed?

WILDE: *What other requirements are needed to become a comedian? How about a good memory?*

BISHOP: It depends upon the type of comedian you are. Now a good memory would be a shortcoming to me, because it would prevent me from creating. Others are mechanics. A memory is very important for them, to go into a file thing in their minds and yank it out.

WILDE: *Is it important to be well educated?*

BISHOP: Again, we are getting back to curiosity. Well educated could certainly never be detrimental. It can't possibly hurt you, because you have more knowledge. I think what's most important is to never *stop* learning. Whether you have an education or not, you must continue to learn.

WILDE: *It appears that an emotional rapport with the audience is stronger and longer lasting than an intellectual appeal. Why is that?*

BISHOP: Well, an emotional appeal can act very well as a reminder and everybody shares in it. You'd have to be an intellect to share in an intellectual approach. Let's talk about poverty. You're gonna remind ninety-five per cent of your audience of either some relative that was poor or that they were poor. If you speak about intellect you may not remind them of anything. It is kind of an affair that you have with the audience. Many times if you say, "I know you married men out there. . . .", well, you've already gotten a group. That's why mother-in-law jokes are so strong. Each guy knows exactly what you are experiencing. If you were to speak about your dean at college, you would have a very small percentage who would remember that they also had that kind of a dean.

WILDE: *Performers who do comedy are known by various titles; "comic," "mimic," "humorist," "story teller," "impressionist." . . . Is there a difference?*

BISHOP: Yeah, there's a vast difference. A comic and a mimic are not necessarily both in the field of comedy. A mimic does not have to be funny. He can be brilliant as a mimic but not funny. Frank Gorshin, I'd consider a brilliant mimic. As a matter of fact, you will find that most of the mimics do terrible monologues. I've never heard Rich Little do a funny line. Never. The exception, of course, would be Sammy Davis. A humorist is more of a Sam Levenson. I think the humorist takes the audience and reminds it of things that we take for granted. Will Rogers did it with politics. Sam Levenson did it with large families, Herb Shriner did it with rural type of people. They are what you call reminders. You have Pat Buttram, Minnie Pearl, Homer and Jethro, who are excellent musicians and humorists.

WILDE: *What is the difference between a "comic" and a "comedian"?*

BISHOP: Well, there is the old cliché that a comic says *funny things* and the comedians say *things funny.** I think of a comic as being more physical than a comedian. Red Skelton, for example, is more physical than Jack Benny.

WILDE: *Isn't Skelton referred to as a "clown"?*

BISHOP: He's referred to as a "buffoon," a "clown," right. But it's because of the physical, see. The physical comic resorts to moves, à la Jonathan Winters.

---

* An epigram created by Ed Wynn.

WILDE: *Would you call Winters a "physical" comic?*

BISHOP: Yeah, sure. . . .

WILDE: *Rather than a "satirist" or a "wit"?*

BISHOP: No. He can be witty too, don't misunderstand. That's what makes Jonathan Winters so great. He can do anything. And if what he says doesn't get a laugh, there is a physical gesture or physical move that will salvage it for him.

WILDE: *What is the difference between a "stand-up" comedian and one who "sits-down" and is funny?*

BISHOP: I don't know. I guess the budget for upholstery. It's the same difference between a stand-up singer and a sit-down singer. It's purely attitude. If one's monologue is such that it is very laconic and is enhanced by what appears to be a laconic attitude, then he's a "sit-down" comic. If one is more forceful and finds he has to move he's a "stand-up" comic.

WILDE: *Is it possible that someone like Jack Carter could do a routine sitting down?*

BISHOP: Yes, he could. He's done it on panels. And he's very brilliant when he does it. But the irony is that Jack Carter sitting down looks like he's standing. Jack Benny standing up looks like he's sitting down.

WILDE: *Is it an informality—a conversational delivery?*

BISHOP: I don't know. I really don't know. I don't know why someone would want to sit down and do a routine, unless they think that perhaps it is the epitome of success.

WILDE: *On the TV talk shows today, including your own,*

after the comedian does a stand-up spot, he will sit down on the "panel" and continue to do material or lines that he would normally do in his stand-up act.

BISHOP: But now you're not dealing so much with the comedian as with the quantity of whether he's known or not. See, to take someone who's completely unknown and have them join you at the panel without having been funny can be the kiss of death for him.

WILDE: *He's got to establish himself?*

BISHOP: Right. Taking someone who's already known and sitting them at your panel, there's no problem.

WILDE: *When Alan King sits down, he can do any one of his routines. . . .*

BISHOP: Yeah, but don't kid yourself into thinking for one minute that if you do a routine sitting down and it is a *routine,* if that audience doesn't believe you . . . if they think it's a *routine,* you're in a lot of trouble. You better make it look like it's not a *routine.* It'd better not have the polish. I warn comics that do stand-up spots, "When you come and sit down, talk at half the tempo you just did your act in." See, one is overpowering and one is overheard. That's a difference.

WILDE: *How does working in a night club differ from working on television?*

BISHOP: In my case, there is none. I'm just being myself. Whether in the environment of a night club, or a temple, or church, or television—I don't change myself. There is very little difference between my sitting here on this couch and being on my show in my attitude. I'm dressed, that'd be the only difference . . . and if we had three or four performances here, I'd be the same as I am tonight.

WILDE: *Is this image of a friendly attitude and an unforced, honest delivery you have, a technique that you plan?*

BISHOP: No. You can't plan a technique, 'cause you can't fool people for so long. It's something you have to feel. It's as though I were to ask you, "Can you plan to be pleasant coming over here?" You *could* plan to make a pleasant entrance, but somewhere during the course of this interview, if you're not a pleasant guy, it's going to come out. It has to.

WILDE: *You're considered to be one of the sharpest ad-lib comedians in the world. Is this a talent you were born with?*

BISHOP: I don't know if I was born with it, but I remember always having an answer when I was a kid. I think it's a defense mechanism which is very true in all comedy. For example, if I was going to fight with a guy—if it came to a fist-fight—if I could get myself out of it with humor, I did. There was no question that this guy could knock my brains out. I would say, "I just want to warn you, if I hit you, I'm gonna go down."

WILDE: *Then this ability can be developed?*

BISHOP: Any way of life can be developed, and it's purely a way of life. For example, if my wife were to walk in here now and say, "I had two flats"—the average guy wouldn't do humor but the comedy mind would try to appease her. We would find some kind of humor in the incident. Maybe, "So that's the way we live, and when they come and take the house away, it'll be fine." Whereas the serious person, who does not delve in comedy all the time, would say, "Well, let's call up somebody and find out what we can do." It becomes a catastrophe. We try to avoid catastrophes—it's a way of life which is accepted as comedy.

WILDE: *Is it possible to actually create a spontaneous joke, or are all ad-libs joke plots that have been consciously or unconsciously switched?*

BISHOP: You can suck a guy in. It's like boxing. You can feint the guy and the guy'll lead, and you'll counterpunch him. It's the same with ad-libbing. When you are ad-libbing you are really, strangely enough, fighting for time . . . if your mind isn't right there. So you can take anything and use words in sentences to give you that time. It still sounds like an ad-lib, although you are not doing a stock joke.* Once they're waiting to hear what you've got to say, when you come to a period, they'll laugh . . . if you've got them waiting.

WILDE: *What is it that allows you to ad-lib as well as you do?*

BISHOP: Peace of mind. Yeah, a complete vacuum up here. A freedom. Nothing clogged up, nothing cluttered. And I know how to unclutter it.

WILDE: *Is it the power of positive thinking?*

BISHOP: No, I don't think it's that. I think the power of positive thinking is when you are looking for a kind of security. The power of positive thinking comes from negative thinking, in order for you to make it positive thinking. You convert that which is negative to positive. But if I'm not negative to begin with, what am I converting?

WILDE: *Is this a God-given gift?*

* A joke that has been done many times by most comedians.

BISHOP: If it's a way of life, then I guess it's a gift from God. I see guys that are failures that are writing stuff . . . their writers are writing stuff. I go there with nothing. I stole a show one night with two words. They were honoring Samuel Goldwyn and they did jokes about him and everything. I stood up and said, "Thank you, very much. Mr. Gold*man*. . . ." and it was the end of the night. How the hell can you come to honor a guy like Sam Goldwyn and not even know his name?

WILDE: *Did you come prepared with that line?*

BISHOP: I knew about five minutes before. There were twenty seven comics—Danny Kaye, Groucho, Berle, everybody. I was the twenty-seventh, so I had to leave my mind uncluttered. There were times when I got a thought pattern and somebody else had something like it. But I said, "What will make me different?" "Who is the only guy here who has no right to know Samuel Goldwyn?" Me. That's my thought. . . . and from that I went to Mr. Gold*man*!

WILDE: *Then it was a conscious effort?*

BISHOP: Not an effort. An *effort* to me reeks of—attempt. I think if I couldn't have used that, I would have gotten to the dais and said something else. It's like a faucet. You know there's water there and you just turn it on.

WILDE: *You must trust yourself.*

BISHOP: Right. You don't think, "If I go there, will there be rust, will there be hot water? Will there be cold water?" You go to the spigot, you turn the spigot on, and you get water. That's kind of a reservoir up here. I've a mind that is channeled that way, and I know that when I hear my name they've turned a spigot on and something is going to come out. Whether it's the introduction that the host gave me, where I might say, "I want to thank you for that introduction. If I'm a hit tonight, I owe you *nothing!*"

WILDE: *Can you ad-lib better today than you did twenty years ago?*

BISHOP: No. I think that they're waiting more to hear the ad-lib today. Because twenty years ago, who could distinguish whether it was an ad-lib or not? Who knew that it was not a "stock"? It is over a period of years . . . you get to a point where you can do a stock and they say, "He ad-libbed it." Because they are tuned that way.

WILDE: *Is it important for the comedian to know all the stock jokes?*

BISHOP: No. No. I think knowing stock jokes is a lack of development. It'll get you by an audience but it won't get you by some guy who's coming in to catch you. The guy'll say, "What'd you send me there for? I've heard fifteen jokes he's done before. Is he supposed to be original, clever or what?"

WILDE: *You're credited with helping the careers of Buddy Hackett, Phil Foster, Corbett Monica. . . .*

BISHOP: No.

WILDE: *Lou Alexander. . . .*

BISHOP: No, I didn't.

WILDE: *People in the business credit you with—*

BISHOP: I know, but it's wrong for me to—I hate to have somebody feel that way . . . think that way. I didn't help Buddy Hackett. . . . or Phil Foster. I didn't help them.

WILDE: *Was that something you derive personal satis-*

faction from, or do you feel their talent is so great it had to be exposed?

BISHOP: Well, I feel what's wrong with our business today is that no one takes the time to use talent correctly. It's a big curse in our business. Either you have to make it before somebody gets interested or you can bomb and it's all over. If a person has talent, there has to be some niche, some place he can fit. In this industry today, they don't take time to find out where they fit. We get talented people and all of a sudden they get offers, only because somebody used them correctly. I had Glen Campbell on my show. I said, "I predict before this summer is out you'll have your own summer replacement show, then you'll have your own show." And he shrugged it off. He's replacing the Smothers Brothers. All I had to say was this guy would be a hell of a host for a variety show—goodlooking bastard, sings like a son of a bitch, plays great guitar, dimples—Charlie All-American. Nobody took the time. Or Simmy Bow. Same principle. Nobody had enough intelligence to say, "Here is the author of a thousand unfinished books. . . ."

WILDE: *If your son or a close relative decided to become a comedian, what advice would you give him?*

BISHOP: I wouldn't give him any advice. I think he'd have to find his own way. If he wants to be a comedian he'll find a way. I would just say, "Don't do anything in bad taste."

George Burns

George Burns was born Nathan Birnbaum on January 20, 1896, in New York City. One of fourteen children, Burns left school when he was thirteen to help support his family. He organized a group of child singers called the Peewee Quartet, the members of which took turns passing the hat in taverns and backyards after performing.

During the following years he appeared in vaudeville acts with many different partners. In 1923, he met Gracie Allen. They formed the soon-to-be-legendary comedy team of Burns and Allen and soon were playing the nation's top vaudeville houses. They were married on January 7, 1926, in Cleveland.

Their first full-length motion picture was *The Big Broadcast of 1932*. Many others followed, including the delightful *A Damsel in Distress*, with Fred Astaire and a Gershwin score. They also made a total of fourteen comedy shorts (two-reelers).

In 1933 they were signed to do their own radio show and remained on the air without interruption for seventeen years. The transition to television was made in 1950. When

Gracie retired in 1958,* George appeared as a single on the "George Burns Show" for NBC. Since then he has been making TV guest appearances and night club engagements.

Mr. Burns is the author of *I Love Her, That's Why* (Simon and Schuster), the autobiography of Burns and Allen, and is currently a producer of several television shows.

A Burns and Allen comedy routine

GEORGE: Well, Gracie, Halloween is day after tomorrow. What do you think we ought to do?

GRACIE: What's the difference? No matter what we do, it'll be here day after tomorrow anyhow.

GEORGE: I mean . . . how are we going to celebrate it?

GRACIE: Oh. . . . Well, when I was a little girl we'd go around the neighborhood ringing doorbells and run away before the people came out.

GEORGE: Well, I don't think I can do that. It might tire me out a little.

GRACIE: Then why don't you stay home and ring your own doorbell?

GEORGE: That I could do, but only one ring. I'll bet you played some awful tricks on people when you were kids.

GRACIE: Oh, we did. For instance, we'd take a wallet, put a five-dollar bill in it, and leave it on somebody's doorstep. Gee, that was funny.

GEORGE: What was the trick?

* Miss Allen died on August 28, 1964.

GRACIE: Well, we didn't put a name in the wallet, so the person who found it would never know who to return it to.

GEORGE: That was quite a trick.

GRACIE: If you think that was a trick, how about the one Aunt Clara played on her husband, Uncle Harvey.

GEORGE: Even better than yours?

GRACIE: Oh, yes. You see, every Halloween he came home late, after celebrating with his friends.

GEORGE: He would celebrate with his friends?

GRACIE: Yes. So she got a skeleton and put it in his bed.

GEORGE: Skeleton, huh?

GRACIE: Then we all waited outside his door and listened.

GEORGE: I'll bet he yelled his head off.

GRACIE: No, he just said, "Clara, I know I've asked you to take off some weight, but this is ridiculous."

GEORGE: I'll bet he was disappointed when he found out that it wasn't Clara.

GRACIE: He was. But he got even. The next Halloween he played a trick on her. He dressed up in a white sheet and locked himself in a closet and started groaning like a ghost.

GEORGE: Did it scare Aunt Clara?

GRACIE: Oh, yes. When she found him in that closet three weeks later he didn't look so good.

GEORGE: You Allens went all-out on Halloween, huh?

GRACIE: One year we had a big costume party and Uncle

Otis came as a jack-o'-lantern. He won first prize, but he was very unhappy about it.

GEORGE: He won first prize and he was unhappy?

GRACIE: Yes, he had a lighted candle in his mouth, but when they slapped him on his back to congratulate him, he . . .

GEORGE & GRACIE: [*Together*] Swallowed it.

GRACIE: Yeah.

GEORGE: Say good night, Gracie.

GRACIE: Good night.

Upon MY ARRIVAL at George Burns' office at the General Services Studios in Hollywood, Mr. Burns was seated at his huge desk, which was surprisingly cleared of all paper. The room, expensively panelled and tastefully decorated in walnut, exuded an air of hospital neatness and careful organization.

Mr. Burns wore a dark blue beret, gray slacks, gray tweed sports jacket, and gray sports shirt. He complained of a cold and made it clear that he would not have come in that day except for our appointment.

He was gracious, frank, and outspoken. At one point he expressed a strong opinion of two comedy stars who did not "impress" him and then requested that his remarks not be printed. I have adhered to his wishes.

WILDE: *How long after you started in show business did you begin doing comedy?*

BURNS: Well, I couldn't answer that. I always had a natural sense of humor—even when I sang with the Peewee Quartet when we were kids. I was able to get laughs on the street corners but not on the stage. I was self-conscious about being on the stage. If I was invited to somebody's house—to a party—I was very good. Prepared stuff was hard for me to do. A lot of people are very funny if they don't have to stick to the words—if they have to stick to the words it's another ball game.

WILDE: *Did you ever do a single?*

BURNS: I did all kinds of singles. I did anything to stay

135

in show business. If it had to be a single, I'd do a single. If it had to be a two-act, I'd do a two-act. If I had to sing with a quartet, I would sing with a quartet. If I had to work with a seal, I'd work with a seal. I wanted to stay in show business.

WILDE: *You were considered the straight man of the Burns and Allen team, yet many of the laughs came as a result of your split-second timing and comic attitude. What is the real function of the "straight man"?*

BURNS: Well, anybody can be a straight man if he hears well. You just have to wait for laughs. A straight man just repeats the questions and the comedian gets the laughs and you just wait for them and don't let them die completely at the tail end of the laugh.

WILDE: *Is that what is meant by "timing"?*

BURNS: Yeah, that's timing.

WILDE: *What is the difference between doing a monologue and feeding lines to someone else to get the laughs?*

BURNS: The difference is that the monologist has no help —you have to get up there on your own two feet and tell your jokes. I use the cigar for timing purposes. If I tell a joke, I smoke as long as they laugh and when they stop laughing I take the cigar out of my mouth and start my next joke.

WILDE: *Have you always used it?*

BURNS: I thought if I smoked, I would look like an actor. So I started smoking cigars when I was sixteen and I have been smoking them ever since.

WILDE: *When you and Gracie Allen first did an act, you*

were the comedian and she was the straight man and then you switched roles. How did the characterizations you both developed come about?

BURNS: The audience really finds the character for you. When we first started, *I* had all the funny jokes and Gracie had the straight stuff, but even her straight lines got laughs. She had a funny delivery. Very sharp and quick and cute, and they laughed at her straight lines—and they didn't laugh at *my* jokes. If she asked me a question, they would laugh and I didn't expect a laugh there. While I was answering her, I talked in on her laugh so nobody heard what I had to say. I knew right away that there was a feeling of something between the audience and Gracie. They loved her, and so, not being a fool and wanting to smoke cigars for the rest of my life, I gave her the jokes. Then I finally found out that certain jokes were not good for her. The audience would tell you. They would resent certain jokes—maybe a sarcastic joke. They didn't want sarcasm from Gracie. And the first thing you know, the audiences picked out a character that she was off-center, and then that's the material I got. I used to dig it out of magazines—*Whizbang* and *College Humor*—and I always had a sense of being able to take a joke and switching it. I am sort of basically a writer, so I was able to always find material, and then when I could afford it, I bought material. I have always been a big believer in paying writers for material—if you don't buy material you can't stay fresh.

WILDE: *You and Gracie did an act called "Lamb Chops" which launched your careers into the big time. How did that come about?*

BURNS: Well, the big jokes in those days were *eating* jokes. "Do you like to love?" "No." "Do you like to kiss?"

"No." "What do you like?" "Lamb chops." "A little girl like you, can you eat two lamb chops, alone?" "Not alone, but with potatoes I could!" We had a routine about lamb chops, so you would title the act "Lamb Chops." The entire act went seventeen minutes . . . not wholly about lamb chops . . . it consisted of everything. Our opening at that time (it was a great opening, by the way . . . they stole it from us) . . . We used to walk out—I would hold her hand (we were very young in those days—it was a boy and girl act—we weren't married) and she would look off stage and there would be a man there and she would look at him and she would kiss him and he would kiss her and he would say goodbye and she would say goodbye and she would turn around and say to me, "Who's that?" It got a very big laugh. What made it such a great joke was that it set up her character in one line. You knew right away that she was a little on the screwy side. We did jokes like that, and finally we got into food and did the little routine about lamb chops. Then we came into New York and opened at the Jefferson Theatre and got a five-year contract. That's why "Lamb Chops" was so important to us—it got us started.

WILDE: *What made Burns and Allen such a great comedy team?*

BURNS: It was Gracie. She was a great actress. She was not funny. She was not a comedienne, she was an actress. Gracie could do the wildest kind of jokes and make people believe them—no matter how mad the jokes were, when Gracie told them you would believe they were true. If somebody else told them, you believed the jokes were funny, but you didn't believe they were true.

WILDE: *Is there a difference between being a comedienne and being an actress who can do comedy?*

BURNS: Yes, a big difference. Take Lynn Fontanne. She's a great actress, but she also played a dumb dame in *Dulcy* and she made you believe her. When Gracie played . . . Gracie wasn't dumb . . . in fact, Gracie thought she was terribly smart. Gracie's character was different. Gracie thought everybody was out of step but her. She was always helping people. She was always sorry for you. Like if she would say, "My sister got up in the middle of the night, she screamed, she looked down at her feet and they turned black." You would say to her, "What did she do?" She was sorry for you for asking that question. She thought you were pretty dumb not to know what to do if your feet turned black. "She took off her stockings and went to sleep again." When Gracie would take pepper and put it in the salt shaker and salt in the pepper shaker, she would look at you like you had two heads. Her reasoning was people always get mixed up and now when they do they are right. She knew what she was doing. We called that illogical logic. It makes sense but it only made sense to Gracie.

WILDE: *This characterization evolved with time—you didn't start with the complete concept?*

BURNS: No, in fact when we first went together, half of the jokes didn't fit her at all. It took a good year to get her into character. That doesn't mean it took a year to do a good act, but it took a year to get the wrong words out of Gracie's mouth. Even though you knew some of the jokes were wrong, you couldn't take them out because your act wouldn't be long enough. You would have to leave in some of the wrong jokes until you found the right ones.

WILDE: *What appeal to the public did the act have to remain so successful for so many years?*

BURNS: Well, Gracie had the appeal. I wasn't good for a

lot of years. I was a bad straight man. I knew more about offstage than on. I would just repeat questions. My job was not too attractive. I just timed the jokes for Gracie. Someone had to time them for her because Gracie wouldn't wait for a laugh—to Gracie there was no audience. Gracie's sense of concentration was so marvelous that she didn't know there was an audience. Those were not footlights. As far as she was concerned, there was a wall and even though she looked that way she didn't look at the audience . . . she talked to me. If Gracie had an exit and you were supposed to stop her and say, "Wait a minute, Gracie, I want to ask you something," if you forgot your line, she would go right into the dressing room and take off her make-up. She only remembered her lines if you remembered yours.

WILDE: *Did you always believe that one day you would become a big star?*

BURNS: In the first place, you don't start out to be a hit . . . there's no such thing as that. You don't get up in the morning on the fifth of January at ten minutes after two and say, "I'm going to be a star!" You are in the same business. You must love what you are doing. If you work enough, you must get better. Of course, I was very fortunate that I met Gracie when I was about twenty-seven. I was a small-time actor until then, and I had no idea of getting as far as I did in show business . . . never planned. *You* have nothing to do with it—it's the audience. As I said before, the audience made me find a character for Gracie, and it's the audience that makes you a star even if you don't want to be. They're the ones that do it.

WILDE: *Didn't you have a driving ambition to—*

BURNS: No, what happened was . . . after we played the

big-time vaudeville—two shows a day—we started doing well. Then you get a feel of success . . . then you want to go someplace. Like when we started out to make a short for Paramount in the early thirties. We were just fortunate. We took Fred Allen's place. Offered seventeen hundred to make a short—nine minutes. Well, I never heard of seventeen hundred dollars. We were told the night before at a party that Fred Allen was sick, and could we take his place. So we got over to Paramount and we had to improvise because the set didn't fit our act. We were a street-corner act, and this was the interior of somebody's home. That short turned out to be very funny, and we started making shorts.

WILDE: *When you performed your vaudeville act twice every day, did you have an acting technique that you were able to call upon to re-create the illusion of the first time?*

BURNS: No, you just got out. You've got your life savings —which is seventeen minutes—and you walk out. I told you our opening joke. She would say, "Who's that?" Now if they laughed, it would spark you and you would give a good performance. But a lot of times the same act that was all right at night wouldn't do well in the afternoon. All you've got is a delivery and an attitude, and the audience will either defeat you or you will be a sensation. But when you got to be good—you got above your audience and your audience couldn't defeat you. See, if you got four hundred dollars a week, you could be defeated by an audience but if you got twenty-five hundred with the same act, the audience couldn't defeat you.

WILDE: *You project confidence.*

BURNS: Yes, and the funny thing is, if you are not defeated the audience finally digs it. They might not laugh at your first couple of jokes, but finally you get to them.

WILDE: *They sense your attitude.*

BURNS: Of course. When you walk out and you are important, they know you are important. It's just like Jack Benny—or anybody—I say Jack Benny because we are good friends—Jack can walk out on the stage and not tell a joke but say, "I went in today and I got a piece of roast beef and it was delicious." If he stops after the word delicious, and pauses long enough, they'll laugh. The audience will be afraid that they have missed a joke.

WILDE: *Was it easier to make the audience laugh in a vaudeville theatre than it was in a radio or television studio?*

BURNS: Yes. It is easier to make an audience laugh that pays to come in, because they are paying to see you. They get dressed and they put on a collar and tie and they get in their cars and they pay so much to see you and the fact that they come *in* to see you . . . they like your act. It's very tough to make an audience laugh that doesn't pay, because they are very critical.

WILDE: *Do people laugh more readily today than they did forty years ago?*

BURNS: If something makes you laugh, I think you will laugh as loudly as you did forty years ago. I don't think there is any difference between the volume of laughter.

WILDE: *Are the comedians today—?*

BURNS: I think people are funny today and everybody has somebody that's funny. I don't know . . . maybe *you* are funny to somebody . . . like, I can do anything to Jack Benny and make him laugh, and there are a lot of people that can do anything to me and make me laugh. I've gone to all the night clubs and watched different fellas work. Shecky Greene—it's impossible not to laugh at Shecky Greene. He's so funny . . . and he's clever. He can do anything. He can dance and he can sing and he's wild and he can take falls, but he's basically funny. You see, there are comedians that are very good but they are not funny—to me. There are guys, I look at them and say, "Great mechanic." He knows his exits and entrances and knows music and how to build it up and bring it down, knows how to quiet an audience, knows all the tricks, but he's not funny.

WILDE: *How is the man with the mechanical delivery different from the comedian who is essentially funny?*

BURNS: The guy that sticks exactly to the words. Does it exactly. Recites it. What I call a mechanic comedian. The fellow, you give him directions: "Go to the bar and pick up the drinks." You watch him rehearse it, and after he rehearses it once, you can bet your bottom dollar that he will start on his right foot, pick up the drink with his right hand, turn to his left, and put the drink down with his left hand. But there are fellows that just start to walk. It's either their right foot or their left. They will turn to the left or right, or they will pick up the drink, or they will read the line after the drink. But the fellow that is the mechanical comic or entertainer or performer—he finally gets to the point where he can't think of the line unless he takes the drink.

WILDE: *Was Gracie like that?*

BURNS: Oh, no, just the opposite. You couldn't underline a word for Gracie. She never read anything the same way twice. Jack Benny once came down—we were playing

Newark. She did some joke and he says to Gracie, "This is the third time I've been in the wings watching you. I always come down for that joke." We had to take the joke out after that, because she didn't know why it was so good. She didn't read it the same way. When we told the joke, she couldn't get a laugh—she was pressing to please Jack Benny. So we finally had to take the joke out.

WILDE: *Both Jack Benny and George Jessel said that in your early vaudeville career you refused to do any material unless every word was just right and you had it rehearsed letter-perfect and then broke it in several times.*

BURNS: Well, that went for them, too. I remember when Jack Benny went to play on the road and left his violin here. He got on the stage, did the first two jokes, and he didn't get his first two laughs. He took the orchestra leader's violin and held it. He was frightened if he didn't hold on to something he would fall down. With us, all we had was seventeen minutes, and if you had to do a new joke in the act, you would take it to Wilkes-Barre or Scranton and break it in and then bring it back, because you couldn't afford to take out a good joke and put in a new one in case it didn't get a laugh.

WILDE: *When you break in a line in Wilkes-Barre for the purpose of eventually using it in New York, if they don't laugh at it, does that necessarily mean they won't laugh at it in New York!*

BURNS: No, it doesn't mean that at all. *You* know your own delivery. *You* know if the thing is funny and you know if you say it funny . . . you feel it . . . if your attitude is right. There are certain jokes I tell that I don't think anybody else could get a laugh with, but it fits me. If we went

to Wilkes-Barre and did a joke, whether it got a laugh or
not wasn't the point. We wanted to *know* the joke and *know*
the line so that when we got to New York we could tell it
and get a fair reaction. We had a joke where I said to
Gracie, "What are you doing tonight?" and she says, "I
can't see you tonight, I expect a headache." She didn't think
the joke was funny. I said, "Let's try it." And for two
months in every theatre we played, I would say to Gracie,
"What are you doing tonight?" She would never answer me.
Finally, two months later in New Orleans, she says all right
. . . she said, "I can't see you tonight, I expect a headache."
It got a very big laugh and from then on the joke was in.

But then it worked the other way too. Gracie and I played
the Palace—they called us up and said we would like to keep
you over if Gracie can be mistress of ceremonies, and can you
do a new act? Which we did. So you see, we didn't always
go to Wilkes-Barre or Scranton. When they want to hold
you over and they say will you do a new act, the pressure
forces you to come up with it and you do it. The interesting
thing is we did an act called "Sixty-Forty" Nobody knew
what that meant, but I did—Gracie was sixty per cent of
the act and I was forty per cent. We had a finish that didn't
go, so we had to take it out and put in another finish . . .
and then when we were held over the second week at the
Palace, we put in the finish that was a flop and it was a riot.

WILDE: *Sometimes the material fails because of lack of
confidence somehow . . .*

BURNS: You are doing it better. You *are* better. The
minute you walk out there and say, "*I wonder* if this finish
will work," you're finished. Cooked. But the Palace Theatre
was the easiest audience in the world—the toughest thing
about the Palace was to book it, not to play it. Because they

were all actors in there and everybody knew your life was at stake, so whether you were funny or not they would scream at you.

WILDE: *On an eight- or ten-act vaudeville bill the comedian usually came on sixth or seventh—wasn't the audience pretty well warmed up by then?*

BURNS: Well, vaudeville was too grooved for me. The sad part was, if you did a great balancing act, if you were the world's greatest juggler—I think the world's greatest anything should be a star, but you weren't in vaudeville. If you were the world's greatest juggler, you would open the show or close it. It was wrong. The world's greatest magician— until Houdini came along, magicians would close the show or open it. Later on, they switched the shows around a little bit and then the comedy acts used to close the show. Number two act would be a two-man dancing act and the third act a sketch. The fourth act would be a single woman. The fifth act would be a big act. And then the magician would open intermission, and then the headliner would come on— Sophie Tucker or Blossom Seeley or Nora Bayes.

WILDE: *You supervised the writing of your radio and television shows. What specifically did that job entail?*

BURNS: I knew exactly which way we were going and I steered the writers in that direction. They would write it here—three or four writers—at the typewriter. When writers take work home . . . let's say you have a scene you want to write. You give it to two writers. They bring in the scene, and you've got four writers and you have to rewrite the scene. Sometimes there's a little resentment because you are taking out a joke that's his favorite—that *I* don't think is in character or something. You've got discontent. When you sit down from scratch with four writers, nobody knows

who said this or that. I found out that's the best way for me
. . . for what I'm doing.

WILDE: *Did Gracie help in the writing of the—?*

BURNS: No. She never even talked show business. Gracie
never told jokes offstage. She didn't talk about lighting or
make-up or anything like that. You never knew Gracie was
in the business.

WILDE: *What exactly did you do to sustain the continued
high quality of your weekly shows?*

BURNS: Well, you paid more money to writers so that you
got better material. For instance, we had a sad moment once
in radio—our rating dropped. We were getting, at that time,
around fifteen or sixteen thousand dollars for the package.
That was the first time, the only time, in our career that we
couldn't get a job, and the ratings dropped and dropped and
dropped. Finally, the Morris Office, Bill Murray, said he had
a job for us six months later for Swan Soap on radio for
seventy-five hundred dollars. Well, I took that job. I paid
Paul Whiteman and his band twenty-five hundred dollars a
week. Tony Martin was just starting and I paid him a
couple of hundred per week and I think Bill Goodwin was
our announcer. I paid my writers four thousand dollars
per week and brought in the best I could get. I lost money
that season, but our rating started climbing again, and the
next season we got ten thousand per week. I finally got back
into the money again. I finally found out why our rating
dropped. What happened was that our jokes were too young
for us. You see, Gracie and I had two children then, but we
were still doing a street-corner act . . . and you can't do that.
You've got to be your age in show business. You can't be
any younger than you are suposed to be, nor any older. We
told a lot of jokes that were all right for a young boy and

girl, but not good for a married woman. Like Bill Goodwin coming out and making love to Gracie . . . well, the audience knew we were married and they wouldn't accept it. For instance, Gracie once said to me when she was about thirty-five, "I can't continue to play this character." I asked her why and she said, "Because I'm thirty-five!" I said, "Gracie, if you were silly or off-beat when you were eighteen, what makes you think you would be any smarter when you are thirty-five? The only difference is that when you are eighteen, you can have a little whistle on your wrist and a fellow goes to kiss you and say, 'I'll blow that and the cop will come!' You blow it and say, 'Well, it's broken from last night!' Now that's a joke when you're eighteen, but you can't carry that whistle when you are thirty-five because the audience will come up and get you. When you are thirty-five you tell jokes about cooking, about roast beef in the oven. . . ." When we went on for Swan Soap we were married. We had two children, Ronnie and Sandy . . . and it was a different feeling altogether, and your writing is entirely different.

WILDE: *It seems the top-flight comedians have an insatiable desire to be perfectionists. Why is it so important to be painstaking in doing comedy?*

BURNS: Well, what is a perfectionist? The kids that go out today and improvise . . . they are perfectionists, too. Vaudeville made you a perfectionist. It sort of got to be machine-made, because you did the same thing . . . the same thing. They were perfect from doing it day-in and day-out, so I think that's what made them perfectionists. Like, Jack Benny did the same joke for a thousand years. He used to come out and say, "How is the show until now?" and the orchestra leader would say, "It's great!" And he would say, "I'll stop that." That was his opening joke, and he did it for

years and years and years. He could not get a different opening. He tried all kinds of openings, but he was used to it. It
was comfortable.

WILDE: *You were forced to quit school at a very early age
and yet with this limited formal education you are considered a well-informed, well-read person. How did you
acquire this . . . ?*

BURNS: I did go to school—*my* kind of school. When I
was a kid I went out . . . I was hustling . . . I had a dancing
school when I was fourteen years old. . . and you meet people . . . you talk to them. Anybody says something that
makes sense, it stays with you, rubs off on you. *That* kind of
school . . . you do a lot of reading as you grow up.

WILDE: *Are you an avid reader?*

BURNS: I am a pretty good reader. I read things I think
are important . . . facts. I like biographies. Magazines like
Time and *Life,* all the papers at night, but I wouldn't say I
kill an evening reading.

WILDE: *Does a man's intelligence have anything to do
with his being a successful comedian?*

BURNS: I think so. You don't have to analyze your delivery, but you do have to analyze your attitude. You say to
yourself, "What's funny about this joke?" I don't mean the
wording, but what's the attitude? What's my *feeling?* If you
can't analyze, then you are just reciting—just *telling* a joke.
I hate a pointed joke . . . that's right on the nose. For instance, the funniest routine I have ever done was at a dinner
for George Jessel. I got up and said, "I didn't know there
was going to be a mixed audience. Now that there are ladies
out there, I'm sure there must be a clean anecdote that I can
tell about Jessel." And I kept talking, and I couldn't find

anything clean to say about him, and I didn't say anything dirty either. But the audience knew I had a problem. The audience made it dirty. I said, "When Jessel played Vancouver with Blasky's Redheads, there was this dame in the act—she was a contortionist—and it gets very cold in Vancouver. From there he went to Portland." It was that kind of thing, and it is a good example of what you just said. And you have to have intelligence to work that out.

WILDE: *You once said: "Comedians have no place to be lousy anymore." What did you mean?*

BURNS: I've changed my mind about that. It's a very good thing there aren't a lot of places to be lousy anymore, because if there are places to be lousy, you *stay* lousy. Comedians have to be good, *fast* today. And the kids make it and you don't have to play all the little towns. In the old days, there was no such thing like Bobby Darin coming into show business, a kid of twenty-two, and being a star . . . or Ann-Margret. It happened in pictures—Mary Pickford. You went through it step-by-step. It took seven or eight years. Nobody made it overnight.

WILDE: *You've also said that "your audience can laugh at you and still hate you." Would you explain?*

BURNS: They can laugh at the joke and not like you as a human being. You tell a dirty joke and the people laugh, but they resent it. It's the wrong kind of laughs, and the wrong kind of laughs will kill you. Let's say in a night club where you are doing some bit too risqué—you are shocking the audience into a laugh, a disappointed laugh. I don't want to mention any names but there is one comedian who is real dirty. I went to see him and the audience screamed at him, but I don't think they liked him. You don't love him. There's no affection. You go see Benny, you like Benny. There's something warm about Benny. Jimmy Durante— you want to take him home with you. Bob Hope. But then there are other guys who are great comedians who are funny and they don't have to be dirty but they are.

WILDE: *Perhaps they feel the audience sees only clean comedy on television and comes into a night club looking for something they don't usually get?*

BURNS: But the danger of that . . . is that young fellows like yourself . . . when you go into a night club and you see big business and a guy comes out and he's terribly dirty, you say, "Where does this stop? You say, "I'll go out and tell a few dirty jokes too!" It rubs off. It's not good. The comedian I am talking about . . . the place was jammed, and the words —I never heard such words. But they come back to see him again. It's all right for the night club, but it's bad for the young fellow, because where do these words end? What are you going to do next to shock your audience? If you are telling a joke, "Well, I grabbed her by the ass . . ." well, that's shock laugh. It's shock laugh if you haven't seen the show before, but if you come in next season and say, "grab her by the ass," the guy says, "He grabbed her by the ass last year!" So it doesn't get to be funny anymore.

WILDE: *Do you consider a comedian funny as long as he makes you laugh?*

BURNS: I like comedians that don't sweat. I like guys who take it easy, who look like they're not getting paid. Shecky Greene does it easy. I don't even know him very well, but I go out and see him. I think Buddy Hackett is a very funny guy. Joey Bishop is funny.

WILDE: *Many comedians just starting out are bewildered about which way to turn. Can you suggest anything to make the struggle a little easier?*

BURNS: I'm a big believer in honesty. The biggest mistake you can make if you are eighteen or nineteen . . . you can take Jack Benny's delivery but don't take his words, because his words are for a seventy-year-old man. First you have to have something yourself. You gotta take . . . a little bit of Bob Hope—the way he looks at an audience after telling a joke—or Durante's turns, or Jack Benny's folding his arms, or whatever you want to take, but only if you can do it—so it fits you—it gives you something new—the combination. But don't finish the way they do. Don't open the way they do. Have your own way.

Johnny Carson

Johnny Carson was born in Corning, Iowa, on October 23, 1925. At fourteen, he began entertaining for the Elks and Rotarians in his hometown of Norfolk, Nebraska, performing card tricks and magic as "The Great Carsoni."

After two years in the Navy and four years at the University of Nebraska, Johnny moved to Hollywood and hosted a television show called "Carson's Cellar."

In 1954, while writing jokes for Red Skelton, he took over the show one evening when Skelton was injured and as a result of his performance won the "Johnny Carson Show" on CBS.

Later, he became host of the daytime quiz show "Who Do You Trust?" and made personal appearances on the Dinah Shore, Perry Como, and Ed Sullivan shows. He also became a regular guest panelist on "What's My Line?" and "To Tell the Truth," as well as doing feature acting roles on "Playhouse 90," and the "U.S. Steel Hour." Johnny became a national institution when he succeeded Jack Paar as host of NBC's "Tonight" show.

Johnny and his wife Joanne live in a duplex in one of Manhattan's most fashionable cooperatives.

A Johnny Carson monologue

[*After introduction by Ed McMahon*] I would have let the applause run longer but what profit a man if he gain the whole audience and lose a commercial.

You people who wrote for tickets six months ago, was the thrill you just had worth the wait?

I'd come out now and shake your hands personally but I don't do custom work.

I'm Johnny Carson . . . known to the Indian braves in Nebraska—to whom I used to loan money as a youngster—as great straight arrow. Ah, that's really a translation. What they called me was: Big Shaft.

This is the "Tonight" show. Listed as event number one twenty-seven on the eight-dollar guided tour of New York.

. . . Another good audience. We've had great audiences recently. Ever since we put that line at the bottom of the tickets: Bring Your Own Bottle.

But seriously, folks, we have a real holiday show for you tonight. And tonight's holiday is the massacre at Bull Run.

Great show tonight. Years from now, when you look back on this show and say, "This was Carson's shining hour," remember—you're all drunk.

In keeping with the holiday spirit, why don't you all turn to the person next to you, shake his hand and say, "Howdy there, stranger!" And that goes for you people watching at home in bed.

If I seem a little pooped, I just got back from Indianapolis. And the flight was a little difficult. Just as I sat down, a man came up to me and said, "Are you Johnny Carson?" I said, "Yes!" He said, "You know I was worried about this flight. I was really scared. But seeing you here . . . a man of your importance . . . gives me the confidence to take this flight." Which wouldn't have bothered me but he was the pilot.

It upsets you a little when you look into the cabin and the pilot's got a St. Christopher statue on his dashboard and St. Christopher's got his hands over his eyes.

I want you to enjoy yourself this evening. No need to laugh or applaud. Just forget that I'm the sole support of three apple-cheeked boys . . .

[*Getting hammy*] Forget that I'm pure at heart. Forget that I served my country for five desperate years in a lonely foxhole in the steaming jungles of New Guinea . . . forget all that! [*Near tears*] If you don't want to laugh or applaud, I won't care . . .

I just threw that in—the Emmy Awards are coming up —and maybe I'll have a chance for Best Actor in a Dramatic Role.

You CAN FORGET that "Carson is cocky, complacent, and cantankerous" myth the magazines and newspapers insist on feeding the public. Johnny sat on his NBC office sofa sipping coffee, puffing Pall Malls, and conversing with all the warmth and geniality that can be expected from a man who for years has been the late-night darling of television.

I arrived twenty minutes early (to be able to make another later appointment) and Mr. Carson interrupted his busy schedule to welcome me immediately.

His winsome secretary, Jeanne Tellez, ushered me into the small but tastefully decorated office. Johnny wore a maroon turtleneck shirt and a blue cardigan sweater. He spoke quickly, emphatically, rarely hesitating to answer a question. He smiled often, implying he was not to be thought of as an expert but was simply expressing his opinion.

WILDE: *John, you started as a magician. I believe there are three types of magic acts. First, straight serious magic. Second, straight magic but with jokes and funny comments interspersed. And third, the out-and-out burlesquing of magic, à la Ballantine.*

CARSON: Right.

WILDE: *Which type did you start doing?*

CARSON: I started out doing straight tricks, to fool people, and then very quickly it came into comedy magic—magic to entertain rather than to fool somebody.

WILDE: *You started doing it at about fourteen, for money?*

CARSON: Yeah, in school—three dollars a show—the Rotary Clubs, Ladies' Aid, church groups. . . .

WILDE: *Great experience.*

CARSON: Greatest in the world. Little by little it became centered around the audience participation type of magic . . . jokes . . . tricks would occasionally go wrong. So it was essentially comedy-magic.

WILDE: *At what point did you eliminate the magic and concentrate completely on comedy?*

CARSON: That was after the . . .

[Jeanne Tellez enters with coffee]

CARSON: Thanks, honey. I also get an antidote with this. I did the magic along with the comedy—all throughout the service. I also did straight "stand-up" in the service. I was probably one of the few officers in the Navy that entertained the enlisted men. It's usually reversed. I was an ensign, and I remember performing on troop ships going over with mainly enlisted men audiences. Any time you did jokes about the officers, as an officer, you had something else going for you. So the magic was really through school—I didn't do it much after I got out of the service. I went into radio then. I keep it as a hobby now. I don't do much with it anymore.

WILDE: *Approximately how many years was that, John?*

CARSON: I did magic for about ten years—where I was quite active in it. Like any kid, I was writing the column for the school paper in humor, in junior high school. Magic was actually just an interest that I picked up along the way. But people ask, "Where did you start to become funny?" No one can really pinpoint it, if you ask any comic. You find out that you can get laughs, when you're a kid . . . either by doing silly sounds or impressions or acting up or whatever it is. The magic actually came after you found out that you could be amusing in other areas. It just became a hobby. But because of the desire, I guess, to get laughs, or finding out that you could get laughs, the magic was a good adjunct thing to have, because you could tie it in very easily.

WILDE: *Where did you get the jokes that you used during that period?*

CARSON: I think you steal, mainly, when you first start, like everybody does. You listen. You subscribe—I suppose like everybody did at one time—to Billy Glason. You read all the gag files. You know you can go to libraries and find jokes that they are still using today. You watch Rowan and Martin in their "Laugh-In" and they are doing stuff to a new audience that hasn't heard it before. They're doing the old blackouts, the old cross-overs, the old two-way jokes. There is no such thing, you know, as an old joke. It's just somebody hasn't heard it . . . it's just as fresh. It's all in the telling. So when you first start, you find your material from all kinds of sources. Then you finally reach a point where you find you can construct your own or you can make them up or you can find topical things and switch them around. It's mainly construction anyway.

WILDE: *Later you became a comedy writer. What made you turn from performing to writing?*

CARSON: I was doing both at the same time, actually, Larry. Even when I was in radio in Omaha, I wrote most of my stuff as a disk jockey. I did a show for an hour and a half every morning . . . you write your own stuff. You pull it out of the papers. I never actually gave up the performing for writing. It was just something that I was doing while I was on the West Coast. I wrote for Red Skelton for about twenty weeks. I wrote monologue stuff but I was still performing. Often I would appear on Red's show and I was doing a local show in California at that time, so it just went hand in hand. If you can *write* for yourself, it is a hell of an advantage.

WILDE: *Comedy writers, in discussing their craft, use phrases like "cadence," "rhythm," "formula jokes," "non-sequiturs,"—the basic tools of the profession. How did you learn the technique of joke construction?*

CARSON: I think, by observing, by listening, and watching somebody else's work. I grew up, probably like you did, listening to the comedians on the radio—the late thirties and forties. As a matter of fact, in college I did a thesis on comedy. I taped excerpts from the various radio shows and then tried to break them down and explain what kind of construction they were using. But I think you learn construction by reading . . . watching . . . listening. Pretty soon you find the formula for jokes, you learn the construction of jokes—whether they are two-way jokes, single jokes, topping jokes, running gag jokes, change of pace jokes. That's all formula stuff. Most discussions of comedy are very dull, I find. Because once you try to explain comedy, it loses the magic that it is supposed to have.

WILDE: *Robert Benchley, S. J. Perelman, James Thurber, and others have authored many comedy classics. What is the difference in the humor that is written to be read and that which is spoken?*

CARSON: Well, Benchley always read better than he performed. I think today Benchley would probably be much more accepted than he was when he was doing those little vignettes in movies. He was almost ahead of his time. He was doing very subtle, dry, things that a lot of people didn't quite understand. The written word gives you a chance to read it again. Perelman is awfully funny when you *read him,* because of the vocabulary, the construction—it's difficult to tell in *jokes.* He forms word pictures. Fred Allen, very often, is almost funnier to read than he is to listen to, because of his construction when he writes, I think. And most writers, like Benchley, Thurber, were not particularly good performers. Perelman, on interview shows, does not come across half as well as he does on paper. Even Art Buchwald, who is probably one of the best comedy writers per se and social commentators, doesn't come across as well in person as he does on the printed page. Maybe it is the personality of the individual—it doesn't translate as well. Sometimes things have to be read and re-read and digested. I think when you do verbal comedy, you have to get to it a little quicker, because the audience doesn't have the chance to mull it over and re-read it, so it has to be a little more direct . . . when you're doing a joke in front of an audience, you have to get to it fairly quickly. You can't encumber it with a lot of vocabulary.

WILDE: *The shortest distance between two points?*

CARSON: Generally, I think so, yeah. So it doesn't muddy it. If an audience has to sit and analyze the joke and say, "What is he trying to say?" I think it's a little difficult.

WILDE: *John, you mentioned the thesis you did on comedy writing, in college. Were you fairly sure then that comedy was going to be your life's work?*

CARSON: No, I can't say that. Again, when people ask, "Where did you make the transition?" I don't think you really know. It happens! It's a gradual changeover. As you work, you feel comfortable with certain things, but I don't think you say—maybe some people do—"I'm going to be a comedian." I knew I was going to be an entertainer. I didn't know for sure if it was going to be "stand-up" comedy but I realized that if you have an ability to get laughs, or if you can write funny things, it's gonna take a direction, and whatever happens, usually kicks you off into the next thing.

WILDE: *Was it in the service that you first began doing a stand-up act—without the magic?*

CARSON: Well, I had done that in college, even in high school. You know, you're involved in school plays . . . they called them *skits* then. I was always involved in that type of thing.

WILDE: *Were there any comedians, when you were getting started, that you admired?*

CARSON: Yeah, practically all of them on the radio. Fibber McGee and Molly, Don Quinn, who just died a couple of months ago, I admired tremendously because he could write comedy so well. The Benny show, the Hope show, Fred Allen—all of the comedy shows that were on the radio at that time—you had to learn from them.

WILDE: *What were some of the things you learned?*

CARSON: I think, you learn . . . first of all, the most important thing to me, in comedy—it always sounds like such a dull discussion when you discuss comedy—I think the greatest thing that a performer can have if he is going to be successful, is an empathy with the audience. They *have* to like him. And if they like the performer, then you've got eighty per cent of it made. And if you don't have that, it's damned difficult to get the audience on your side. If they resent you or if they don't feel any empathy with you or

they can't relate to you, as a human being, it gets awfully
difficult to get laughs. Bob Hope can walk out on a stage and
people are laughing before he gets there. A lot of it is conditioning. There may be funnier men in the world who are
quicker on the ad-lib and say funnier natural things in a
given moment . . . but I still think the most important thing
is the like-ability, the rapport, and that again is that indefinable thing . . . you don't study for it, you don't learn it,
you don't take a course in it—it is either there in the individual or it is not. When I see comics performing on a
stage . . . you can tell very quickly whether the audience
likes them—not so much *what* they are saying, as *how* they
say it. *How* they relate to the audience . . . are they just
throwing out one line after another and saying, "Hey, folks,
here come the jokes." Or does the audience really *dig* them.
As a guy.

WILDE: *When you were the host of the quiz show "Who
Do You Trust?" you often had to ad-lib and create spontaneous humor. Was there anything special in your background or training that you believe prepared you for that
kind of an assignment?*

CARSON: That again is difficult to answer. As you know,
people misunderstand the term "ad-lib." Very often they
think it is coming up with a new, completely original line at
the time. It's not. Very often it's memory. Very often it's
switching something. Very often it's something you have
used before. The trick is to have it at the right time. I think
it's the recall, the ability to take the situation and create
something or to make a comment on what is happening
that is really more important than having to create a brand-
new line. I think it's a natural thing, I don't think you learn
it—to ad-lib as such. Now, Milton Berle of course . . . people

say, "Does Milton ad-lib or doesn't he? Does Milton remember?" I'm not being patronizing. That is one way that people ad-lib . . . sometimes it can be a total recall. Morey Amsterdam can give you a joke for any subject that you want to come up with. That may or may not be ad-lib.

WILDE: *Then it was just your general training, your interest in jokes, in their construction, that gave you the foundation to be able to handle that show?*

CARSON: I think it's more than that. And again, I say, this always sounds serious. I think there are some people who *think* funny, who think off-beat. I remember once NBC had a comedy workshop school on the Coast, which was never successful. I think you can teach fellows to write comedy construction and jokes—a formula joke: "It was so cold that . . . ," "She's so fat that . . ."—and you come up with a funny word picture. You can teach formulas for writing, but I don't believe you can teach people to *think* funny. I don't think you can teach somebody to be a Jack Douglas or a Woody Allen. Their minds work in a little bit different areas than the normal mind works. Mel Brooks— you don't manufacture a Mel Brooks—it's there, the off-beat mind! What the background is that produces somebody who thinks funny I'm not sure. That could be a whole study in itself. Where do the comedians or the guys who get laughs— what do they have in common in their background that produces that kind of a mind?

WILDE: *It's amazing how very similar all the backgrounds of comedians are.*

CARSON: Yeah, even though they may have come from different ethnic backgrounds, different racial backgrounds, different stratas of income, basically they have that ability

I think, to see the ridiculous in a normal situation . . . that the average person would just look at. The comedian looks at it in a little bit different way and makes a comment on it.

WILDE: *And you don't believe it's possible to learn that?*

CARSON: No, not really. I don't think you can teach somebody to be a comedian. I think you can learn timing to a certain extent, stage presence, what material is good and bad, but I don't think you can create the overall attitude that makes a successful performer. I think there has to be something in the psyche that is there.

WILDE: *But it's an intangible?*

CARSON: Yes. You just can't define it. I have to go back to Stan Laurel. Somebody asked him, "What's comedy?" and he said, "How the hell should I know?" What makes people laugh? *I* don't know what makes people laugh. I know *devices* that make people laugh, but I don't know *why* people laugh.

WILDE: *And the very devices that you use may not work for somebody else?*

CARSON: Certainly. That's true. I don't think anybody knows *why* people laugh. George Burns says, "If they laughed at it, it's funny." Everything is relative in comedy. Tragedy no. If you see a serious play, everybody that sees that serious play will come out with almost the same reaction. If something is sad, it's sad. If you have a scene in a play where somebody is dying of cancer—that's sad. And that will affect everybody in that audience pretty much the same. But when you walk out and do a piece of humorous business, it's not going to affect everybody the same because it is all relative to their own individual experience with it— how they relate to it. Everybody has a sense of humor. So, when somebody says, "He's got a great sense of humor," . . . in relation to what? Hell, I know people who couldn't stand Fred Allen and people who *loved* him. I know people who hated Laurel and Hardy, couldn't see anything funny that they did, and other people who think they are the greatest. So that's what you are dealing in when you talk about what makes people laugh. It's all relative.

WILDE: *John, when you ad-lib a line that you feel will get a laugh, does that sentence actually form in your mind before you deliver it, or does it just come out?*

CARSON: Sometimes you are ahead of it and sometimes you just say it very quickly. Sometimes without even thinking. Sometimes you'll be formulating a line, if you can see where the conversation is going and you think you might get to that point, then you are kind of prepared for it. Other times somebody will say something and you react immediately. For example, the other night we had a fellow on the show, weighed five hundred pounds . . . a writer . . . big fellow. One of the guests on the show, a girl, said, "I wanted to be a nun." And this writer who was sitting there said, "I always wanted to be a monk." And I said, almost without thinking, "You could be a monastery." Now that may or may not be the funniest joke in the world, but at the time it was perfect. I didn't stop and think. It just came out. But it was funny because the guy was huge and it made a funny picture—and it was just that fast. It may or may not be an original line, but it fitted.

WILDE: *When the writers submit the jokes each day for the monologue, in addition to their being funny, are there other ingredients that you look for, such as specific subjects or types of construction that you feel more comfortable with, etcetera?*

CARSON: Yeah . . . when the writers come in and they submit stuff, you have to go with what you feel when you read it. I will edit the material. I'll put it in a certain order that fits—for me. I may change a line or a joke, I may change the construction of a joke, I may put the specific in rather than the general. Since I do the show every day, I like to talk about things that are going on in the news . . . the political situation . . . whatever is happening. It is difficult to make jokes about the Vietnam War . . . but it is easier to joke about the politicians. Yeah, I do look for certain constructions, certain phrasings that are funny, because a joke does not have to be a joke to get a laugh. A line can be funny because it *sounds* funny. It comes out funny. The content of it is strange . . . it's good construction and yet it's not a joke as we look at a joke.

WILDE: *It's conversational, it has a feeling of believability?*

CARSON: For my style, yeah. I can tell jokes or comment on things. I do both. I don't think you should ever shy away from jokes. I think Mort Sahl started to do this—and I have a great respect for Mort—when Mort first started, he was very, very funny. And then he started to take himself a little serious and he started to comment on things and become a reporter. And very quickly the sense of humor leaves you. I wouldn't shy away from jokes. Woody Allen—as casual as Woody looks when he performs—is very well constructed. He knows exactly where he's going. Even Buddy Hackett, who has a great ability to look like he's creating . . . most of the performers know that Buddy has certain things that he does very well. He makes it sound spontaneous, but he knows exactly where he is going. So construction is very important. Things have to fall together, they have to *build*. You have to keep your audience off-balance. Woody is probably as well constructed, comedy-wise, as anybody. He's a good writer. But he delivers it not as bang, bang, bang, bang. He comes out and he says, "Oh, I want to tell you about what happened," and it's a great feeling. The delivery, I think, is as important as the material very often. Your delivery can save you if the material isn't up to par and your *reaction* to it. It always amazes me when I see guys working in front of an audience and they are not going—they don't seem to realize it. They plunge right on doing the routine, like, "I'm going to do this folks, come hell or high water," rather than change it and going into different areas.

WILDE: *John, what is the approximate number of jokes that make up one of the opening monologues?*

CARSON: Oh, that's hard to say. It may be seven, eight, nine, ten, depending on what I have that day—what the guys come in with.

WILDE: *About how many minutes does that run?*

CARSON: It can run seven, eight minutes.

WILDE: *How many jokes do you and the writers have to come up with in order for you to finally select those ten?*

CARSON: Well, a lot of times, the fellows don't write jokes. They may write observation. So "jokes" is a bad word to use.

WILDE: *Funny comments?*

CARSON: Yeah. We may come up with six or seven pages of things. Maybe twenty-five or thirty, out of which I may take ten or a third of them.

WILDE: *Sometimes when a joke gets no reaction, or worse*

a groan from the audience, you get a big laugh by your follow-up comment, verbal or visual. Do you ever create such a situation purposely?

CARSON: No, you don't create it purposely because that becomes obvious. There is nothing I hate worse than somebody on a stage when jokes don't go, to start to use what we call "savers" or "toppers"—and then they have a "topper" for the "topper." The device becomes obvious. Nobody likes to die. I would much rather go with a joke that's funny than to tell a joke and then try to figure out how I can recover from it. An audience doesn't mind seeing you in trouble, if you have fun with it . . . and take the laughs on yourself. But it is attitude again, and how you do it.

WILDE: *Is it easier to come up with a new topical monologue night after night than to perfect just one as a permanent part of your night club act?*

CARSON: It is more difficult for this show because of the demands. Every night you're there. It is difficult to come up with a good monologue if you are out once a week on television. But when you do it every night, five nights a week, it gets more difficult. Some nights you'll be good, some nights you'll be so-so. But I like it because it is an integral part of the show—gives me a chance to be out there and talk to the audience for a while and see what kind of a mood they're in for the evening. And as you know, once you get a good monologue for a night club you can use it for a long, long time with changes . . . and that's why I very seldom do on television anything that I do in clubs, because it takes too long to create a good *chunk* of material.

WILDE: *A "stand-up" comedian working night clubs builds his act step-by-step, through trial and error. If a line doesn't work he replaces it, until the routine is solid. . . .*

CARSON: Right.

WILDE: *Since you have to do a new show every night, how do you decide if a joke or a line or a sketch is funny?*

CARSON: You go on your own judgment. There is no other way. Sometimes you may be wrong, sometimes you may be right, but I think if you're a professional, you are going to be right more often . . . you *should* be right more often. First of all, you have to analyze and see if it's comfortable for you. Do you feel comfortable with it? Do you think you can give enough to it that will make it funny? Sometimes you go in with reservations and you may pull it out. But I think it becomes a personal decision.

WILDE: *Is this a skill that can be developed and that you get better at as the years go by?*

CARSON: You should. You should get better at it. Also, there is another thing we haven't discussed and that's *acceptance*—acceptance by the audience. You can take the funniest man in the world who is unknown and put him in front of an audience that has not yet accepted him because they don't know him . . . it makes a big difference in the reaction he's gonna get. I'm accepted now much more than I was five years ago, because I've had tremendous exposure on television . . . as Jack Benny had in radio and motion pictures and Bob Hope has built up over the years—the acceptance that a Sinatra has. Someone who might be a fine singer can go out and he's not going to have the magic and he's not going to have the acceptance that a Sinatra has because the audience doesn't know anything about him yet. So I think that's tremendously important.

WILDE: *Does that make it easier for the comedian?*

CARSON: Oh, sure. The confidence. Once you have the confidence and you know the audience is there to see you, you've got to come out ahead—rather than walking out and saying, "I wonder if they're going to like me tonight?" . . . 'cause you're not known. But if you're known, and you have the reputation that you have built up or else you've earned, you are way ahead of the game when you walk out on the stage!

WILDE: *There's a tremendous amount of overlapping here. . . . Bob Hope is known as a one-liner comedian, Jack Benny as a character-situation comedian, Jackie Gleason as a sketch or book comedian. How would you describe the kind of comedy performer you are?*

CARSON: Well, it's a combination. When I work in night clubs, I do "stand-up." I go out and I do an hour, an hour and ten-fifteen minutes. Part of it is monologue. I finish with a physical sketch. Now we are back to tags again, which are kind of dangerous. When people give me an application for something, I just put down *entertainer*. I do a lot of things on the "Tonight Show." I do "stand-up," "sketches," "blackouts," "interviews," I get involved with the acts, etc. It is an *attitude* I guess, more than anything in what I do. I like to work topical. Most of my comedy is built around things that people identify with. If I go someplace . . . I will talk about going to the Mayo Clinic. Not just a doctor routine with jokes, but it'll be an in-truth thing with an attitude and a point of view. It's not easy to sit down and *describe* what I do. It just comes naturally. I've always hated tags, you know.

WILDE: *You are considered to be one of the masters of the "take," or "non-reaction." Would you define what a "take" is?*

CARSON: I'll try. I don't know if I can. A "take" is not completely natural. It's an unnatural thing. It's an exaggeration, I suppose. You have to probably get somebody like Ben Blue . . . we'll go back to Oliver Hardy. Those things were not thought of in advance—the long stare into the camera that he did, the frustrated, the anxious, exasperated take. That came out of . . . when they were making a movie, he didn't know what to do, so he did this stare into the camera and they found it served as a great device because it gave pacing to their comedy. It gave the audience a chance to relish the joke, to laugh, so they didn't overlap into the next laugh. The "tie-twiddle" thing, where he twiddles the tie, it came out of accident. It worked for them. I've found, over a period of years, certain things work for me. Like, just doing a *deadpan,* holding-still "take" or just an "eyebrow" thing . . . I don't know really how you explain it. Benny, of course, is known for his *long* pauses and looks. Gleason does great, great reactions in his sketches. They're reminiscent of Oliver Hardy or Edgar Kennedy and all the people who do reactions. In certain instances I am a reaction comedian, because of this kind of a show where I am playing off of people. Very often you get more out of it by your *reactions* to things than doing jokes. If you get some nutty dame out there, sometimes you can get more out of it by just doing exasperated reactions or takes. But to explain a take is kind of difficult. I'm not trying to beg the issue, I don't claim to analyze it that much. It's something that I feel and I do and is comfortable and works for me.

WILDE: *Charlie Chaplin in a* Life *magazine story said, "You cannot be funny without an attitude. Being without an attitude in comedy is like something amiss in one's make-up." What exactly is a comic attitude?*

CARSON: Well, you can use different words for it—a *form.* It takes a certain form. Generally, it is your outlook on things. It is, in a way, an extension of your personality. But

I think it has to have discipline. That's another word that
sounds corny in comedy, but discipline—and I hate to be
patronizing to other comedians so I won't use any names—
there a couple of fellows working today who are tremendously funny, but they have no discipline. They have great
natural ability and talent but they haven't learned how to
confine it, how to edit it. They haven't learned—as far as
I'm concerned—what is good and what is bad for them. And
they continue to do things they really shouldn't do—either
somebody can't tell them, or they don't realize it themselves.
The way you are looking, I would guess you know who I am
talking about. They don't know how to edit, they will go
twelve minutes when they should go six, but they don't seem
to realize they have gone six minutes too long. I can usually
tell if I'm on too long, or if I should get off, or if I should
go to another subject—that's something you have to feel.
So I think that shapes your attitude. Your attitude is an
expression of your relationship to things, and the way they
affect you and the way you talk about them or react to them.
It comes from your experience and your upbringing. And
the way you feel about things.

WILDE: *You mentioned before that you don't do anything
in a night club without its having an attitude and a point
of view. Is a "point of view" an extension of the comic attitude?*

CARSON: Yeah, in a way. You can take a very common
situation and your point of view or your attitude toward it
and what you see in it may be completely different from
what somebody else sees in it. They will comment on it one
way, you may take a completely different approach to it,
and this is where the humor comes out—your specific look
at something the audience hasn't thought of.

WILDE: *Is that like someone telling a funny story and the other person says, "I heard it another way"? It's the same joke but from a different point of view?*

CARSON: That's right. Yeah. "Form," "attitude," the shape that the comedy takes. Now I don't know what my attitude is because I am not strictly a sketch comedian, I don't deal in just the one area, nor do I deal in just standing up and telling a hundred and twenty jokes à la Henny Youngman. Henny has an attitude in his comedy, very definite. You know what you are going to see if you go see Youngman. I like to stay flexible enough to be able to change, because I think attitudes in comedy change. I don't think you can do comedy now that you could do twenty years ago. People's tastes change. If you looked at stuff now that was big in burlesque and vaudeville, you'd think it was terribly corny. They didn't think it was then, but it would be terribly dated today. Smith and Dale would be dated now. And Weber and Fields. I think you have to change with the times. And television has been responsible for a lot of that. The guy sitting in Omaha or out on a farm in Nebraska has seen all the comedians. He knows what's going on. You have a hipper audience, a more sophisticated audience today, because they've seen so much stuff in movies and television. And you have to keep up with that. I don't think you can just stay in one bag all the time.

WILDE: *Does a comedian's pride or vanity play any part in being able to evoke laughter from an audience?*

CARSON: Well, I think anybody who's in show business, who appears on the stage has a certain vanity and ego to fulfill and that is the desire to be liked. It is just that simple. You wouldn't be up on that stage . . . most people get stage fright if they have to get up and address the PTA—so there must be something in the make-up of an entertainer that says, "I want to be accepted. I want to go in front of this audience and I want to hear the applause and the laughs." I think it's that basic. You got to have that vanity, and if you don't have it, you shouldn't be out there. You are always raised as a kid, you know, that you should be modest. But, unfortunately, in the entertainment business that does not work. If you don't have a certain amount of ego—now that doesn't mean cock-sureness, it means confidence in your own ability. "I know what I do, I do it well, and when I walk in front of an audience, I know that I am good." And if you don't have that attitude, you shouldn't be out there.

WILDE: *Does "sex appeal" have any direct relationship to a comedian's popularity?*

CARSON: I don't know, really. Not necessarily. You look at Durante . . . now if that is what you mean by sex appeal, that is rather a nebulous . . . I think you have to have both sexes like you, which is a form of sex appeal. It is just like when Sinatra sings, the men envy him and the women want to jump in the hay. There is a certain amount of that, yeah, and especially television gives you a closer identification because it comes right into the home. So, there probably is a certain amount of that sexual transference.

WILDE: *There seem to be many psychological reasons why someone becomes a comedian—need for adulation, overcoming a feeling of insecurity, etc. Have you ever thought about your motivation for wanting to make people laugh?*

CARSON: I suppose it goes back to acceptance. Everybody wants to be loved, no matter what they do—even if you are a shoe clerk. Everybody wants to feel that somebody likes them, that they're accepted. I think, by the fact that you find you can get laughs when you are in school—and this is where most of the guys start, when they are growing up in the neighborhood—they're jerking around, doing silly things, interrupting the class. It's an attention-getting thing, and that, in effect, is saying, "Hey, look at me, folks, I'm getting your acceptance." I'm sure that's part of it, to any performer—they *like* me, I'm *accepted*. So it is a form of love that you are looking for from the audience. I don't think that necessarily means or follows that all people who do comedy are hostile, bitter, unloved people striking back at society.

WILDE: *There are some comedians who fit that description.*

CARSON: Yeah, but that does not necessarily mean that to be funny you have to follow that pattern. It has always been kind of a standard comment—comedians come out of impoverished backgrounds. Yes, there are some that have. There are some that haven't. Bob Newhart is an extremely funny man. I don't think Bob came from the Lower East Side—Bob was an accountant in Chicago. A lot of comedians did years ago . . . but I think that now there is a new brand of comedy. You have the Sahls, you have the Newharts, maybe the Carsons, I don't know—who didn't have the same background but nevertheless it comes out the same.

WILDE: *Ralph Waldo Emerson, in his essay "The Tragic," suggests that out of insupportable pain and certain death, there is a mysterious counterbalance in life of composure and cheerfulness.*

CARSON: I thought Jack E. Leonard said that. Was that Emerson?

WILDE: *Is it possible, John, that philosophy could be the basis for all comedy?*

CARSON: Well, again, there's that old cliché that tragedy and comedy are just a hair apart. You can read all those symposiums or articles on comedy . . . as somebody said, "You could probably find something unpleasant in all humor if you dig far enough." If you do a joke about divorce . . . divorce is unpleasant, it is painful. Broken marriages, drunkenness, alcoholism—there's pain and tragedy there. Why do people laugh so hard at jokes about death? Adultery is not basically a funny thing—it's something that is supposed to be immoral—and there are more jokes about sex, adultery, death, murder, so forth, than anything else. That's an interesting observation, Larry. Max Eastman points out that old joke in his book, *The Sense of Humor* . . . the old man falling on the banana peel and everybody laughed. That's unpleasant. A man slips on a banana peel and breaks his ass—it's only funny relatively. It is not if it happens to *you*. A guy walking along and falls in an open manhole. People laugh at that. That's unpleasant. I mean, if you come right down to it—somebody hitting somebody with a two-by-four, you can laugh at it, but there's physical pain involved. So I am sure comedy and tragedy are closely intertwined philosophically.

WILDE: *John, there is a show business axiom that a comedian has to have closer rapport with an audience than a singer, a dancer, or an actor. Why is that?*

CARSON: Well, because you watch a dancer, you observe, you're a spectator, so to speak. Not so much a singer. A singer has to have a little more communication with an audience and that is why the good ones *do* have that indefinable rapport with an audience. A singer is telling a story. A dancer is telling a story, in a way, but you are more of an observer . . . what you call the *dumb* acts, like the jugglers in vaudeville. A comedian and a singer are communicating on a more personal level. You're trying to work on a person's emotions and thoughts—the way they feel about things—so it's a very close relationship. Before people are going to laugh you have to get them in a frame of mind —you have maybe five hundred, six hundred, eight hundred people in a room—or maybe ten thousand—you've got all kinds of senses of humor . . . different responses to what they find amusing. So it becomes a transference, a personal give-and-take with the audience. You're giving something and they are giving something back to you. As you know, there are performers that have no contact with the audience. They perform mechanically. They don't have that transference. And as I said before, I think you have to have that . . . the likeability . . . that the audience relates to when you are on the stage. It is a very personal thing, comedy. With me, anyway.

WILDE: *How much does the audience's receptiveness affect your performance on any given night?*

CARSON: It affects me quite a bit. Maybe I'm overly sensitive. That's good, though. Keeps you sharp. When I'm out there and things are not going my way, I start to switch and fool around, but I'll do something. You have to work your audience. Of course, being on television every night you can't do that all the time. I realize I am playing to ten or twelve million people and there are only two hundred and fifty in the studio audience. So you can't be overly concerned about your audience reaction. You still have to play the show basically for your home audience, which consists maybe of five or six people in a room. When I'm out on a night club floor or in concert dates, that is a little different —now they are all there!

WILDE: *Do you find it easier to make people laugh in a night club than on television?*

CARSON: You have a little better contact with your audience there. In a television studio there are many distractions. You've got to remember when people come to see a television show, most of them have never seen one before and they are rather entranced with what is going on. They see all the cameramen, the lights, the technicians scurrying around—so they have a lot to obscure their vision. When you are in a night club, you are there, you've got them and they have to look at you if you àre talking.

WILDE: *Most comedians have a theory or two as to why an audience can be more responsive on certain nights than others. What do you think the reasons are for this phenomenon?*

CARSON: I don't think there is any reason. I have never in my life yet learned how to tell on any given night what kind of an audience it's going to be—and I don't think any other performer can either. Let's take our show. We have two hundred and seventy seats. On any given night, you are going to have two hundred and seventy different individuals from different parts of the country, with different senses of humor—human beings. Now, that's reason enough. Theoretically, suppose I do the monologue and I get great reaction. Then we clear the studio and I bring in two hundred and seventy new people. I come out and do the monologue the same way—same timing, same inflection, same delivery. I'll get a different reaction. All of a sudden it's not playing as well or it's playing better. The simple fact is that you've got two hundred and seventy people in there. I've played Vegas, where you'd think Friday and Saturday would be gang-busters—your audience can change. You may turn out on Monday night, and all of a sudden you've got a completely hysterical audience. Whether there is a certain rapport within the audience, I don't know. I have never been able to analyze it. They just change. On holidays you can be a little more sure. Especially during Christmas—people get a little tired . . . they've been out shopping.

WILDE: *I find working in a resort area—where people have come for a vacation—they seem more relaxed and respond easier.*

CARSON: That's very often true. Again, in Las Vegas, people get surfeited with entertainment. They'll see a dinner show, they'll see a lounge show—maybe three lounge shows —another show. They may have been there for three days. Now that's a completely different audience from an audience, for example, that goes to a concert on a Saturday night—they haven't seen six other shows. It's something they have looked forward to—they've planned. You are going to get a completely different reaction.

WILDE: *Many comedians complain about the Borscht Belt audiences. They've seen five other comics that week before you come out to. . . .*

CARSON: That's right. They've seen the guys all week. They've been playing Simon Sez and *tummuling* and now as you say, you are on on Saturday night and they say, "Okay, fella, let's see what you can do!" Now it becomes a challenge. There is really no accounting for audiences, outside, as we say, of the resorts. They may be in a mood. I never know how to figure them.

WILDE: *Sometimes you'll be doing the show and maybe not getting the volume of laughter on the material you got the night before, but that audience has enjoyed themselves just as much, and very often will give you a big round of applause.*

CARSON: Oh, yes. I only played the Concord once, and I went up there and I didn't think that I was doing well. I don't know why—maybe I didn't hear it or something—and I walked off to a standing ovation. I came back and they were still standing, I went off and I came back and they were still standing. It was tremendous. I thought while I was out there that I wasn't reaching them. It's like working in a Veterans' Hospital. You are never going to get a lot of laughs. They appreciate it tremendously. You walk off sometimes to little nods or silences and then the guys'll come back later and they'll say, "Gee, you don't know how much the show meant!!!!" But it can be kind of depressing when you're out there. So you have to learn to read that.

WILDE: *Very often, comedians will use borderline jokes, taboo subjects, or blue material. Is that a sign of the times, John, or is it a calculated technique to loosen up the audience?*

CARSON: Well, Larry, I think you have to draw a definition to what is off-color . . . blue . . . and out-and-out dirty. And again, I think, we have to take into account who is doing it and how it's told. This becomes a degree of shading. I don't do anything in a night club that I wouldn't do in front of my own kids. Yet some of it might be termed risqué. Well, risqué is a long way from being dirty. And it depends on what you mean by "blue." I think it depends on the way in which it is said and the way it is delivered There are some fellows who can do a line and it comes out dirty. It sounds bad . . . it is said in an attitude . . . you know what they are trying to say. Joe E. Lewis can come out and do a line that somebody else couldn't touch with a fork and get a laugh with it, because of the manner in which he has said it, the *attitude* in which he said it. It's the kidding on the square. That to me is more important than the material. Guys who deal in dirty material are constantly going to homosexual jokes. They just don't have the material, so they're going for the easy jokes they think will get laughs, and they *will* in a certain room. I have always gone by a rule of thumb—I will throw out any joke that I think is going to cost me . . . at the end of the show. If I have any feeling about a joke, that it may offend, I will throw it out. Any joke is expendable. No joke is important enough or big enough that it can hurt something I'm going to do. It's awful for people to leave at the end of a performance and say, "He was funny but I wish he wouldn't have been so dirty." That's bad. You are only hurting yourself by doing it. So when it comes to blue material. . . .

WILDE: *You've been accused of that.*

CARSON: I've been accused of it on this show, but again comedy is relative. The word "pregnant" may offend some people, or the word "naked."

WILDE: *Will Rogers once said that "comedy can be a dangerous weapon . . . ridicule can sway people." Have you ever done material in the hope of swaying public opinion on a particular subject?*

CARSON: No. Will Rogers was something different. He was mainly a writer in those days and he didn't have the forum they have nowadays. I don't do it . . . oh, as they say, I stick pins in pomposity, which people like . . . but never at the expense of being cruel. But I think you can ridicule. I think the greatest ridicule line ever said in politics was about Thomas Dewey. "He looks like the groom on a wedding cake." Which was a devastating thing . . . to say about anybody. It is ridicule, but it is a very funny line. But I don't consciously go out to ridicule . . . ridicule is not humor. You can poke fun, give somebody a little *zinger* —but again it depends on the attitude with which you do it. Will Rogers got away with a lot, because he was a likeable man . . . again. As much as I like Shelley Berman and some of the things he does, sometimes he does it with too much hostility and people resent it. Bob Newhart is very likeable, and he get's away with a lot of things, because Bob is a likeable guy and he does some real zinging things. So again, it comes to the manner in which it is said, the context in which it is said at the time, and who says it.

WILDE: *John, psychologists claim that you can tell a lot about a person by the sort of jokes he laughs at. By making people laugh, do you feel you have a better insight into human nature?*

CARSON: That's difficult again. Now you are getting into the psychology of humor. I suppose you can. I'm sure if you have a battery of tests—with a hundred, one hundred and fifty jokes . . . all those tests, of course, are built on many thousands of surveys—like, Rorschachs and anything else, and I'm sure you could get a profile on the person by the type of thing he laughs at—because of certain kinds of jokes. I don't know that that gives me greater insight. I think as a performer, you learn to . . . or you should learn, anyway, when you are working, to *read* an audience. To *feel* their attitude toward what you are doing and react to it. When I work, I am conscious of the rapport and the feeling and how I am working and the reaction and if it goes a certain way, I'll go a certain way and if it goes another way, I can change with it.

WILDE: *In a* Look *magazine story on you, Harriet Van Horne said, "a star must be sufficiently common to permit the audience to identify with him and sufficiently uncommon to convince them he is special, unique, and loves them for all their commonness." Would you say those qualities are the basic requirements to become a successful comedian?*

CARSON: Yeah, I think there is a certain amount of validity in that . . . it goes back to what I was saying before about likeability—which means they can identify with you. Again, I think the most important thing is the acceptance and the likeablity . . . especially for the performers who work live—not so much in motion pictures because you are playing a role up there—but when you are standing out naked on a stage, so to speak, you are in front of an audience, there is where it comes down to the nitty-gritty. And if they like you . . . it's amazing what you can get away with and what they will accept from you. Laurel and Hardy were extremely likeable guys if you analyze their comedy. Under all their hostility toward each other, you always knew they were kidding, and that they were nice, likeable dumbheads. And you know, the old psychology: everybody thought they were smarter . . . people identified. They liked each other and you felt the by-play. Like, Carney and Gleason—when they yell at each other, you know that underneath there is a genuine respect and admiration. They can hit each other and thirty seconds later it's back to "Hiya pal," and that . . .

WILDE: *Alleviates the hostility . . .*

CARSON: Absolutely. The audience knows it's all in fun and that they're kidding.

WILDE: *John, comedians are often thought of as men who have made their way to the top without any formal school-*

ing. Would you say that your college education was a significant advantage or disadvantage in your career?

CARSON: That's hard, again, to analzye, Larry. I don't know. As I said, I think with the change in comedy and the awareness of the younger element . . . kids nowadays are hipper to what is going on in the world. They've seen a lot more than we did when we were kids. I think it gives me an advantage with the type of material I do. I try to keep abreast of what is going on. Certainly education has helped me in that it has made me aware of different areas I can go into and comment on. It's true many comedians have not had formal schooling. . . . That doesn't make them any less funny. I think comedy is constantly changing and the attitudes . . . I think if Ed Wynn went on television today, he probably wouldn't be accepted, he would look old hat. . . . Not that he wouldn't be funny, I think the era has kind of gone past the props and. . . .

WILDE: *Funny costumes.*

CARSON: And the funny costume type of comedy. Things change. It's a little more modern now. That doesn't mean you have to go out and be Mort Sahl. I would like to see more physical comedy. I love good physical comedy—Lewis, Skelton. I love to do physical sketches occasionally . . . because a good physical sketch, if it is done well, is high comedy. I think an education can help in anything. In the show that I do, it has been a great advantage, in that I have to work with so many different people. One night with Vice-President Humphrey . . . the next night I may have Margaret Mead . . . the next night I may have Jastro from NASA . . . so naturally that helps me. Otherwise, I would sit there, not knowing exactly what I am talking about. So I don't think having an education precludes the fact that you can be funny.

Maurice Chevalier

Maurice Chevalier was born at Menilmontant, Paris, on September 12, 1888. At seventeen he joined the night club act of Mistinguett, the legendary French star, and together at the Folies-Bérgère they became the rage of Paris. During the First World War, he was captured by the Germans and while in a prisoner of war camp he learned to speak English. This has enabled the Frenchman to communicate with audiences on two continents.

Chevalier made his first American film in 1929, *Innocents of Paris*. His recent successes have been equally divided between movie and television screens and personal appearances tours all over the world.

His best remembered films include: *Love in the Afternoon*, *Gigi*, *Can Can*, *Pepe*, *Fanny*, and *In Search of the Castaways*. Among his best-selling records for the MGM label are: "Maurice Chevalier Today," "Maurice Chevalier Yesterday," "Maurice Chevalier Sings Broadway," and "A Tribute to Al Jolson."

In Paris, Chevalier lives at Marnes La Coquette, a showplace filled with paintings and other treasures and considered one of the most magnificent private homes in France.

A sample of Chevalier's humor

Each time a journalist asks me, "How does it feel, Maurice, to be nearing eighty," I always answer, "Well, considering the alternative, I like it."

I FIRST MET M. Chevalier backstage at the Alvin Theatre (New York) where he had just finished his one-man show. He entered the little sitting area outside his dressing room wearing a white terry cloth robe, with a blue towel tucked in around his neck. I was entranced with the clarity and sharpness of his sparkling, blue eyes. His skin tone was of a man half his age in perfect physical condition. He stood so erect, I instinctively straightened my own posture.

Chevalier agreed to a meeting and three days later I arrived at Suite 1405 of the Delmonico Hotel. François Vals (Chevalier's manager) ushered me into the living room.

I prepared the Uher 4000-L and in a few minutes Chevalier, smiling, hand extended, entered and greeted me warmly. He wore rimless, orange-tinted glasses. His still abundant hair was almost white. He had on a dark blue suit with a vest, a blue and cream-colored tie. His cuff links were emerald green, as were his stick pin and a ring he wore on the little finger of his left hand.

He looked so distinguished he could easily have been taken for a bank president instead of one of the world's greatest entertainers.

Having been an admirer of his for many years—I had seen him in person twenty-six times—I must admit I was nonplused. He further complicated my attempt at being relaxed by saying, "I don't know your work, but I have heard of you. Exactly what do you do?" I told him, and the interview was underway.

CHEVALIER: How old are you, thirty?

WILDE: *Thirty-one.*

CHEVALIER: You look terribly like a French . . . a very fine, young star called Gilbert Beacaud, very much . . . very much. The same kind of dark and charming face. So now, what can I do for you?

WILDE: *Monsieur Chevalier, the majority of the American public has known you through motion pictures, television, and records as an acting and singing personality. Whereas people who have seen you in person know you are also a very fine comedian doing some very funny monologues. Have you ever thought of yourself as a comedian? In the American sense of the word?*

CHEVALIER: I tell you . . . I started when I was a boy as what we call in France a "low" comedian, you see, a red-nosed comedian. I was putting make-up on my face, I was dressed in funny clothes, and I started by singing, dancing and saying monologues, like that . . . It was only later that some women friends told me that I was not bad-looking and why should I make myself ugly. They said, "You could do exactly the same kind of jokes and the same kind of songs and monologues but well-dressed, as you are lucky enough not to be too bad-looking." And I did that . . . I started to sing in a tuxedo and a straw hat . . . and I found my real style. But my foundation was "low" comedian.

WILDE: *Your clothes onstage are more simple than the conventional American entertainer's wardrobe—with attention to shirt cuffs showing, high collars, and severely styled suits. Is this intentional?*

CHEVALIER: Yes, yes! I want, especially since I have been lucky enough to be strong enough to do those one-man shows. . . . You see, at that time in my career, I had always wanted everything to be as simple as possible. It is almost a sort of an exaggeration for me, you see. I have no music before I

come on the stage. It's a very simple set, just a piano. I come
without warning . . . I want everything to be as pure as
can be and as simple as can be because I think that a very
old artist like I am has got to be very simple and good
enough to be simple. That is not a real tuxedo,* . . . that's
sort of a compromise between a real tuxedo and a blue suit,
you see. But when I had a tuxedo it was a nice, fine tuxedo
from London. But I don't believe in trying to be too fancy
when you come on the stage because I don't see why you
should dress yourself so fancy as that when you come to
entertain the people . . . be well-dressed but not with a false
elegance, you see.

WILDE: *Performers today are very concerned about how
they appear to the public. What do you think your image is?*

CHEVALIER: I don't know . . . I don't know . . . I am exactly myself. . . . I have always been really myself and went
through the years just keeping in accord with myself, but
I have been evolving with the years. And I go on . . . I'm
an old man but I'm a man of our times. I am interested
by everything that is happening now. I have my own judg-
ments. But I am an old man . . . not one who says only,
"Oh, in the old days—the old days. . . ." No, the old days are
gone! We are living some new days and there will be some
new days later. So, I am trying to be on key with all the
periods of times that I am going through.

WILDE: *Performers who do comedy are known by various
titles. what is the difference between an "entertainer" and
a "comedian"?*

CHEVALIER: I cannot explain that very much. An "entertainer," they call that a "fantasist." A fantasist is a sort
of light comedian. At times improvising, light, charming—

* The suit he wears in his one-man show.

funny at times. I don't see the difference between an entertainer and a comedian. Both try to make people happy and laugh and to me there is no difference. A comedian may be only a man who tries to be funny, funny, funny—and an entertainer tries to charm the people, maybe a little more. But they called Jolson an entertainer. He was more than an entertainer, he was a great popular singer and something much more. An entertainer seems to be a kind of light name for something that is not light, something that is very artistic.

WILDE: *Bob Hope and Jack Benny are referred to as "comedians," but Danny Kaye is called an "entertainer."*

CHEVALIER: Yes, because he sings and he does different things. Maybe that is why they call a man an entertainer. When he does many things as you are doing . . . as I am doing myself. A little dancing now and then, some singing, some talking, some funny. . . .

WILDE: *Has singing and dancing always been part of your act?*

CHEVALIER: Yes, yes, until one day I was brave enough to do the one-man show as I do with just the piano. It was very brave because it was terrible risky.

WILDE: *How would you describe the kind of comedy you do?*

CHEVALIER: I don't know. I always have been working more instinctively than *thinking* very deeply about what I should do and all that . . . I feel instinctively the things and I try to get the tempo that I feel is right with the songs— some of them are touching, some of them are light, some of them are very funny. I feel that this year, at seventy-seven —that's a terrible and wonderful experience—I feel I am more on my real style this year. I am more happy with my style than ever. I never force at any moment. But the songs have always done . . . there are little moments when they hit right.

WILDE: *I love "Mimi la Blonde."*

CHEVALIER: "Mimi la Blonde" is a charming song. [But the audiences] do not understand one word, they do not know what I am saying. I just say it's a middle-aged French courtesan and the music—which is very fine music—and the antics and all that makes it very satisfying.

WILDE: *There is a theory that most comedy comes from anger or hostility and yet you get laughs out of warm, loving situations. How do you account for that?*

CHEVALIER: Because I think it's the only way to look at it when you become very old. You have to take the whole thing with a smile as you cannot change it. You can get laughs by things that would be sad if you did not take it that way.

WILDE: *Do you study people or human nature in perfecting your comedy?*

CHEVALIER: I don't study. . . . I never study. . . . It's kind of instinctive. I look at people. I'm learning a lot of things from people. I have a new gag, which was given to me by a fellow who said, "How do you work when you are in a very bad mood?" and I say, "I've never been in a . . . we have not the right to be in a . . ." It gave me the idea of trying to show a fellow who had been so bothered the whole day that he would be in a really bad humor. . . .

WILDE: *Your charm and magnetism are so powerful, people are not aware you are an indefatigable technician.*

I've heard that you refuse to do anything in front of the public unless you have rehearsed it to perfection.

CHEVALIER: Oh, yes . . . oh, yes . . . or sometimes not. . . . Even this new gag about the fellow who is absolutely disheartened and has to sing, "When You're Smiling," I am making it night after night with the audience. I tried it three days ago and now I'm going to polish it every night with the audience.

WILDE: *Is it really an advantage to rehearse each song or routine?*

CHEVALIER: Yes . . . but after that, it is still with the public that you make it, you see. Because you rehearse it— you try to think of the best things you can but it's still the public that tells you that's right and that's not right.

WILDE: *Can you tell immediately if the audience will be receptive?*

CHEVALIER: It seems that from the first laughs, from the first entrance, from the first way they receive you, at the beginning, that you know it's going to be a nice evening or you will have to make them get warmer.

WILDE: *What do you do if you sense that they are not receptive?*

CHEVALIER: You try not to think that they are so bad and do the best you can to convince them that you want to please them, that you want to make them spend a good evening.

WILDE: *Do you work harder, do you try harder?*

CHEVALIER: Not harder, but maybe a little bit more warmth. Because, after all, in a case like that it's a question that you have to win them, to make them get warmer than they are, you see.

WILDE: *Is it difficult to make an audience laugh?*

CHEVALIER: It depends on the material. With some material it becomes very easy. When the material is not quite neat enough it may be difficult. When you don't laugh easily they are very cold.

WILDE: *When you say, "not neat enough," do you mean that it doesn't fit the comedian or that it is still in rough stages and hasn't been polished enough?*

CHEVALIER: Yes, yes, sometimes. . . . Very often I almost improvise a gag or something like which I want to try and I explain it badly and after that I know I have to polish the way I present it, you see. . . . But it's the public who indicates it to me.

WILDE: *Last night you came out and immediately told two or three stories for laughs. Two years ago at the Ziegfeld Theatre, you came out and you sang first and didn't attempt to get laughs until later in your act.*

CHEVALIER: The laughter came . . . yes . . . about that picture, *I'd Rather Be Rich*—the gag between Sandra Dee and Sophie Tucker. I knew it was very funny and it's true. Very often I find my material in things that happen, you see.

WILDE: *Most authorities agree that it is harder to make people laugh than to make them cry. Has that been your experience?*

CHEVALIER: Yes, yes, but still all depends on the quality—on the sentiment . . . things sentimental . . . on the quality of laugh, you see. You have some fellows who make people laugh and at the same time simply because they laugh doesn't mean that it's good, you see.

WILDE: *Do you also do your comedy routines in French?*

CHEVALIER: Oh, yes . . . and more and more even in France, I'm becoming French-American. The last time when we celebrated my [seventy-fifth] birthday, I did the whole world—New York, London, South America, Brazil, and I did about thirty concerts and finished in Paris in the Théâtre des Champs-Élysées and it was almost half an act in French and American. Because now, first of all, they speak much more. English in Paris and they've learned to love those rhythms, those songs . . . and as my real work has really become French-American, since I came to America, I told them in Paris, I said, "I'm going to do exactly something like I do in New York and London because that is my profession. I'm not only a French singer, I'm an international singer and I have to use both languages"—and they liked it very much.

WILDE: *Has your style of comedy changed through the years?*

CHEVALIER: No, I don't think so. You see, it depends on what you have to do and what kind of comedy you have to use for a sketch or for a joke or for a monologue. No, I think it has always kept something that has been between Paris and Broadway, you see. Since I was a kid I have been inspired by the American showmanship. And at the same time I want to keep my truth which is to be a Parisian.

WILDE: *Many comedians have ways to prepare themselves before they go onstage. They jump up and down backstage, dance, talk to themselves. . . . What do you do?*

CHEVALIER: Nothing, because my evening starts quietly

by talking with people and then singing and then, I am warming up on stage . . . to tell the truth. But I understand that some people try to *warm up* like some dancers do, and some acrobats do. They have to warm up before getting into their show.

WILDE: *Is there a difference between a night club audience and a theatre audience?*

CHEVALIER: Definitely, definitely. Those I've been doing lately have been fine night clubs . . . like the Americana in Puerto Rico, the Diplomat in Miami Beach. When you sing, for example, at the Palmer House in Chicago, or the Empire Room here (Waldorf-Astoria, New York) . . . these are night clubs of quality with always the risks of having somebody having drunk a little more . . . but still it's a very nice and easy and in fact, in Puerto Rico and in Miami, very often they would give me standing ovations, which is very rare in a night club. I think you have some night clubs that are more difficult in America . . . because you have some hecklers and some people who talk to you and annoy you when you are working. There is surely a group of very first-class night clubs where you can still do your work very easily.

WILDE: *What is the length of your program in clubs?*

CHEVALIER: Well, it lasts between fifty minutes and one hour. I think when you do a night club . . . as big as you are . . . one hour is plenty. To do more is, in my view, a mistake. It's better to give them a good solid, fine, first-class meal but not overfeed them.

WILDE: *What qualities are needed to become a comedian?*

CHEVALIER: You cannot explain those kind of things. They should come naturally. You have naturally a way of saying your jokes and you know that you can become a comedian before you start being a comedian. You do not learn that on the stage, it has to be in your blood.

WILDE: *What must a comedian have to become successful?*

CHEVALIER: [Chuckling] He needs to have luck. . . . He needs to understand what the people like . . . and it seems to me that every artist can learn from the qualities and from the defects of all the other artists . . . by looking over and trying to see when they are right and when they are not right. You cannot explain those things, you *feel* them.

WILDE: *Is it necessary for a comedian to be educated?*

CHEVALIER: In these days, I think they need to have a sort of culture. But in my case, I had no culture at all, you see. I became a comedian and learned everything on the stage and learned everything going through my life, you see.

WILDE: *In your biography (With Love, by Eileen and Robert Mason Pollack*), you said, "Montaigne was becoming a friend of mine, so were Tolstoy and De Maupassant . . . the immortal authors . . . that I was meeting for the first time at the age of forty-three and I had never read anything outside of the daily papers." Then you really began to read very late in life?*

CHEVALIER: Yes, yes. I began reading when I was in Hollywood and became very friendly with Charles Boyer, whom I knew from France . . . whom I knew was the best young actor in France and we became great pals in Hollywood, and he is the one who taught me what I could get from reading. Because up to then . . . it's even a miracle that

* Little, Brown and Co.

I kept on top in France because I never read, I had no education, I had no culture. It was only instinct, you see . . . a sort of personality or something like that. But since I have been reading all those great writers I must say that it has helped me to become old much more beautifully than I would have become if I had not read them.

WILDE: *If someone wanted to be a comedian, what advice would you give?*

CHEVALIER: Well, there is no advice to give, you see. If he has the talent, he has to show it to the public. He must have courage, he must be able to be funny when he feels like crying. You've got to love it very much or you better do something else because it's not always very funny for a comedian. There are some nights that are not funny.

[*At this point a* Newsweek *reporter telephoned. He wanted Chevalier to describe what had taken place the previous night when Mrs. Jacqueline Kennedy attended his one-man show with her sister and brother-in-law, Stash and Lee Radziwill (the Prince and Princess).*

Chevalier explained that during his performance, he looked at the former First Lady sitting in the second row and without mentioning her name said, "Madame, with all the love, and admiration and respect my people have for you, I would like to say . . ." and he sang, "You Must Have Been a Beautiful Baby." It brought the house down.

After the show, Chevalier, Mrs. Kennedy and the Prince and Princess dined at El Morocco. The group discussed many subjects but the highlight of the evening, Chevalier revealed to the magazine correspondent, came when Mrs. Kennedy said to him. "You were so much at ease on the stage, you looked so peaceful and happy, I wanted very much to be you!"

Then Chevalier said to the reporter, "That was quite a complement coming from one of the greatest ladies in the world. It was one of the most memorable nights of my life."]

CHEVALIER: [*Putting the phone down*] Now let's get to the end, because I'm getting tired talking too much.

WILDE: *Have you ever had any voice training?*

CHEVALIER: Voice! I've never had any voice. . . . I had my tonsils operated on when I was younger and since then it has given me a better voice but before I had my tonsils operated on I was always. . . . easily hoarse, you see.

WILDE: *What about dancing?*

CHEVALIER: No. Each time I can see a good dancer and he can help me with a little routine, I always do it.

WILDE: *Two years ago at the Ziegfeld Theatre, you had a cold and you said, "I have a cold, so my voice is not too good. But that is all right. When I don't have a cold my voice is not too good, either." Was that an ad-lib?*

CHEVALIER: I always said that. It came to me in America long ago. I was singing at the Paramount Theatre in 1930, I think, and doing four or five shows a day and I had the flu. So I had a very bad voice . . . and I used to say at the beginning of each show, "My voice is very bad, I have the flu—but don't worry because, after all, when I have no flu, my voice is not very good either!" It's a good beginning. And it's true.

WILDE: *What is the hardest thing about being an entertainer?*

CHEVALIER: It's to keep your heart in the mood. That's the hardest thing.

WILDE: *What do you do to keep in good physical shape? Diet? Rest?*

CHEVALIER: Well, moderation. Only one word, moderation. Especially now at my time. To come and do two hours alone on the stage . . . with that responsibility, so I'm almost like a boxer. I drink very little, I don't smoke, and I don't eat too much. I gave up smoking almost thirty years ago. I was a very *big* smoker.

WILDE: *Which medium do you prefer? Movies, television, records?*

CHEVALIER: No, I think my real profession is to be on the stage . . . but in our times when you make a good picture it's also wonderful because it goes all over the world without you moving. It's like a visiting card that goes all over the world for you. Television can be very, very strong. And I still hope when I retire from the stage to do some television from Paris for America as sort of a bond.

WILDE: *What efforts have you made to remain a star for so many years?*

CHEVALIER: I never thought of doing anything particular. I just love it more than anything else and so I just went on as long as the public was with me.

WILDE: *What about publicity?*

CHEVALIER: Oh, no, not a bit. I have never had a publicity agent. Only when I was in Hollywood, because the studio did it. I believe in not running too much after success. I believe in meeting it half-way.

WILDE: *Of all your accomplishments in show business of what are you most fond?*

CHEVALIER: Well, probably what I am doing now. To be able to do that after sixty-six years in show business and to still be a major attraction all over the world . . . that I think is what I've done the best.

WILDE: *And this above the memorable movies you are famous for?*

CHEVALIER: Yes, in a movie, you see, you depend on so many others. The director, the story, you depend on so many things. When you are alone on the stage you depend on yourself only. That is my biggest pride. But when I can make a movie I am very happy about it, too. . . .

WILDE: *I want to thank you. . . .*

CHEVALIER: You're welcome. . . . I have spoken to you longer than for any interviewer I have ever met. Good luck!

[Mr. Chevalier died in Paris on January 1, 1972.]

Phyllis Diller

Phyllis Diller was born in Lima, Ohio, on July 17, 1917. Until she became a professional comedienne, Miss Diller was a housewife and mother of five children. Her husband, Sherwood, encouraged her to get into show business and since her first engagement in a San Francisco night club in 1955, Miss Diller has become one of the world's leading female stand-up comics.

She has appeared on every major television show as well as her own series, "The Pruits of Southampton" and as star of "The Beautiful Phyllis Diller Show" for NBC.

Miss Diller has recorded four comedy albums on the Verve label as well as "Phyllis Diller Sings Like She Looks" for Columbia.

Her movies include, *Boy, Did I Get a Wrong Number, Eight on the Lam, The Private Navy of Sergeant O'Farrel,* and *Did You Hear the One About the Traveling Saleslady?*

In the literary field, Miss Diller's books have been noted on the best-seller lists. They include: *Fang, Housekeeping Hints, Marriage Manual,* and *The Compleat Mother.* The last three were published by Doubleday & Company.

Some Phyllis Diller humor

Most people get a reservation at a beauty ranch—I was committed.

Am I a bird watcher? You kidding! Birds watch me!!

Fang never learned the alphabet til he started taking vitamins.

We owe a lot to Thomas Edison. If it weren't for him, we'd be watching television by candlelight.

Fang got his father's tooth and his mother's lip.

You know why this dress looks so wild and live? It's a skin graft.

My mother told me how to cure Fang's hiccoughs. "Hold his head under water."

Fang applied to the SPCA for a divorce. Claims he married a dog!

Fang loves crowds. He's not gregarious. He's a pickpocket.

I never made *Who's Who* but I'm featured in *What's That?*

Fang has that lean look—every time I look at him he's leaning on something.

I'm looking for a perfume to overpower men—I'm sick of karate.

I've turned many a head in my day—and a few stomachs, too.

I made up my mind to show the world—and they're afraid to look.

I'm a back seat driver . . . I don't tell people how to drive —I have long arms.

I'm studying karate and I've finally gotten to the point where I can break a board in half—with my cast.

Fang brought home a dozen flowers—three bottles of Four Roses.

This dress hides the eighth wonder of the world.

I'd do my ironing—but I can't find the refrigerator.

I must be mixed up—I call my husband Fang and the dog "Honey."

My advice to brides: Burn the toast so he won't notice the coffee.

Fang has two hobbies—at the beach it's bikinis, at home it's martinis.

Talk about boozing . . . Fang never goes out on New Year's Eve—he calls it Amateur Night.

When I got my first job I thought a filing system had something to do with fingernails.

I don't know if he said "There's nothing like a dame"—or "A dame like you is nothing."

He said he'd carry a torch for me—but he's afraid of fire!

Our TV man had to take our set back to the store for an adjustment—it needed three back payments.

I was arrested for taking a four-way cold tablet on a one-way street.

When Fang wants a hot meal—he knows where he can go.

Once I fed a stray dog and he never left—he couldn't move.

To Fang—a good year for whiskey is the year he drinks it.

If I looked like this on purpose—it would be "art."

Talk about old—she has a jar of lard made from dinosaur fat.

Fang says '68 will be a banner year for us—if it is, you know who'll have to carry it.

If I were a building—I'd be condemned.

Have you ever seen a soufflé that fell?—nature sure slammed the oven door on me.

I had to give up exercising—I can't stand the noise.

I decided to have my ears pierced—and Fang is so cheap he said he'd do it. He started out by sterilizing the ice pick—

Fang has scads of socks—six pair that match and twenty-seven singles.

THIS INTERVIEW took place in Miss Diller's suite at the Waldorf Towers. She greeted me wearing a black muumuu, leather sandals, and no make-up. It had been several years since we first met but she remembered the circumstances and we talked about those days for quite some time. Phyllis looked absolutely ravishing. Her eyes sparkled and she offered her opinions eagerly, quickly, often anticipating questions before they were framed.

WILDE: *Phyllis, when did you realize you could make people laugh?*

DILLER: When I was in grade school. It sounds like I was a trouble-maker, but it wasn't that at all. I was always a pro—even as a little teeny kid. I was an absolutely perfect, quiet, dedicated student *in* class. *But* outside of class I got my laughs. I've always been able to control myself and be disciplined and follow the rules. . . . There are people who have absolutely no way of shutting themselves up. You've seen them on TV panel shows where they keep butting in and finally you just wish they weren't there at all. This doesn't happen to me because I have a great sense of timing and a sense of when to speak, when not to speak, and so it was a professional attitude toward comedy right from the start . . . when I was simply doing it for kicks and had *no idea* that I would ever become a comic. It was just a natural thing. To me, it's a great attitude toward life: Laugh! Laugh it off.

WILDE: *Your first professional job was at the Purple*

Onion in San Francisco in 1955. What did you use for material?

DILLER: Well . . . every day I worked on material. . . . I had a guy that worked with me. . . . He was one of those French-type people—part decorator, part gallery owner— you know the kind—part show biz and part actor. He was one of those people that have a nice bright mind—very quick—and when things were slow at his gallery he would go through back issues of the *Reader's Digest* looking for decent jokes. I would go through *Vogue* and *Bazaar* and find pictures that were ridiculous and I would paste them on a cardboard and hold them up that night and talk about them. I would take a full-page ad—I'll never forget one ad of Joseph Magnin's for a hundred-thousand-dollar sable coat—I'd hold the ad up, tell 'em the cost and I wrote a whole bit about how ridiculous it is . . . you have to get an appointment to try it on . . . and then two guards are there . . . you know, the whole thing. It was my kind of comedy . . . new, not the old jokes . . . 'cause anyone can tell jokes anyway. That was just a matter of desperation.

WILDE: *When you knew you were going to open you must have had some idea . . .*

DILLER: Of what I was going to do?

WILDE: *Yes.*

DILLER: Oh, I had an act . . . I auditioned my act. But the problem is I only had *one* act and it's four shows a night there.

WILDE: *What did that act consist of?*

DILLER: A musical act. It was sing—talk—sing—talk— sing—talk. It took me a long time to stop singing and to stop using props. I had funny glasses, I had funny stoles, I had funny furs—I borrowed furs from the audience and did bits. I couldn't do a thing without a funny prop.

WILDE: *Until then where had you worked? What had you done?*

DILLER: To get the thing congealed?

WILDE: *Yes.*

DILLER: Oh, well, I'll tell you. . . . I was thirty-seven when I opened there and I had five children. I was married . . . a suburban lady and I had been doing things for church groups, for little Kiwanis groups, for the Navy—Alameda Naval Air Station, they had a little thing for the sailors. They'd invite me out and give me seventeen bucks and a live turkey. How's that for pay? Don't ever accept a live turkey! [*Laughs*] Gee, they're mean—mean sons-of-bitches. Anyway, things like that . . . which was rare . . . but just the fact that I had been in front of somebody *ever*—it's amazing how it falls together—it falls into place. Then when you know you're going to open . . . I had been working on this act . . . trying to get it ready. . . .

WILDE: *Prior to the Purple Onion how long had you spent developing?*

DILLER: I worked a year on an act because my husband kept nagging me to do it and I finally decided, "What the hell! I'll do it."

WILDE: *And this was in between taking care of a house and family?*

DILLER: Plus a full-time job with a radio station. I never did anything talent-wise. I was in the office end. I was in press, continuity, advertising, and merchandising—that sort of thing. They would never let me in the other side of it. They didn't think I had any talent—the idiots! I auditioned—they said, "No good!" They were wrong. It's just that they couldn't see me because I was an office girl to them. They couldn't see me at all.

WILDE: *As a female were there any particular problems you had to overcome on stage?*

DILLER: Yes, of course, because being a woman, right away you walk out to almost total rejection. Almost nobody wants you to be a female comic and they give you a lot of static just because of your sex. It's almost the same as they don't want a female President. There's an old cave-age saying: "Keep women in their place—in the cave—back in the cave with a spoon in their hand." Men have this silly, witchy, witchcrafty attitude that a woman who is a comic has lost her femininity. Now it's not necessarily so. It frequently is true but then I still had to go through the onus of that even though I was never unfeminine—'cause I'm a feminine person.

WILDE: *How did you overcome it?*

DILLER: By simply being feminine and by understanding it and not hating them for it. I just bided my time and lived perfectly patient and waited. Just waited for them to come around.

WILDE: *Until you found your comedic character did you feel any resentment or antagonism from the male segment of the audience?*

DILLER: Oh, absolutely I did. I certainly did. The first group that supported me insanely were faggots. They were my maddest fans. The next group that I rolled up into a nice little ball were housewives . . . when my material stopped being chi chi and music and talk . . . when it became more talk and it became more center-based in my world—home, children, family, sex, autos. Then I picked up all the women. Then through the women I got the men. Then through my Snowy Bleach commercials and my "Pruit" series I got the kids. You would not believe the kids—what fans they are.

WILDE: *What about the female comedians—Martha Raye, Lucille Ball, Eve Arden? Did any of them influence your work in any way?*

DILLER: I doubt that very much. I think I have been *more* influenced by the men. Now, let me tell you why. I'm a stand-up comic. None of those girls are. Those girls that you mentioned are all comic actresses. Therefore, they always work within a framework as a character. *I* am a true —and the only—female stand-up comic. Therefore, I could be likened most to Bob Hope—who was always my idol—and I have just automatically studied him. There is a great similarity in our delivery and the way we work.

WILDE: *Were there any specific things you learned from watching other comedians work?*

DILLER: Oh, when I first was new in the business I very carefully avoided going to see anyone work because I knew that automatically I would copy and I didn't want to do this—I wanted to develop my own style. I wouldn't copy their mannerisms, I wouldn't copy *anything* about their psyche. Now, I always try to understand how everyone works . . . to understand their approach to comedy. From the moment I walked on stage in 1955, I carried that cigarette holder without having any idea why. I just knew that was part of what I was going to do and it was at least five years later . . . I'll never forget the night where it happened . . . it was at Dick Kollmar's Left Bank here in New York—Dorothy Kilgallen's husband—I gave that thing a little tap for an imaginary ash and I realized that was *it* —it's a punctuation mark.

WILDE: *George Burns and his cigar. . . .*

DILLER: Right! I got to it all by myself. I carried it around for all those years and didn't know what the hell to do with it. It gave me an excuse to hold up one arm. Right? Now the male comics, they touch their kidney—or whatever's there—their liver. But for a woman it's a great thing to be able to always hold up one hand because you get attention. What does a cop do? Holds his hand up. Stop. Look and listen. Right?

WILDE: *How did the housewife character and the ghoul- ish laugh come about? The wigs, the grotesque costume. How did all that happen?*

DILLER: Well, you see, the grotesque costume is now what America is wearing. It's just that I started it. Now I can walk in any store in America and buy what used to look odd. My dog collar's now the latest thing—the big diamond Queen Victoria crown jewel dog collar. Watch for that. This wild hair-do that I've created will be in next—with crazy wild curls all over. Remember, I came out of a group of comics that were, at that time, in the beginning, called "off-beat." Mort Sahl, Elaine May, Mike Nichols, Milt Kamen, the Smothers Brothers . . . all those people were called "off-beat." It's just that we were ahead, baby. We were going to make everything else look old-fashioned. Woody Allen would be considered off-beat—that genre of material—'cause we were the ones that were right. We needed a whole new approach to comedy and we did it. But we had to go through that thing like Fulton with his boat

. . . they stood on the river and stoned the boat . . . they laughed at the Wright Brothers, they laughed at Henry Ford. . . .

WILDE: *What about your laugh?*

DILLER: That's my own laugh. When I laughed at first in my act, I'll bet anything I was laughing because *they* weren't and I was trying to prime the pump . . . and it worked. Then, later, a lot of people would criticize . . . say, "Oh, she laughs too much. I don't like that silly laugh." But I then became absolutely famous for the laugh. And I've gotten big, rich commercials out of—cause all they wanted was the laugh. So you don't listen to anybody. You listen to the small voice within. You know what you're doing and if you don't, get out.

WILDE: *Is there any one particular type of joke that you've found gets a bigger response than another?*

DILLER: Yes, yes! The closer it's based to absolute, solid truth, the funnier it is because you bring out a funny attitude in a great truth. Let me give you a couple such examples. "There's one thing about the business that really frightens me, the bright lights—because when I was a housewife, if I ever had this much light on me, when I woke up, I had another kid." See, it's so true! If you've ever seen an obstetrician deliver, my God, it's bright, white tile and the light . . . and what makes this great is that it's the most self-conscious, worst situation a woman can get herself into. With her bare ass out and seven people looking and they know she's committed a sex act—that's why it's good. There's another such line: "Why is it when a couple has reached their fiftieth wedding anniversary, he looks like a little old lady and she looks like a little old man and neither of them knows the difference?" Beautiful? 'Cause it's abso-

lutely true. You've seen those fiftieth wedding anniversaries
—you can't tell them apart. By the time they've lived together fifty years, they look like twins.

WILDE: *Did you always do the short, punchy, one-line
jokes?*

DILLER: I've always had the knack of building one. . . .
I'd lay something out and then top it . . . because silence
makes me so nervous. You wouldn't believe it. Therefore, I
always have these little phrases—one word, three words,
four words—that at the end of each line is a laugh. Now,
I'm building to a big punch or maybe I've given 'em a big
punch and I add, add, add, add, add, topper, topper, topper,
topper, topper . . . that's one of my biggest things. It makes
me different.

WILDE: *Did all these toppers grow gradually or were they
written?*

DILLER: Right out of me. Those are all mine. You can't
buy those. Those all happen on the floor. . . . I get the line
and then as I'm out there it grows, just grows, grows. One
night I'll think of a silly thing and add it and then it stays
in. Or if I add it and it doesn't work, it comes out.

WILDE: *How long does it normally take to perfect one
routine?*

DILLER: Oh, it could happen in—well, you say *perfect*—
that sometimes I work on forever. Mine always change.
Some people get 'em and leave 'em, but I don't. It could take
anywhere from two weeks to four years.

WILDE: *Why is that?*

DILLER: Well, a routine can always be better. That's my
attitude. One could be all there in two weeks . . .or I've al-

ready had one grow right on the floor in one night. Example: If it's wild and it was funny, something that just
happened and you're *on* and you're terribly creative, your
channel is open. I went to my first sukiyaki dinner place in
San Francisco with a group of people—sat on the floor for
the first time and it was Saturday night—the big night at
the Purple Onion—went right down there and on the floor
that night a great big *bit* grew. I probably tinkered with it
for two weeks but it was solid 'cause it had just happened.

WILDE: *Approximately how many jokes are in each piece?*

DILLER: Each piece? My pieces are all different lengths.
I couldn't say. I'll tell you one thing which you may be interested in. Bob Hope goes for six huge *boffs* a minute and
he says that his writers have clocked my work and he claims
I get twelve. Course, I talk faster and my material is geared
differently. I work more frantically than he does. I work
wild—like a woman would. *He* lays it right out and then
looks at you.

WILDE: *How many jokes have to be written and then
tried to then wind up with a polished end result?*

DILLER: How many jokes? I don't ever count anything
like that?

WILDE: *Often, in order to get two jokes that work you
have to write five. . . .*

DILLER: Oh, of course! Well . . . excepting that I don't do
that anymore because I now know what's funny and what
isn't. I didn't use to. I don't have to try 'em anymore. I
know. I just came across a line today which I bought, which
is a great line, and I'd forgotten even ever having read it—
of course, I'd read it or I wouldn't have bought it. "Fang
decided that blondes have more fun so he bleached his hair

and asked me for a divorce." That's funny. No doubt about it.

WILDE: *In addition to writing some jokes yourself, you're noted as being gracious enough to buy material from hundreds of free-lance writers.*

DILLER: True.

WILDE: *How do you go about handling this vast number of submissions?*

DILLER: Well, this started about six and a half years ago. When I was less busy, I read *every* bit of the material that was sent to me, because then it was not in such vast volume. I discovered my top writer—a woman who lives in Jamesville, Wisconsin. Her name is Mary McBride. She's absolutely a genius. Same situation: Five children, mother, housewife—she's got a laboratory there. She's brilliant. She's a diamond mine. Now, from all those years—six years —I must have had submissions from, oh, maybe two thousand different people. However, toward the end . . . toward this section of my life with the fantastic schedule I have to keep, I found I could not possibly go through that volume of material myself. . . . I hired a couple of editors and when it got beyond them and beyond me, I had to close my market. However, I can still discover new writers if they're talented. I started getting an awful lot of material that people had just heard and were going for a fast buck or thinking, *unrealistically,* that they were comedy writers. A lot of people were copying jokes out of old joke books. I never was worried about being sued because I opened all the mail, I read it all, and then I *bought* or sent it back and said "no sale." They always got their original manuscript back . . . and they got a typewritten copy of what I bought and a check. It was all very clean.

WILDE: *Then you've actually developed your own writers?*

DILLER: Yes ... I've trained some. I wanted 'em. I wanted
'em to improve. I've taught them editing, I've taught them
the use of words. Let me give you an example. I have a line
where I'm talking about my mother-in-law, Moby Dick ...
she's a fat ... and I was with a writer who was writing a
movie for me and he heard the act and I'd say the only way
that I can describe her is Jell-O with a belt. Now, he said,
why don't you say, "Jell-O with hair"? Do you hear the
difference. It doesn't work. I tried it and then I thought to
myself "Why"? Jell-O with a belt—*belt* is a *pow* word.
Jell-O with *hair* is soft and lovely—it lets you down. So
that's one thing—you can learn about words.

WILDE: *The importance of the sound ...*

DILLER: Sound of words ... it's an audio medium. You're
appealing to the ear. They're hearing it. They're getting it
first through their ear—something through the eye, but
mostly ear—if you're a *talk* comic. Then there are things to
learn about writing—like editing. When someone has talent
and has great ideas, I teach him how to write one-liners.
I explain to him that's all I buy and that's all I use. It sounds
like I talk like that but I don't. It's a thousand one-liners put
together. So then I teach them that a one-liner or a gag is
not the same as a joke. A gag or a one-liner is a set-up,
pause, pay-off. That's the simplest form.

WILDE: *How about an ex—*

DILLER: Example: "The year I finally lost my baby fat
I got middle-aged spread." You see, set-up, pay-off. That's
not a strong gag but it's a perfect example of what I mean.
They can't meander ... The funny word must be at the end
of the sentence. See, these are all technical things. Anybody

can learn them. If you put the funny word here they don't hear the rest of the sentence 'cause if it's really funny they're gonna laugh right there. Another rule of mine: I work right in the center—food, sex, clothing, everyday things—I never predicate a gag on the audience having had to read something or having had to see a movie or having to have traveled to a certain place. They can be idiots and I reach them because I speak right to the center. I know they eat and sleep and they got a car . . . if they don't, they've seen a car. Right? So, therefore, rule: If every person in the audience doesn't get it at the same moment, I don't want it. Because I only want boff, boff, boff, boff! I don't want giggles. I don't want twitters, because I can get that on the street with my clothes.

WILDE: *Do you find it easier to make people laugh in a night club than on television?*

DILLER: Not at all. I find it's the same problem no matter where you are. You either make 'em laugh or you don't. I love to play tents, I love radio, I love television, I love club work, I love theatre, I love it all.

WILDE: *Some students of comedy feel that a comedian is in reality a mass psychologist. Is it necessary to have a keen insight into people's behavior and to be a student of human nature in order to cope with large and highly diverse groups?*

DILLER: Absolutely. You've gotta be an expert.

WILDE: *How do you learn that?*

DILLER: Well, from the way you're born and raised and educated and your sensitivity to people and your observations of life all through your life.

WILDE: *Then this is something you can train yourself to do?*

DILLER: Oh, every human being who doesn't do it is a *clod*. But a lot of people don't bother to develop themselves or pay attention to other people or observe people. That's a terrible thing. That's awful. But it's true. There are people who are insensitive, and it's a shame because think of all the lovely things they miss. . . . You read books about yourself, understanding yourself. You read books on how to get ahead. There was one I read that absolutely shot me into outer space. If I hadn't read it, I'd still be washing the laundry by hand. *The Magic of Believing* by Claude Bristol. It's a Prentice-Hall book. It's one of those self-help books and I got it when I was on the bottom—flat on my back, on the bottom—and it absolutely turned me into a dynamo.

WILDE: *Experts estimate that there are probably less than two hundred first-rate comedy writers and not even a hundred top-flight comedians in America. . . .*

DILLER: It's probably true.

WILDE: *If there's such a shortage why is it so difficult for a new comedian to get recognized?*

DILLER: Because of that thing we were talking about—rejection. A very few people have the guts to stick to it in the face of rejection and unemployment and poverty. But if you can make it the riches are so rewarding. But that's life. Anything that's worth this much is very difficult to do or to attain. It means you made an extra effort. That's why it's worth so much. Nobody's higher paid than a great comic . . . because there are so few. They'll never be enough. So the money's there. But very few people can take it and believe me, till you're there *you take it*. I once wrote a line and I love it. I gotta play it on you. People ask, "How did you do it, now that you're up the ladder?" and I say, "I ate shit!" And then the tag is: "I still take a spoonful a day for fear I'll lose my taste for it." [*Laugh*] That means you gotta stay humble.

WILDE: *Why are there so few women comedians?*

DILLER: Because of the same thing: *guts*. It takes so much to make it. Once you've made it, you're the queen and life is beautiful and everybody wants your body and they want to give you gifts. But man, before you make it, *you're nothin'!* You're negative nothin'. You're below zero and you know it. You feel it. However, the secret is don't accept it. It's there, but you never accept it. You wear this little white feather psyche around you . . . completely around you . . . you've heard of water off a duck's back? . . . this little white feather and nothing pierces it. You stay cool inside. Keep that equilibrium. Most people just panic, they get jangled and they get ugly, they get hostile. They get a bad audience and they get hecklers and they talk back and they get evil and every time they do that they're weakening and being unprofessional. And every time you're unprofessional, every time you're undisciplined, it's easier to do it again. First thing you know, they've lost everything.

WILDE: *There are many psychological theories why one becomes a comedian: need for love, recognition, etcetera. Can you put your finger on what it was that drove you to make people laugh?*

DILLER: Poverty. Same thing that drove Beethoven and Brahms and Bach to writing great music. Everybody wants to eat. It's just that I picked this field because I'm a natural. Because all my life I have used a light attitude toward small tragedies. I remember one time I was present when a woman got news of her mother's death. She fell apart. She cried . . . and after she got a little of that out of her system, it wasn't ten minutes after, I got a big hearty laugh out of that woman. Now, I feel that's like doing a doctor's work. I feel that's a great thing to be able to do—to make people laugh. So, you see, I have, all my life, had that attitude. That was my work—to make people cheerful, to make their life less burdensome, to show them that it can be fun when you can laugh at that crap. You stay healthy, you don't let it pull you down . . . so that was just my attitude and I translated it into being a pro.

WILDE: *Most comedians have achieved success by years of developing delivery and timing and acquiring material and experience. Is there such a thing as a "natural" comedian?*

DILLER: You gotta be a natural, first. Steve Allen in his book, *The Funny Men* (Simon and Schuster), made a statement that if by the time you are twelve, you aren't, don't even consider it. That's what it is to be a natural. Now, I'm a natural comic. . . . I'm certain that all the successful ones —maybe not all of them—I do know people who are completely technical—who aren't the least bit fun offstage . . .

WILDE: *Is it possible for anyone to learn to be a comedian?*

DILLER: Nope. Nope.

WILDE: *What are the prerequisites . . . ?*

DILLER: That comic *attitude*. An enjoyment of being in front of people. An enjoyment of being a leader and taking them where you want 'em to go. You're the troop leader— the scout master. Enjoyment of being set apart, being up there instead of one of them. You gotta recognize that. It's an egoistic thrill. You've gotta have a very strong, healthy ego. Sometimes it's a very strong, sick ego that drives people . . . then you get a different kind of humor. You get a different kind of reaction to the person. But there's nothing wrong with having a good solid ego. . . . And it's a wonderful thrill to be able to do something like that.

WILDE: *Is it possible to define that extra-special quality that allows a comedian to see humor in that which appears to be a serious situation to others?*

DILLER: That can be developed. That is something that happens over the years and gets stronger and stronger and stronger. Once you're a pro you actually look for the funny angles and then that becomes material if you're working. For instance, we're sitting here in this room full of flowers —they're getting a little stale and old—and the line is: "I know a guy who is so allergic he sneezed when they played *Star Dust*."

WILDE: *What percentage of a comedian's ability is a gift he was born with and what per cent the mastery of his craft?*

DILLER: I'm not too good at percentages. I would say, well, look, here's the reason you can't cut that into percentages. If you aren't born with it you got no percentage, so then how do you know what percentage was hard work? You *gotta* be born with it or you're not going to make it. Therefore, that other percentage, plus being born with it, you gotta go a hundred per cent. All that hard work and strain and attention to detail and being really fabulously interested, dedicated to your work, you can't do it half-assed, it's gotta be all the way.

WILDE: *What specifically does one do to discipline or dedicate himself?*

DILLER: You work your ass off. You do everything you can right up to the point where if you got any health problem, you don't dare do something. . . . That's when you start saying you can't do this, you can't do that. You go everyplace and you do everything you're asked to do until the law of cause and effect takes over and reduces it so that then you're doing things for more money and you can't do the lesser things, so it balloons upward that way. Onward and upward—that's my password.

WILDE: *Is there a standard number of years a comedian must spend in order to become successful?*

DILLER: Not necessarily. . . . In the case of Bob Newhart, he became fabulously successful very quickly through records and then was quite ill at ease onstage in front of a large audience because he simply did not have the experience. It's one thing to put brilliant material on record in a studio by yourself and then it's an entirely different thing to get up in front of people. That takes . . . simply habit . . . just a lot of experience to be comfortable in front of people.

WILDE: *Then it's a different number of years for different people?*

DILLER: That's it. That's it. You see, *he* [Newhart] was an overnight success although it had taken him quite a while to produce the material but then once it was heard, right away he was big. And then other people will be around twenty years and finally make it. Buddy Hackett—he never made it big until Paar presented him. I think Mimi Hines and Phil Ford had been around many years before Paar— Paar threw a nice spotlight on a lot of people. Joey Bishop had been around a long time.

WILDE: *How much of a comedian's success depends on his agent or manager as compared to his own efforts?*

DILLER: None. None. Your act sells you. Your agents don't sell you. It's not possible to sell things like that. You create the demand—you must create the demand. You have to do all the work. You do it out onstage in the lights. That's where all the work happens. They answer the phone and they handle the paper work and they take care of the contracts. They can see that they've got you in the right places and they can steer and they can route you so that you're in the right places at the right time. There are agents who are brilliant at that and there are some who are dumb.

WILDE: *They're only interested in booking you for their ten per cent commission?*

DILLER: Right. If they go for the money instead of where you oughta be they're doing you a disservice. My agents have always been understanding of me, because I trained them. I told them, "I don't want money. I want career." Because in the end, that's where you get the money. Never go for present money—go for present rightness. . . . It's too delicate a situation . . . it's too tremulous a thing. No one should criticize you and you should never ask for criticism in this field—ever—'cause you're going to get it. You're the one who knows . . . inside . . . you know. And remember, criticism is worth exactly what you pay for it.

WILDE: *What about some of the comedians who are becoming nationally known—Jackie Vernon, Jackie Mason, George Carlin?*

DILLER: I've never seen Jackie Vernon in a club—only on television and you really don't get a flavor. You've gotta see it live. I've always enjoyed him. Jackie Mason is very funny. Just to hear him talk makes me laugh. He wouldn't have to say anything funny—that very thick Russian-Jewish accent just makes me fall down. And then . . . George Carlin . . . he was Burns and Carlin and now he's out on his own, alone. I haven't seen him lately. . . . Woody Allen's material just absolutely ruptures me. . . . I heard a new guy on the Merv Griffin show that I'd never heard of— Rodney Dangerfield. He's funny as hell. He's adorable . . . with a name like that you'll remember it.

WILDE: *Is there a relationship between a comedian's physical fitness and his abiliy to sustain a high level of performance?*

DILLER: In exact ratio. It's that scientific. A person must be in absolute Olympic form because it is exactly like running a race every time you go on. You must be in top shape, physically and mentally, hopefully. And then your performance is the exact ratio of the physical fitness you're in.

WILDE: *Do diet, exercise, and rest have any effect on the efficiency?*

DILLER: Darling, everything you learned in the first grade applies. If people would just learn it when they're six years old, take it to their graves, they wouldn't go to their graves so fast. Eight hours sleep a day, eight glasses of water a day, outdoor exercise, say your prayers, keep your conscience clean no matter how you have to do it. Some people go to a shrinker—psychiatrist. No matter how you do it, don't keep garbage from the day before or guilt or anything that went wrong. Throw it out. You wouldn't let physical garbage pile up in your kitchen 'cause you couldn't stand the odor. Well, some people let their odors pile up until you can't hardly stand them. They have kind of a psychic odor and you sense it. You don't want to be around these people. They make you sick. But these simple rules—and good diet: fruit, vegetables, protein. Eat all that and do all those things and love. Fill your life with love and happiness. You can't miss in *any* field.

WILDE: *Can you make any suggestions to someone who might decide to become a comedian?*

DILLER: You can't *decide*. . . . They must first know they *are* then they can decide and do it. But a person just can't look at somebody who looks successful and rich and say, "That's the way I'm going to do it." You can't do it. It's gotta be inside with a great drive behind it.

WILDE: *No matter what the drive comes from?*

DILLER: No, it doesn't matter. It doesn't matter what the motivation is. It's good to have a healthy motivation. My motivation is that when I was a little girl I read fairy stories and I always wanted to be a princess and live in a castle and have a prince on a white horse to kill the dragon. I always pictured that. Now I got my castle and I'm Queen of the May—*my way*.

WILDE: *Is there any advice you would give to someone who has made the decision to become a comedian?*

DILLER: Hmmmmm, Larry, I'm glad that came up. I've written an elongated answer to that so I will make sure you get a copy of it because it is apropos of what you are doing.

[*Author's Note: Miss Diller was kind enough to send along her views on this question, of which the following are excerpts.*]

People who think show biz is all glamour sometimes think there is nothing to it, excepting just walk out and be gorgeous and sing or dance or talk. Into all branches of show business go years of work, experience, or training, or all three. When it looks *easy* you're looking at art!

To get started in show business, start where you are. There are those who think you have to go to Hollywood or New York to get into the business. I say, a trip around the world starts with the first step and the first step can only be taken in one spot: where you're standing right now.

Once you're working, *taste* is as important as talent. A lot of people who are loaded with talent have no taste. They can't possibly ever make it. Believing in yourself is completely imperative. Every doubt you have weakens you. You have to be able to face humiliating failure. You have to have great stamina and excellent health.

People have a completely mistaken idea about "breaks." There is no such thing as "breaks." If you're looking for "breaks" you've got your eye on the wrong thing. Many people turn down opportunities because they are usually disguised as "hard work." You'd be amazed the people who will not go out on a limb or progress, or change and hurt a little for a while, to expand their powers. Most are prone to take the easy way, the comfy way. If you're not hurting a little, you're not growing.

An entertainer should never give up onstage. No matter how badly things are going, you keep right on as if everything was all right. A performer who consistently blames "the audience" will never make it. There is no such thing as a bad audience, only a bad performance.

After all, they're there. They paid to see you. You're supposed to be the leader and take them where you please. You should not be affected by them, they should be affected by you. If they aren't, you're not strong enough to be up there in the white hot lights.

Summing up my advice:
1. Start where you are.
2. Work steady.
3. Read *The Magic of Believing*.
4. Realize you're not going to have "help."
5. Don't ever give up.

Jimmy Durante

James Francis Durante was born in New York City on February 10, 1893. As a youngster, he took piano lessons and soon began playing in the neighborhood saloons.

While working at the Club Alamo in Harlem in 1915, he met singer Eddie Jackson (who is still his partner and close friend) and then later, when Jimmy opened his Club Durant in 1923, Lou Clayton joined them and the legendary Clayton, Jackson, and Durante comedy team was formed.

It was Clayton who coined Jimmy's world famous nickname, Schnozzola, and later became Durante's business manager, until his death in 1950.

On Broadway, Mr. Durante appeared in Cole Porter's *The New Yorkers* (1930), and in *Strike Me Pink* (1934), *Jumbo* (1935), and *Red, Hot, and Blue* (1937), the latter with Ethel Merman and a new comic named Bob Hope.

His earlier screen credits include: *Roadhouse Nights* (1929), *Get Rich Quick Wallingford* (1931), *Her Cardboard Lover* (1933), *The Passionate Plumber* (1932), and the *Phantom President* (1933), with his idol, George M. Cohan —the only film Mr. Cohan ever made.

Later, Jimmy appeared in *The Man Who Came to Dinner* (1936), *It Happened in Brooklyn* (1943), *Two Girls and a Sailor* (1944), *Music for Millions* (1945), *Two Sisters from Boston* (1946), *Ziegfeld Follies* (1946), *On an Island With You* (1948), *The Great Rupert* (1950), *The Milk Man* (1950), *Jumbo* (1962), and *It's a Mad, Mad, Mad, Mad World* (1964).

After years as a radio headliner on NBC with Garry Moore, Jimmy entered television in 1950. He starred on "All-Star Revue," "Colgate Comedy Hour," "Texaco Star Theatre," and "Hollywood Palace."

In 1960, Mr. Durante married Margie Little. They have an adopted daughter, CeCe Alicia, born in 1961. The Durantes live in Beverly Hills, California.

Jimmy Durante's best-known comedy song

Inka Dinka Doo*

Inka dinka doo
A dinka dee, a dinka doo
Oh, what a tune for crooning
Inka dinka doo
A dinka dee, a dinka doo
It's got the whole world spooning

* Copyright 1933 by Bourne, Inc., New York.

To PARAPHRASE Will Rogers, there's never been a man who met Jimmy Durante that didn't like him. After four and a half hours with the indestructible Schnozz, I left knowing I had been with one of the great human beings of our time.

At the Hollywood Palace Theatre, Mr. Durante opened the door to his expensively decorated duplex dressing room. (It contained several armchairs, a sofa, thick red carpeting, mahogany bar, RCA color TV, Sony stereo tape recorder; bath and bedroom on the second floor.) He greeted me warmly, and said. "You came all the way from New York, justa talk ta me?" "Yes, sir!" I answered. He shook his head, removed the ubiquitous gray felt hat and said, "Okeh, wot d'ya wanna know?"

Unfortunately, because of an incredibly tight schedule (rehearsing for the "Hollywood Palace" television show with Lisa Minelli and comedian Jerry Shane) he never spent more than ten minutes in the dressing room, which made rapport and continuity of thought practically impossible.

I waited patiently, however, my Uher 4000-L warmed up, microphone in hand, prepared to resume questioning. When he did manage to sit down, eager to talk, the telephone interrupted with calls from friends requesting tickets for the taping, his William Morris agent offering a night club booking, a request to do a benefit and a long distance interview with a Boston reporter about the Blinstraub fire. (The famous supper club had burned to the ground two nights before Mr. Durante was scheduled to open).

WILDE: *When you were a boy, how much piano training did you have?*

235

DURANTE: Well, I started to take lessons when I was about twelve years old—ten or twelve—I can't remember. And, you know, you had one of those professors who wants you to be an opera piano player. But I was crazy about the piano and I wanted to be a great, great ragtime piano player.

WILDE: *Which was the style of the times.*

DURANTE: Yes, yes. Sure, and in my neighborhood—I was born on the East Side of New York, on Catherine Street—that starts Chinatown, goes down to the East River. And they used to have clubs there—the athletic club, this club and that club—and they used to run dances every week, every Saturday night and finally I got to play in them for two dollars. After two, three years of piano playing, I marveled at the piano players that played in the other joints. I'd take a walk up to Chinatown and look underneath the pushing doors—they used to have concert halls then—and I'd say, "Geeze, if I could only be like that," you know? George M. Cohan's tunes at that time were so great. "Give My Regards to Broadway," "I Was Born in Virginia. . . ."

WILDE: *You were just a teen-ager then?*

DURANTE: Oh, yeah, about fifteen.

WILDE: *And all this time you had been practicing the piano?*

DURANTE: Practicing, yeah . . . but not what that teacher gives you [*chuckling*]. . . .

WILDE: *You had your own ideas.*

DURANTE: That's right. And many a time, I'd be, you know, going around to publishers trying to get some professional copies . . . the music publishers then was around

Fourteenth Street, you know?

WILDE: *Which was then considered* uptown?

DURANTE: That was uptown, that's right . . . then it moved up to Twenty-fourth and then went up to the forties and fifties.

WILDE: *How old were you when you began playing the piano professionally?*

DURANTE: Seventeen.

WILDE: *So you had about five years of training?*

DURANTE: Yeah, yeah.

WILDE: *Did you have an act then?*

DURANTE: No, no, I was a piano player. Just a piano player.

WILDE: *Did you sing a little?*

DURANTE: No, no, I used to sing later on. I did a lot of singing. You know, my first job was down at Coney Island . . . at seventeen . . . just a kid.

WILDE: *Is that when you met Eddie Cantor?*

DURANTE: A year later, yeah. Because at that time, there was no dancing in cafés, you know, just entertainers. In some joints you'd go into there'd be singing waiters and a couple of regular singers . . . they'd all have a cue—"Oh, How I Hate to Get Up in the Morning" . . . and you'd play for them.

WILDE: *Were you able to play in any key they sang in? Suppose Eddie Cantor wanted to sing?*

DURANTE: Transpose? No! That baffled me at the beginning. Yeah. It was a terror when a guy came up there and I had to play in his key. To this day, I only play in C, D flat . . . B . . . give me anything in A natural, you know.

WILDE: *When you and Eddie Cantor worked together at that time did you have any idea that one day you would both become internationally known?*

DURANTE: [*Chuckling*] No, *God* no. I wanted to be a great piano player and Eddie wanted to be a great actor, you know. He really wanted to be a great actor. But he was a comedian then, you know? I liked him . . . both of us sure had some fun. We'd make up something if a guy asked for a song we didn't know. Eddie'd make up the words and I'd make up the music to a song as we went along. Sometimes it'd work, sometimes not. When the customer'd shout, "That ain't 'South Nebraska Blues,'" we'd answer innocently, "You mean there's *two* 'South Nebraska Blues'?" Eddie never played a café after that. No, he went with an act called, oh, geeze, a big, big act . . . Bedini and Arthur.

WILDE: *Then how long did you work in Coney Island?*

DURANTE: Well, Coney Island was just the summer. Then the next year I went to Chinatown at the Chatham Club. Then back to the Island—that's when I met Cantor—at every joint there was a pimp and a girl on the outside and upstairs . . . so they closed down these joints. But then we used to play after hours. They closed the doors, took away the chairs, and then they used to dance, nice and soft . . . just you alone playing the piano.

WILDE: *At this time you still had no idea of doing an act?*

DURANTE: Noooo. Then I went to Chinatown and that was a great experience. Chinatown at that time was like Broadway and 42nd Street—at three in the mornin' . . . oh, sightseers and, oh, gee, across the way was Nigger Mike's. . . .

WILDE: *Was it during this period you found you were able to get laughs?*

DURANTE: No, no . . . I went years after that. Irving Berlin used to come around . . . he used to sing his own songs. . . . And the song pluggers used to come around . . . they'd come in sing their songs and leave . . . boy, that used to be a shame to go back to the piano after they played— geeze, I wanted to be a great pianist. So now, I went back to the Island, like I told you, and after that year, I went up to Harlem, place called The Alamo. Now, instead of being alone, at that time . . . the Dixieland Jazz Band came out in Rizenwebers . . . so I went down to New Orleans and I got myself a band—what a clarinet player, Oh, Christ, great jazz men. And now, that's where I thought everybody loved me . . . I used to get up, while they're dancing to this dixie- land . . . and while they were dancing you'd kid around with the people . . . get up at the piano and the guy at the drums was shimmying. . . .

WILDE: *You're putting on a show. . . .*

DURANTE: [*Tapping foot, singing, and snapping fingers*] "Somebody wants my gal. . . . Sing it, Jimmy boy!"—while they're dancing, never nuthin' alone, you know. And Eddie Jackson was working up there . . . and from then on every place I worked I took Eddie. . . . I worked up there for seven, about eight years . . . and the first break came when—that's when I first knew people loved me—I went down to the Nightingale on Broadway, my first job on Broadway, with a six-piece band.

WILDE: *By then you must have been in your twenties?*

DURANTE: Easy. Yeah, oh, yeah. I think I was twenty-eight. I brought Jackson in there and that's when we had the fun with the customers. . . . I used to get up and announce the balloon game and I used to kid around. . . .

WILDE: *How long did you stay there?*

DURANTE: Three years. Then we opened up our own joint. That's the break.

WILDE: *Was that the Club Durant?*

DURANTE: That's right. I didn't want to go in it. I said, "I'm doing all right, I'm making enough money—a hundred and a quarter—what do you want off me?" They said, "You're very popular, Jimmy. . . ." Then Jackson got to be a partner in the Club Durant, then Clayton come in.

WILDE: *Did Clayton do an act?*

DURANTE: Clayton was one of the big acts of his day. Clayton and Edwards . . . remember Ukelele Ike? He was headlining in vaudeville and every show, I think, that Shubert ever put on.

WILDE: *Was he basically a dancer?*

DURANTE: Basically a dancer. And a great straight man.

WILDE: *So he became a partner in the club?*

DURANTE: Yeah, after we had opened about a couple of months. And that was the turning point of the whole thing.

WILDE: *After he joined you, how long did the Club Durant stay open?*

DURANTE: A year and a half. . . . Well, now it's our *own* joint . . . I was playing piano for them, right? So I says, "I'm a boss." So I went and got a piano player and that's where I'm doing everything with them. Kidding them as they're dancin' and I get out on the floor and that's how I started. Now, if I didn't go into that club, I don't think anything'd ever happen. I woulda had a band though. I mighta been a Harry James. . . .

WILDE: *Up to this point you had never done a single on the floor?*

DURANTE: No, never sang a song on the floor. Never sang a single alone. I sang with the band while they're dancing . . . I'm like the girl that was in front of the bandstand. . .

[*Stage manager beckons Durante for rehearsal*]

. . . Now, no more than the club opened—Clayton, Jackson, and Durante—they started singing and I started kidding at the piano, with the band, always with the band. That's why I'm lost without a band in back of me, I mean, in a night club. You gotta have them in back of you, I can't have them over there. . . . I started to write songs: "I Ups to Him," "Can Broadway Do Without Me?", "Who Will Be With You When I'm Far Away?", "Wood."

WILDE: *The comedy done on radio, television, and in the movies is for the most part clean and in good taste. However, some comedians working in night clubs feel the need to do risqué or off-color material to stimulate the audience. Is that really necessary?*

DURANTE: No, No! So help me, God. I never seen a comedian be a big success with off-color jokes. No, in all the years we've been in cafés I've never told an off-color joke—even in cafés I've never told one. I wouldn't tell one. Never. You know why? I want to give you an instance of this.

[*Again the stage manager beckons for rehearsal*]

. . . Remind me to tell you. . . .

[*Later*]

DURANTE: The big number in Clayton and Jackson's day was known all over the world . . . a number called: "Wood." Used to get all the wood, put it on the stage. . . . "You've got a head made of wood," "So I've got a head made of wood," "Well, wood is a substantial thing—it built the railroads, it built the schools, the houses. . . ." At the end of the thing, after bringing all this wood out, I brought out a toilet seat . . . that was a big, big laugh. Irving Berlin was in the audience and I remember he came back and he says, "Jimmy, you've never used an off-color joke in your life." I says, "Is that off-color?" He says, "Yeah, don't use it!" Since then I never . . . now this is fifty years ago. . . . I never knew an entertainer, comedian, that ever got anywhere using off-color material.

WILDE: *Is this taste you have in material something you were born with or was it developed?*

DURANTE: I really think you gotta be born with it and I also think a good, smart comedian will realize if he's doing off-color material. But as they get up and up and up, they get rid of it.

WILDE: *Has the comedy form—what people laugh at— has it changed much since you first began entertaining?*

DURANTE: Well, it's changed a little . . . but comedy is the same. Just bringing it up to date and change in locales and . . . comedy never changes . . . it's the same, I think, for the last hundred years.

WILDE: *People laugh at the same things?*

DURANTE: Yes, yes . . . but there's a different kind of

comic coming up today—in the last few years—the stand-up comedian . . . not the "physical" comedian . . . a guy who talks mostly. But I advise any comic . . . they never get anywhere imitating anybody. There's never been an imitator that ever got to be a big star—that I know of.

WILDE: *I once saw you at Copa City in Miami Beach and toward the end of your act you were smoking a cigar. You took a deep puff, looked directly at the audience and blew smoke at them. It got a tremendous laugh. How do you explain something like that seemingly simple piece of business getting such a big reaction?*

DURANTE: Well, I think I must've made some kind of a cute face with it, you know, laughed as the smoke went out . . . or maybe I imitated an aristocratic guy. But it had something to do with the face. You know, I'd grimace or do something like this [*looks shy*]. Now that would get a laugh.

WILDE: *You made a facial expression?*

DURANTE: Afterwards, yeah.

WILDE: *When you decide to do a comedy song, what are the ingredients you look for?*

DURANTE: Now, here's where your jokes come in. I never use a comedy song that I don't stop and put jokes in . . . put funny lines in . . . because there's no comedy song that's strong enough by itself because you keep going on and the audience loses the lines. I was the first one to do that. Take for instance, "Who Will Be With You When I'm Far Away?" I'm singing along and then it goes out . . . and I'm telling a joke. Now as soon as the catch line comes—". . . the manager!"—the band comes right in on top of that joke. And if the joke don't go—you havn't been hurt.

[*A telephone call comes from a Boston reporter asking Durante to comment on a night club fire. Durante says: "That was a wonderful spot . . . you felt at home in that place. I don't think the kitchen would be right unless Blinstraub was in there cooking French fried potatoes. He's a wonderful man. I don't think I've ever worked for anybody I liked as much as Stanley Blinstraub. I loved working in Boston, it's like a second home. . . . That was a catastrophe . . . that fire . . . I lost six valises of costumes and music. . . . I wouldn't go to work for anybody else up there if they gave me ten thousand dollars more than he was giving. . . . Give that guy a hug and a kiss for me. Thanks for calling."*]

WILDE: *We were talking about comedy songs. . . .*

DURANTE: Yeah, if it's good—if the lines are good, and the verse, you know, if it's a good song, then we have the writers put in jokes—not jokes, lines—but it's got to be related to the song.

WILDE: *When you get a song you like, how many performances do you try it out before you decide to keep it in?*

DURANTE: Well, if you use it and try it seven or eight performances—you keep it in . . . but you better it. You better it.

WILDE: *You've never tried a number that didn't work?*

DURANTE: Oh, certainly. But that's very seldom. You get the number and I like it and you put a better joke in . . . that's been my experience. Now, I think I'm a champ at putting things together. . . . .

[*Another phone call interrupts*]

WILDE: *You've been referred to as a clown, an entertainer, a comedian—which title do you prefer?*

DURANTE: Oh, I don't know. I like "Portrayer of Songs." It's nice to be known as a comedian and called a comedian, cause a comedian makes people laugh and that's one of the greatest things anyone can do for his fellow beings. . . . People laugh, they forget their troubles. When you're out there and you see two thousand people laugh—like at Blinstraub's or the Latin Casino—you pray to God it never ends. It's wonderful.

WILDE: *You were the contemporary of another great entertainer—Al Jolson. Audiences have the same love for you they had for him. Are you and Jolson the same in any way?*

DURANTE: Well, I think we are, a little bit. He's a portrayer of songs. He put over a song . . . a lot of heart . . . and that's my forte, too, I think, songs.

WILDE: *Through the years you've built up a love relationship with your audience. Is that quality essential for a comedian to maintain?*

DURANTE: Yes, definitely. The audience today can— through television—spot a phoney in a minute. The minute they look at him they know if he's sincere. . . . if he's not sincere. And if people are not sincere that television set sure brings it out. They know right away. It's like D. W. Griffith said to me once, "The minute a performer comes out on the floor, they either got it or they ain't."

WILDE: *The critics say your enormous popularity comes from an emotional rapport with your audience. They talk about the magic that happens between a performer and the audience. Is it possible to explain what that magic is?*

DURANTE: I don't know. You come out with the band playing and try to get the feeling on the floor that it's a party. . . . You try to make them feel they're sitting in their own homes, having a lot of fun . . . and they're part of it . . . and you like to get intimate. The intimacy between you and your audience—that's what counts. There's no phoney business about it, you know. And I can tell you we're having as much fun as the audience. It's no phoney . . . and the audience is with you a hundred per cent.

WILDE: *Do you think the audience can sense that you're having a good time?*

DURANTE: Yes, oh God. That's the first thing they always say—"You seem to enjoy yourself as much as we do." And you know something? We never get a heckler . . . never get a heckler. The only kind of hecklers we get yell, "Hey, Jimmy, sing it there. Come on, Jimmy."

WILDE: *Most comedians came from poor families and had unhappy childhoods. Do you think these emotional and psychological scars were the reasons they became comedians?*

DURANTE: No. Let's place bets. Now, I was born in back of the barber shop on the East Side of New York . . . washroom is out in the yard . . . my dad owned a barber shop. But we wasn't what you call poverty-stricken. My dad made a nice living . . . we never wanted for bread or a meal. I went to work when I was a kid, selling papers—I worked after school. But that don't mean we were poverty-stricken, that we didn't eat. And I don't think Jolson or Cantor . . . they didn't have riches, but I think Eddie's grandmother made a nice living.

WILDE: *Some psychologists believe that we are all motivated by feelings of inferiority. They say, for example, that Eddie Cantor was driven into show business because he was short and because he felt terribly insecure. Or that Sophie Tucker—because she was fat. Or W. C. Fields, because he was unattractive. Is it possible that you became a comedian because as a boy you suffered humiliation and torment over your nose?*

DURANTE: No. No, when I was a kid, naturally they made fun of your nose and had many a fight over it, and busted my nose . . . you wouldn't call that . . . my ambition, like I told ya, was to be a great piano player—a ragtime piano player. And I'd have become a great orchestra leader, like Harry James—I repeat—or Guy Lombardo or any of them.

WILDE: *You don't feel there's any psychological reason for having . . .?*

DURANTE: No, there's no psychological . . . I like to have fun. I love people. I had fun playing the piano, you understand? Since I been a kid. . . .

[Another telephone call]

WILDE: *Gene Fowler in* Schnozzola*, *his biography of you, wrote that you did a great deal of exercise to keep your legs in shape. Do you still do that?*

DURANTE: Yeah, I exercise . . . not a great deal. Every mornin' . . . kick up, swing 'em around and do about . . . fifteen, twenty minutes, that's all . . . and do a lot of walkin'.

WILDE: *What is the greatest quality a comedian can have?*

DURANTE: Heart. He's gotta have heart. Otherwise he's nuthin'.

[Call for dress rehearsal]

WILDE: *Before you go, Mr. Durante, do you have any special diet or . . .?*

DURANTE: Yes, I can't eat anything fried. Everything's gotta be broiled . . . nothing fried. Let me shake your hand, I gotta go.

* The Viking Press, New York.

Dick Gregory

Born October 12, 1932, in the slums of St. Louis, Richard Claxton Gregory started running away from his environment as soon as he was old enough to walk. One of six children, the Negro comedian quips in his autobiography, *Nigger,** ". . . Geegobs of kids in my bed, man. When I get up to pee in the middle of the night, gotta leave a bookmark so I don't lose my place."

Gregory became a crack track star in high school and won an athletic scholarship to Southern Illinois University. After two years in the Army where he displayed comic skill in talent contests, Dick moved to Chicago and embarked on his theatrical career.

Excerpts from a Dick Gregory monologue

I understand there are a good many Southerners in the room tonight. I know the South very well. I spent twenty years there one night. . . .

Last time I was down South I walked into this restaurant

* E. P. Dutton & Co., New York.

and this white waitress came up to me and said, "We don't serve colored people here!" I said, "That's all right, I don't eat colored people. Bring me a whole fried chicken!"

About that time these three cousins come in, you know the ones I mean, Klu, Kluck, and Klan, and they say, "Boy, we're givin' you fair warnin'. Anything you do to that chicken, we're gonna do to you." About then the waitress brought me my chicken. "Remember boy, anything you do to that chicken, we're gonna do to you." So I put down my knife and fork, and I picked up that chicken, and I *kissed* it.

Segregation is not all bad. Have you ever heard of a wreck where the people in the back of the bus got hurt?

There's no difference between the North and the South. In the South they don't care how close I get as long as I don't get too big and in the North they don't care how big I get as long as I don't get too close.

To be honest, I'm really for Abraham Lincoln. If it hadn't been for Abe I'd still be on the open market.

They asked me to buy a lifetime membership in the NAACP, but I told them I'd pay a week at a time. Hell of a thing to buy a lifetime membership, wake up one morning and find the country's been integrated.

Wouldn't it be a hell of a thing if all this was burnt cork and you people were being tolerant for nothing?

I'm going to cut my show short tonight 'cause I'm gonna leave here early in the morning, fly down to Kansas City, Missouri, to help out a friend of mine. A white cat that just moved into an all colored neighborhood. Some colored bigot just brought a watermelon on his front lawn.

THIS INTERVIEW was arranged by comedy writer Edwin Weinberger, a mutual friend, and formerly employed by Gregory, then Johnny Carson, and now with the Bill Cosby company.

Weinberger brought me to Gregory's dressing room at the Village Gate night club in Greenwich Village. I explained the project and Gregory suggested I telephone him at nine the next morning to set an appointment.

I confess I felt I was being put off, for it seemed terribly early to call someone who would not finish working until two A.M. and probably not get to sleep before three. However, I complied and was astonished to have Gregory answer the telephone—wide awake.

One of the basic requirements for success in show business is having an overabundance of energy. The Chicago comedian undoubtedly meets that qualification.

Gregory welcomed me to the living room of Suite 1726 at the Beverly Hotel. The five New York newspapers were strewn about the floor. He wore a T-shirt and undershorts. The following exchange took place.

WILDE: *Just to get warmed up, Dick . . . what made you decide to become a comedian?*

GREGORY: I went into a night club and listened to the M.C. and I think this is what made me . . . for no other reason. I never had no show business. The fact that I was a very good athlete, I stayed out of clubs. I was born in 1932 and never went into a night club till 1958. The M.C. just fascinated me. I would say that had more to do with it than anything.

WILDE: *When did you first realize you could make people laugh?*

GREGORY: Oh, I've been doing that all my life.

WILDE: *Even when you were young?*

GREGORY: Yeah, until I went into show business . . . then I found out you couldn't make people laugh. It's like you have a baby that plays beautiful piano and you say, "Come by the house and listen to my three-year-old play the piano." That's fine but come to Carnegie Hall and pay five dollars to hear her and it's a different thing. This is when I learned how unfunny I was.

WILDE: *Many comedians come from poor families and have had very unhappy childhoods. Do you think this is why they became comedians?*

GREGORY: I think it has a lot to do with it. I was born and raised on relief and I can be the world's biggest billionaire and I can tell jokes about being poor whereas if Rockefeller's son decided to . . . he couldn't.

WILDE: *Does coming from an impoverished environment enable the comedian to see things funny?*

GREGORY: No, I think the funniest humor comes from the guy in the street, who's not in show business. To be a comic is another form of being a whore. The housewife has sex relations, she's not a whore . . . a prostitute is, because she's selling what everybody else is doing for free. Humor is everyday life, and the funniest thing you're gonna hear is from the cab driver or the soda jerk or the guy in the factory. But there's something about the comedian that makes him able to get up and sell it . . . present it in a certain way.

WILDE: *What is that?*

GREGORY: I can't explain it. I don't think there's too many people who can. . . . I think the guy that would explain it wouldn't be a comedian; he'd be in the field of psychiatry or a sociologist.

WILDE: *Does the Negro have a different sense of humor from the white man?*

GREGORY: Oh, yes, because the Negro has a different set of values from the white man. The white man lacks humor . . . we laugh at him . . . we've been laughin' at him for years. Everything he seems to do we think is silly. You go to a Negro movie house and you think the Negro is loud, boisterous, ignorant, and uncouth, but he's not . . . he's laughing at white folks. His biggest form of entertainment has been the American white man . . . the silly things he does.

WILDE: *When you started, did you do essentially Negro humor?*

GREGORY: More so Negro humor, but it was satire on a local level. I didn't know anything but Chicago.

WILDE: *Were you doing ethnic humor . . . Negroes, their problems . . .?*

GREGORY: Yeah, but I think it would go deeper than ethnic humor because it goes deeper than just a race. It goes into the economic . . . food . . . clothing. The biggest humor you have is the "put-down," whereas the white folks use it for us, we just take it and laugh at it.

WILDE: *Like what?*

GREGORY: I get a big bang talking about watermelon because the white man eats more watermelon than we do. We get a big kick talking about switchblades cause the white-man got all the missiles and declared war on everybody on the face of the earth and we have yet to declare war on anybody. He stole us . . . come over here and kicked the shit out of the Indians and pushed the switchblade rap on me. He gives us credit for inventing the word "mother-f——r" like he's never read *Oedipus Rex* . . . that's who invented "motherf——r." So we twist everything he's used.

WILDE: *Do you change your material when you work for an all-Negro audience now?*

GREGORY: Definitely.

WILDE: *What is the difference in what you would do for an all-Negro audience as compared to a mixed group?*

GREGORY: Well, for one, the Negro don't care about the stock market. He's not worried about the financial page . . . he's trying to pay his rent. You can have brilliant jokes about finance and they wouldn't mean a thing. He reads the paper and hears the news in a certain way.

WILDE: *Slanted towards himself . . .*

GREGORY: . . . Yeah, how does this affect him. . . .

WILDE: *Do people have to read the newspaper and be up on the latest news to appreciate your humor?*

GREGORY: Oh, yes, definitely, they have to be well in-formed.

WILDE: *Wouldn't that tend to limit your audience?*

GREGORY: No, because you can always water it down. But I go across the country and it's amazing how tremendously the American is informed. Although sometimes not as sharply in one area as another.

WILDE: *Were there any comedians you admired or patterned yourself after?*

GREGORY: Yes, I'd always admired Rochester, Amos and Andy, Redd Fox, Slappy White. My knowledge of comedians was very limited because I didn't go to night clubs and before television there just wasn't that many [Negroes] to break through . . . other than on radio. Bob Hope had always been a favorite of mine. And Red Skelton. As you get into the game, you spread out and learn to appreciate many more and then you find that comics are like whiskey—wine, ginger ale, bourbon, Scotch, beer—and that no two are the same . . . each one is in his own brand. . . .

WILDE: *Were there specific things about the performers you liked that you studied or tried to . . . ?*

GREGORY: No, since I didn't have the money to go to night clubs I was never able to see too many comedians. And the few minutes you're given on TV doing an act . . . three minutes don't give you enough time to do it at all.

WILDE: *Now that you have the chance, what do you learn by watching other comedians?*

GREGORY: I never watch them. I never have . . . I'm so wrapped up in them and what they're saying I could never learn anything. . . .

WILDE: *How do you explain that Negro comedians like Redd Fox, Slappy White, and Nipsey Russell, who have been around for years, couldn't make it and yet you came along and in a comparatively short time became a national success?*

GREGORY: Well, I think it was because I stayed in Chicago. Had I been in New York, I don't think I would ever have made it.

WILDE: *How long did it take you from the day you put together comedy material until that moment when you broke through?*

GREGORY: 1958 to 1961.

WILDE: *It took you about three years to "find yourself" and what you wanted to do?*

GREGORY: In '58 when I decided I wanted to be a comedian I walked into a night club and paid the guy five dollars to put me on and I was the funniest thing in the world, but when I got the job there two weeks later I wasn't that funny anymore. I really had to work hard for my laughs. I had steady work from '58 to '61 but I spent a lot of time figuring out what makes people laugh . . . this I didn't know. If young comics only knew that when there's a little bit of hesitancy on laughing from the audience it's because you got a streak of brilliance and that's resented. They resent you without being a big name. Power makes people laugh. L.B.J. can tell unfunny jokes. Your boss can tell unfunny jokes. Power . . . there's a certain amount of surprise you get out of humor coming from power. This is why when the boss took you aside and told you an old silly assed joke that never made any sense . . . you laughed.

WILDE: *Is that the reason the new comic doing fresh material with a different point of view has the more difficult row to hoe?*

GREGORY: You have it. Because when you come through with the mark of brilliance, you have the challenge, especially if you're not a big name . . . you're upsetting something inside someone.

WILDE: *You strike home . . .*

GREGORY: Yeah. The audience is a very funny animal. He'll be ever so sympathetic to you when you're dying and

once you get him laughing you have him. There's a loyalty
people have to comedians. It's just unbelievable.

WILDE: *If you find an audience unresponsive, do you have
any tricks or gimmicks to start them laughing?*

GREGORY: No, it's almost impossible for me to get an
audience like that. Because I'm so strong outside the field
of show business that the power itself when I walk on the
stage . . . I can just look down and there's X amount of
people that's frightened of me. . . . I just wink and that
makes them laugh. It's amazing the effect power has on
people.

WILDE: *When you say "power," do you mean an inner
strength that you project to the audience?*

GREGORY: My power lies in civil rights and although I'm
a very good comedian I have this extra thing going for me.
Consequently, I never have to worry about walking out and
an audience not laughing. Sometimes I say to myself, "For
ten minutes I'm going to try and not get a laugh." It's
impossible. Deliver the material backwards, jump over the
punch line, and you still get a laugh.

WILDE: *You've been to show business what Jackie Robinson was to baseball, that is, the first Negro to break through
on a national level. As the pioneer, what were some of the
problems you encountered?*

GREGORY: Oh, I didn't encounter that many because I was
in Chicago and I never knew Negroes couldn't work in top
white night clubs and all I was trying to do was work well
enough to make twenty-five dollars a night. When I broke
through I became aware of the problem of the Negro comedian working in a white night club . . . then I basically
figured out most of the problems myself before I ever went
to work. I knew that the white comedian . . . when the white

woman got up to go pee, he's always made a comment about it, so you look for it. So when I'm onstage and see she gets up to pee, it's not only that I can't make a comment about it, the fact that I *wouldn't* make a comment still is obvious, because in every other club in the history of night clubs there's been a comment. So for me *not* to make a comment leaves it sticking out, you know?

WILDE: *How did you solve that?*

GREGORY: The minute she'd get up to go to the washroom, I'd start talking about my kids and that's something everybody can relate to . . . and it worked. Another problem was . . . the drunk heckler. What happens if a guy calls you a nigger and the audience ends up embarrassed? They can't laugh at you anymore because humor is nothing but a disappointment with friendly relations. . . . All these things I had to work out on paper before I . . .

WILDE: *You actually sat down and figured them out?*

GREGORY: Oh, yes, because I knew they would come up. For six months I told my wife to yell insults at me. I never got my reactions right until one day I was at the house and was very aggravated about something . . . I looked at my wife and said, "What would you do if from this day on I started refering to you as 'bitch'?" And she said, "I'd just ignore you!" The way she said it was the attitude I wanted . . . the tone of voice . . . and once I had that tone the rest was easy. Of course, later on I found funny ways to overcome problems. If a man yelled "nigger" up at me I would say very politely, "According to my contract, the management pays me fifty dollars every time someone calls me that. Please do it again."

WILDE: *Do you think the civil rights movement also helped you progress as fast as you did?*

GREGORY: Oh, yes, no doubt about it.

WILDE: *A performer doing comedy is often referred to as a comedian or a comic or humorist. What do you consider yourself?*

GREGORY: Comedian ... social satirist ... maybe a clown. The true clown knows all the social problems. When I first hit it big people said, "You remind me of Will Rogers," which they considered a compliment. But one guy, real hip, said, "You remind me of Mark Twain." *That* was a compliment because Mark Twain didn't pull any punches. I think the greatest social commentator of our times ... and the only man I know that could equal Mark Twain is Lenny Bruce.

WILDE: *Why this great admiration for Lenny Bruce?*

GREGORY: It's his brilliance. Here's a man can do three hours on any subject. I'm not talking about three silly hours —three manufactured hours. Lenny Bruce, two thousand years from now will be one of the names that will still be remembered. He's to show business what Einstein was to science.

WILDE: *Why do people laugh at you?*

GREGORY: 'Cause, for one thing, I'm funny, and I use very powerful stuff, and I jam it right.

WILDE: *What do you mean "jam it"?*

GREGORY: I place it right where I want it to be placed and know exactly when to drop a thing. It's like a guy boxing. When you're sparring, you roll to his punch. It's the same thing with that laugh, you roll to it. . . .

WILDE: *When a writer submits material to you, how do*

260 The Great Comedians Talk About Comedy

you decide what's funny and what you think the audience will laugh at?

GREGORY: I never read new material until I'm in the dressing room, five minutes before I'm ready to go on. If it's funny it'll be with me and if it's not, it's not there. That's the way I decide.

WILDE: *Then it's instinctive.*

GREGORY: I key myself . . . my feelings . . . to their laugh machine. I've read a lot stuff they would love coming from somebody else . . . but when I look at material I have to look at it for me and hear my tone on the stage sayin' it. A lot of stuff I don't use. I throw away enough stuff from my writers to make ten million comedians in America cause they are funny lines to begin with, but they're just not lines I can use.

WILDE: *They don't fit you . . . they're not right for you . . .?*

GREGORY: Yeah.

WILDE: *What percentage of the material is usable?*

GREGORY: It varies. . . . If I can get one good joke with power . . . they don't have to send me nothing for six months. That's what I look for—the power.

WILDE: *Is an education important for a comedian?*

GREGORY: I would say it is. But there's so many outside elements involved in being a comedian. . . .

WILDE: *Like what?*

GREGORY: Being aware of social problems and social conditions and of people. The more education you have the better comic you'd be.

WILDE: *Is a comedian born or made?*

GREGORY: I think they are made. Of course, kids are naturally funny because they say things we adults would not say because of convention, society . . . my daughter was very hip as a little girl. Eight o'clock one morning I said to her, "Be quiet!" "Well, Daddy, we gotta make a deal with you," she said. "If you're gonna go out and get drunk and come in with a headache and don't wanna hear no noise at eight o'clock in the morning then you're gonna have to take us with you every night and get us drunk because it's normal for kids to get up at eight o'clock."

WILDE: *Is there any luck in getting ahead or do you have to make your own breaks?*

GREGORY: There's luck in getting along in show business —just like any other business—but it's not luck to stay up on top. It's hard work . . . very hard work. Constant study. I read a great deal. But even more than that I have a research staff of twenty people set out to probe and get information.

WILDE: *Have your civil rights activities affected your popularity?*

GREGORY: Oh, yes, very much so. I'm probably the voice of America today. I don't think there's anyone in the country that's stronger than me today. Everybody asks me have demonstrations hurt my career. I could make three times as much money outside of show business now than I do in because I go to a night club for five thousand a week and work six nights doing two or three shows a night. But I do lectures about the social problem for twenty-five hundred for one night, one hour of my time. So in two nights I make five thousand dollars, and if I do four lectures I make ten grand.

WILDE: *How important is a comedian's technique?*

GREGORY: That's what makes him. This is the thing he could never sell. This is the thing that material can never do. You can take away the jokes . . . you cannot take away my technique. And if you do and you perfect it well enough . . . then you become a mimic.

WILDE: *Is economic security an advantage to a comedian?*

GREGORY: Very much so. It allows him to chance material he knew was good but was worried about trying. . . . When you go out on the stage worrying about the laughs, or the audience laughing, then you get in trouble. They sense a certain insecurity. They are all there for the same thing . . . to have fun and they gotta see that *fun* look. Economic security means a lot. Like with me . . . last week my lights was cut off from my house 'cause I couldn't pay the bill . . . but still, I know I'm economically secure 'cause I know if I find time to go to work I can make five thousand dollars any given week I want.

WILDE: *In spite of the tremendous success you have had with your books, personal appearances, and so on, you are still in a position where your lights were turned off?*

GREGORY: Yeah, but this is my fault. I don't believe in money. I dump mine. I don't want it. I don't need it. I don't even want insurance. I tell my wife if I die tomorrow and there's no insurance money to raise my kids on she's gonna have to bring them up on wisdom and knowledge.

WILDE: *What kind of jokes get the biggest laughs? Those on the Negro, the political situation?*

GREGORY: Depends on what's goin' on in the news. . . . You know, I thought comedy was the number one savior in the world until the Kennedy assassination and then I realized had it not been for four days of music the country would never have survived . . . 'cause there just wasn't anything you could have said that was funny. We always thought humor was the answer to everything, when everything else failed humor came to the rescue. But I learned with the Kennedy tragedy that music is still the most powerful healer in time of need.

WILDE: *Aside from current events aren't there some jokes you do that have no bearing on what's in the news?*

GREGORY: Yeah, that's because I don't want to be pressed . . . to be forced to come up with lines that aren't funny. . . .

WILDE: *What is an example of something you can always do . . . a neutral joke?*

GREGORY: I say: "I have problems. I'm married and my wife can't cook. How do you burn Kool Aid?" Then I do things on kids which is standard. I don't like to use things that I know are safe. The challenge is to go out and use the unsafe stuff.

WILDE: *Doesn't that come when the comedian has achieved a degree of success and emotional security? Until then he's still looking for the strong, powerful, big laughs.*

GREGORY: When I walk out on stage the audience is not a challenge to me. I don't go out there saying I'm going to make you laugh. I go out knowing they are going to laugh. Not as a threat but as a friend. It's like if I was at your house and asked you for a glass of water, I'd get it. It ain't a challenge. They know you're there. They came to see you. We're not against one another. . . . I'm not scheming against them and this is the attitude I have.

WILDE: *What advice would you give to a comedian just starting?*

GREGORY: Go to the library and book stores and get every book he can lay his hands on and read the jokes and learn as much about comedy as he can. The most important thing is not to be in a hurry. Doing comedy is like money in the bank. As long as you know you're good you never have to worry . . . as long as you are constantly growing while you're waiting for the break. Another thing is knowing people. Watch 'em. Look at 'em. Not just staring at them but figuring them out. There's no school you can go to to learn to be a comedian. It's trial and error. There's more facilities for a man to become President of the United States than to become a comedian. And we need good comedians just as much as we need good leaders.

Bob Hope

Leslie Townes Hope was born on May 29, 1903, in Eltham, England. When Hope was four, his father, a stonemason, brought his wife and seven sons to Cleveland (which Bob now considers his hometown).

In 1933, after several years of vaudeville, doing a blackface act, dancing, and doubling as a saxophone player and scenery mover, Hope hit Broadway, where he starred in *Roberta* (with Fred MacMurray and George Murphy). This was followed by *Ballyhoo, Ziegfeld Follies,* and *Red, Hot and Blue* with Ethel Merman and Jimmy Durante.

In 1938, Mr. Hope began his own radio program and in the same year played in his first motion picture, *The Big Broadcast of 1938.* (This is the movie in which Hope sang "Thanks for the Memory"—later to become his theme song —to Shirley Ross.)

Referred to as "the Will Rogers of the age," by *Time* magazine, Bob Hope made his first appearance on television in June, 1950. He has been a regular ever since.

Aside from the *Road* pictures with Bing Crosby and Dorothy Lamour, Hope's biggest hits were: *Monsieur Beau-*

caire, The Paleface, Sorrowful Jones, My Favorite Brunette,
and *The Seven Little Foys.*

Mr. Hope has written five books: *They've Got Me
Covered, So This Is Peace* (Simon and Schuster), *Have Tux,
Will Travel* (Simon and Schuster), *I Never Left Home, and
I Owe Russia $1200.*

Bob and Dolores (Reade) were married in 1934 and have
four adopted children: Linda, Tony, Nora, and William
Kelly Francis.

Bob Hope has received over 300 awards and citations
for his humanitarian and professional activities. He started
entertaining the troops during World War II and has since
traveled more than a million miles, playing to more than ten
million troops in every corner of the globe.

Random jokes from a Bob Hope monologue

In my family, we were seven boys and one girl. She
died young. She never had a chance at the table.

I used to be quite an athlete—big chest, hard stomach. But
that's all behind me now.

My wife is so Catholic we can't get fire insurance—too
many candles in our house.

I like to see politicians with religion—it keeps their hands
out where we can see them.

Once I was flying in a place that was hit by lightning.
A little old lady sitting across the aisle said, "Do something
religious!" So I did—I took up a collection.

On champagne flights, some stewardesses serve too much.
Once I got on as a passenger and got off as luggage.

Hollywood Catholics are different. They're the only
Catholics who give up matzoh balls for Lent.

Last year I received the Humanitarian Award and this
year "Doctor of Humane Relations." . . . If I can just stay
human for one more year I get to keep 'em.

There's a dangerous side to these honorary doctorates. The last time I was sick I took two aspirins and called myself in the morning.

But I want to tell you, ladies and gentlemen, some friends of mine had a very exclusive wedding. They threw a Chinaman with every grain of rice.

[*As M.C. at the Academy Award ceremonies*] This is the night when war and politics are forgotten, and we find out who we really hate.

ALAN KALMUS, Mr. Hope's public relations director, arranged this interview and was present in the NBC Studios dressing room where it took place. Bob had come to New York to tape a television segment at the Rockefeller Center studios.

At first he joked and kidded and treated our talk as a lark, but he soon settled down and offered some earnest reflections. In preparation for his television appearance, he wore a midnight blue suit, light blue shirt, and dark blue tie.

WILDE: *Mr. Hope . . . when did you first become aware that you could make people laugh?*

HOPE: I think when I was here in New York. . . . I was doing a dancing act and one day I went down in the subway and stuck my head out to look for the train . . . and that was the first laugh I got and I've been funny ever since.

WILDE: *Did you really start doing comedy by accident?*

HOPE: No, not really. I did a dancing act with a girl in Cleveland and we used to do little jokes in between dances . . . and that's how I started. Then the first tab show I was in—a musical comedy which was very popular back in those days—I did blackface comedy. . . . I did all styles of comedy. I did everything on the stage—singing, dancing—and that's actually how I started. I think what you're referring to is the incident in New Castle, Pennsylvania, when the manager of the theatre asked me to announce the show that was coming in and I went out and started doing a monologue. . . . And I'd add a joke or two every time and finally the manager said, *"That's* the kind of act you should do. This dancing act doesn't compare with those laughs you get standing up." That gave me the idea to do my single act. So I broke up the double and I started doing comedy.

WILDE: *From that point, how long did it take you to become aware of the kind of jokes that fitted you and your personality best?*

HOPE: Oh, that was developed in the next three, four, five years. . . .

WILDE: *What did you do for material?*

HOPE: Well, I was master of ceremonies at the Stratford Theatre in Chicago and they used to change the show in midweek so I did two shows a week and I needed a lot of material. . . . So if a vaudeville act would come in I'd say, "Do you have any jokes? You know any jokes I could tell?" I used to do all kinds of dialect jokes. . . . I used to scrape them up from reading *College Humor* and I switched them. . . . I did anything just trying to get material to do. It was a great thing, this job, because I used to have to "save" jokes. . . . Jokes that didn't play so well, I had to play with the audience to save them

WILDE: *How long were you there?*

HOPE: I was at the Stratford Theatre about six months and the audience got to know me. . . . When I started to do a dialect joke—I'm probably the worst dialectician of the world and as soon as I started to tell an Irish joke or a Jewish joke they used to laugh before I got to the punch line because I was so bad telling it. But it was like working to your family because it was the same audience all the time. They'd come back, they knew you, they liked you, so you had their sympathy. Thank God!

WILDE: *That seems to be a very important aspect in the development of a comedian—being able to stay in one place, one club for a long. . . .*

HOPE: I don't think that's important. I think just *work* for a comedian is important, that you go on. . . .

WILDE: *When delivering your monologues you have a very smooth and easy style. Did you always work so relaxed?*

HOPE: No, I learned an awful lot after I was a hit in Chicago. Then I was doing a brash type act and working fast and making it the *audience's* problem whether they got the jokes or not. Then I went down to Fort Worth and I worked the same way and laid the biggest bomb in the world. The manager of the circuit, Bob O'Donald, said to me, "Look, slow down, these are nice people. They're not rushing around. I don't know where you're going—you're in such a hurry." So I said, "That's the way I work. I just tell the jokes that way and if they don't like it, they can lump it." He said, "Well, try it a little slower." So I did— for the next few shows and I started to get laughs . . . which I liked and it woke me up a bit. I said to myself, "Wait a minute now, when you get to these people you got to slow down a little." . . . That's in the days before television, before much of radio. Now today, in my experience, *all* audiences are the same. They're just as fast in Texas or in Oklahoma or anywhere you go because they see all the shows, they hear all the jokes. You're working to the same audience all the time.

WILDE: *Don't you believe that having become an American institution and having so many millions of people see you, that when you walk out on stage they're laughing before you get. . . .*

HOPE: Yes, you've got a head start but you've still got to

come up with it. How long are they going to applaud for you? They like you, that's fine but then you've got to prove yourself.

WILDE: *Jack Benny made a similar point when he—*

HOPE: Oh, sure, because you have to satisfy them. They're expecting a certain quality and you have to come up with it. And Jack Benny, by the way, don't mention his name to me cause he's the *biggest* ham in our business.

WILDE: *He loves you. . . .*

HOPE: Well, that's a mutual thing. Jack's been one of my great friends for years. He said something the other day that tickled me. He called to ask me about his playing in a college and I said, "You'll do marvelous in a college!" He said, "Can I do my night club material?" I said, "You can do *anything*." Because you know he's never been really in bad taste. He does a couple of nude jokes . . . but I said, "I'm going over to London for the Command Performance." And he said, "No kidding, I'm going over to the West End and rent a theatre and do a one-man show!" I said, "Why?" He said, "Well, I just want to show off!" . . . and to me that's a marvelous expression for people, they want to show off.

WILDE: *In the beginning did you study other comedians?*

HOPE: Oh, yes, I studied a lot of people. Jack Benny . . . and I studied Frank Fay a lot. . . .

WILDE: *Were there specific elements that you looked for when you watched them work?*

HOPE: No, not really. I think you have to be gifted with a certain sense of timing and if you have any sense of comedy, you absorb different things just watching.

WILDE: *What are the circumstances or conditions that*

cause a comedian not to get laughs on one particular night?

HOPE: Well, there'd be a lot of reasons for that. I died a lot of times. . . . For instance, I was forced down in Australia in 1944 in a place called Lorryton and these people had seen all my pictures. I was doing a routine that I'd been doing for the troops down there and I knew was surefire 'cause I'd done this material everywhere in the world. I walked out to do this show for about five hundred of these people and they looked up and just smiled at me. I kept telling jokes and they just smiled right at me and they were so happy looking at me they forgot to laugh—they just smiled me right out of town. I finally said to myself, "I gotta do something broad here," and I did a broad joke . . . the oldest joke in the world. I said, "I was in Brisbane and it was raining and this woman was standing with her dress up over her head and I said, 'Lady, you're getting your legs all wet,' and she said, 'I don't care, my legs are fifty years old but the hat's brand new.' " And they liked that and they laughed and I said, "Well, here's Frances Langford," and got off. That'll give you an idea how much of a hero I am.

WILDE: *At a personal appearance, do you have definite opening lines that you use to establish a laugh climate or your character before going into any routine you're going to start with?*

HOPE: No, you got a head start as you said before . . . they recognize you and they know you. You don't have to establish any laugh climate, all you have to do is come up and say something they're going to laugh at. I used to challenge an audience when I first started. I used to just look at them. I told a joke about going into a restaurant, and when I got up to the cash register I said, "Sorry, I left my money in my other clothes in the theatre." And she said, "That's all right, we'll just put your name on the wall and you can pay it the next time you come in." And I said, "But wait a minute, I don't want people to see my name on the wall." She said, "That's all right, your coat will be hanging over it." . . . And I used to just look at the audience for maybe twenty seconds and wait till they all got together and decided that that was pretty funny. I'd just look at them and stare and that was how I established my laugh climate back in those days.

WILDE: *Wasn't that after a number of years, after you had developed the courage and the confidence to wait?*

HOPE: Yes, I should say—after I had a little bread money.

WILDE: *In a* TV Guide *story by Melvin Durslag, he quoted an associate of yours saying that one of the maxims you were guided by was that you felt no audience was an audience as such but a jury. Could you explain that, please?*

HOPE: [*Laughing*] Well, I think that's one of Mel's conclusions . . . that isn't my idea at all, I don't look upon it that way, in fact, I don't even worry about it. . . . There's only one audience that *bothers* me and that's a Command Performance in London where you might have to change the material and switch around. I just experienced that. Now, I'm a *little* concerned at the Academy Awards—it's a long show, like an hour and a half, two hours—I'm *concerned*, but I'm not nervous. But the other night at the Palladium in London I was going on as the last act, the sixteenth act, and there were four or five comedians on, doing every joke in the world . . . and I found myself scrounging around for an act. They had done every subject, every topic, and there was nothing left. Backstage I walked up and down and I said to myself, "Well, I can do the joke about that and I can do this routine and I can do that one. . . ." When I finally got on it was 11:30, the Queen was still there and I said,

"I've been waiting—I've been made up since breakfast" and I got a big laugh. Then I looked down and they put the cards behind the leader, so I said, "Hey, move away from the card," and he didn't know what I meant, so he pushed a button and raised the pit two feet. . . . That always helps your act, when the pit is coming up . . . it looks like the orchestra is going to attack you for something you said.

WILDE: *It was a challenge.*

HOPE: Yeah, it was more than a challenge . . . it was a place for my psychiatrist.

WILDE: *When your writers submit monologue material, what percentage of it are you able to use?*

HOPE: An awful lot of it because you see, I confer with my boys and keep working with them. There's no guesswork. We talk about subject material and what I want to do and they know *me*. Most of them have been with me for . . . my Johnny-Come-Latelys have been with me fifteen years.

WILDE: *Mort Lachman is the oldest?*

HOPE: No, Norman Sullivan is the oldest. He's been with me since 1938. Les White has been with me, off and on, since 1932.

WILDE: *Is there some special secret to keeping such a long, successful relationship with writers?*

HOPE: Yeah, just keep them working and they keep you working . . . it's a mutual thing.

WILDE: *How do you decide which jokes to use?*

HOPE: Well, that depends on your taste and what you want. That's the whole story.

WILDE: *What is the difference in the reaction of an audience composed of armed forces personnel, a TV studio group, and the people who see you at a paid personal appearance?*

HOPE: There's a different routine for all of them. You see, when we do shows offshore for a GI group, we try to point it a little more their way but they laugh at the same things that the TV audiences do . . . as long as they're general routines, general topics.

WILDE: *Common denominator material.*

HOPE: Yes . . . right, right. With a GI audience, every place we play we steer it more to local jokes.

WILDE: *In that article by Melvin Durslag, he said that you believe that no comedian was secure. What did you mean by that?*

HOPE: He said that?

WILDE: *Yes.*

HOPE: What do *you* mean by secure?

WILDE: *Having the courage and confidence to continue in spite of setbacks, bad ratings, bad notices. . . .*

HOPE: Well, Mel's a pretty smart fella . . . maybe he means this: I don't think a comedian should *feel* secure. Whenever you get the feeling that you're the greatest around and you stop being objective, then I think you're in danger . . . and I think that's what Mel is talking about. [*Jack Shea, Mr. Hope's TV director entered and said,* "We're ready for you now!")

WILDE: *One last question. Are there any words of encouragement you can give to a beginning comedian?*

HOPE: Yeah, forget it! We've got enough and stay out of our racket. No . . . they've just got to study and try and get a lot of work. What we discussed before is the most important thing—getting out and working and applying different techniques. Finding out what's best for you to do. You can only do that by experimenting. The greatest thing is to come up with a fresh approach. For instance, Mort Sahl came in with something different . . . Jonathan Winters did . . . that's the thing that will grab immediate attention. Nice seeing you.

George Jessel

George Jessel was born in New York City on April 3, 1898.
He began his show business career in Gus Edwards' "School
Days Revue." Afterward, he did an act in vaudeville, and
then graduated to the legitimate stage when he appeared on
Broadway as the star of the play *The Jazz Singer* (which
later was made into the first talking picture, starring Al
Jolson).

Jessel appeared in several movies and then became a
motion picture producer for 20th Century-Fox Company.
During this period, when not at his desk or in actual pro-
duction, Jessel was making after-dinner speeches. He
started this in 1925, while campaigning for the late mayor
of New York, James J. Walker.

Since 1953 Jessel has been acting as a "good-will ambas-
sador" for the democracy of Israel and is responsible for
over ten per cent of the millions of bonds that were bought
by the people of all religious denominations to help the
economy of Israel.

He appears continually on television—first with Jack
Paar, then Johnny Carson, Jackie Gleason, Dean Martin,

and Pat Boone. He is now starring in his own television series, "Here Come the Stars."

Among Jessel's several books are his best-selling auto-biography, *So Help Me; This Way Miss;* two comedy books, *Hello Moma* and *Jessel Anyone;* and a book on public speaking, *You Too Can Make a Speech.*

His recent publications are: *Elegy in Manhattan* and *Halo Over Hollywood.*

A George Jessel monologue

Operator, give me Imglick 6134 . . . hello, Fineberg's Delicatessen? Mr. Fineberg? George Jessel. How are you feeling? You sprained your ankle? I'm sorry to hear it. Would you mind running up three flights and call my mother to your phone? . . . The place is packed and you're all alone? Well, couldn't you close up for a couple of minutes? You say my mother is just coming into the store? That's a coincidence. I say, it's a . . . it's nice she came in . . . put her on the phone.

Hello, Mama, Georgie. Georgie. Your son, from the money every week. How are you feeling? You still see spots before your eyes? Have you got your glasses on? They're on your forehead? Well, how long does it take to get them down? You got them down. How is it? You see the spots better now.

Say, Mom, how did you like that bird I sent home for the parlor? You cooked it! That's a fine thing to do. That was a South American bird . . . he spoke four languages. He should've said something? Well, never mind. I'm going around to the art shops tomorrow. I want to see if I can get a nice Whistler's Mother. If I do, I'll get a lovely frame and we'll hang it over the fireplace. . . . I say, for the front room, the parlor, I'm gonna bring home Whistler's Mother.

. . . She'll have to sleep with Willy . . . I figured you'd say that. . . .

How's my sister, Anna? Anything new with that fella of hers. You think he'll marry her this winter. . . . Why? He said it'll be a cold day when he marries her. Well, Mama, she's in love and there you are. Let her get as much out of life as she can. You know what Longfellow says, "Tell me not in mournful numbers, life is but an empty dream." I say, Longfellow said that. . . . I shouldn't go around with him, he's crazy. . . . No, no, no . . . Henry Wadsworth Longfellow, the poet. . . . He didn't live next door to us at all . . . that was Lowenstein, a bookmaker.

Well, I have to go Mama, I'll call you tomorrow.

SAM CARLTON, George Jessel's long-time friend and business representative, arranged this meeting and was present in Mr. Jessel's suite at the Hotel Astor. This room, overlooking Times Square, seemed the perfect setting: George Jessel in the very heart of his beloved city.

After a brief wait in the sitting alcove, I was ushered into the "Toastmaster General's" room. He was sitting up in bed, covered by a sheet, wearing a navy blue yachting cap and smoking a huge cigar.

His face, shoulders, and arms were freckled and he looked twenty years younger than his actual age. His warmth and friendliness were overwhelming. He was enthusiastic and delighted to chat. After the interview he telephoned Jack Benny long distance to tell him of this project and to suggest he talk with the author.

WILDE: *Is it true that you began your career as a singer?*

JESSEL: Yes, as a boy singer. Actually, the first time I was seen in front of any public I was the bat boy for the New York Giants, early in 1910. And then I sang when the game was over . . . if the Giants won. . . . I would go into the clubhouse with McGraw and Matthewson and all those fellows and sing. And if they lost, McGraw would say, "Get out of here, you little Jew." And then I'd go to the visiting club . . . and at that time, the Cincinnati Reds had wonderful dark uniforms—dark, heavy navy blue . . . and red caps and I had sort of an ambition to wear that uniform. The manager was Clark Griffith, of the ball club . . . and he was going to take me along to be the permanent bat boy, or mascot, for the Reds. And then the next day, my mother, who was the cashier at the Imperial Theatre on 116th Street in Harlem, knew that I'd been rehearsing some songs with Walter Winchell and another kid by the name of Jack Wiener . . . and she arranged for the manager to hear us sing as the Imperial Trio. And we were engaged there, at four dollars apiece, and five songs on Sundays at ten cents apiece, to sing with illustrated slides. Then we made up our minds that we'd have to have a stage name. No matter what your name was . . . you changed your name. So Winchell, Wiener, and Jessel became Lawrence, Leonard, and Mc-Kinley. He was Stanley Lawrence, Wiener was Jack Leonard, and I was George McKinley. I was ten then. And then in order to get songs . . . to learn songs . . . you had to go down to Tin Pan Alley. And Gus Edwards, he was a famous songwriter . . . and also it was a market for children . . . he had acts with kids in them . . . and he heard us sing and engaged us all for his acts. That was the beginning.

WILDE: *When did you actually begin doing comedy?*

JESSEL: Well, I did a little comedy at the age of ten . . . and some imitations. Georgie Price was the star of the show. He was even younger than I. . . .

WILDE: *The Gus Edwards show?*

JESSEL: Yes. And some places they wouldn't let him go on because he was a child. So was I, but I wore long trousers and had a cigar in my mouth and a phony birth certificate. I bought a birth certificate from some old Hungarian fellow on the East Side. His name was Imril Kazani. According to that birth certificate I would now be two hundred and twelve years old. Some places I fooled them and some places I didn't.

WILDE: *When did you first begin doing a "single"?*

JESSEL: 1917.

WILDE: *That was the beginning of your going out and standing up, so to speak?*

JESSEL: Yeah. That's right.

WILDE: *How did you discover you coula make people laugh?*

JESSEL: Oh, my family, all of us had quite a sense of humor. We were always laughing. My grandmother was funny . . . and my aunt was funny . . . my mother told jokes. We always had a lot of fun. But I wandered around professionally, not knowing what to do. At the age of sixteen and seventeen . . . on the stage . . . I was doing things that were much to precocious and over-smart. I was telling the same kind of jokes that I might tell now. "I just left the bank . . ." and so on, and nobody believed it. Then I met a song and dance man named Al White, who now owns that tremendous big restaurant at the Roosevelt Race Track. And he suggested that I ought to do things . . . in the second manner. I ought to say, "This is what happened" and tell it to my mother. And being young and unafraid, as he told me that, I asked the property man—this was in Mount Vernon—for a prop telephone, and I went right out and . . . that's how I started to talk to my mother. Then in later years I met Sam Carlton and he prepared most of the "mother" monologues for me.

WILDE: *You are generally credited with doing the first telephone routines. . . .*

JESSEL: No . . . that isn't true. I did the first telephone routine to my *family*. But before me there were wonderful telephone conversations like, "Cohen on the Telephone"— that was done by Barney Bernard. And Willis Mann. And Monroe Silver.

WILDE: *Why do you think people laugh at what you say?*

JESSEL: At what I say? Because there's a humane quality. An authentic quality. An honest quality. For example, I told a story last night on the Johnny Carson show. I did it in four minutes and something, because of the time element. As a rule, there's a commercial that comes in. But we cleared the way for it. But when I tell it in the theater or in a lecture, it runs ten, eleven minutes. One joke. It begins, as I say, with an authentic quality, that it actually occurred. And that's always been my method. I was also the first one to tell a story with music behind it.

WILDE: *Once at a Friars Club luncheon you said, "A comedian is a fellow who can make my Aunt Tilly laugh."*

JESSEL: That's right.

WILDE: *What do you mean by that?*

JESSEL: Well, I mean, unfortunately, it isn't their fault . . . there's so little show business today in the United States. And I've just returned from Europe and it's very blatantly seen in my mind. For example, they've got about eleven theatres on Broadway. There's about eighty-seven in Paris. And so the young comedians prepare themselves for a night club and that kind of a thing. Or they do a television show and they're ordered by a client or the advertising company. . . . Now, for example—and these are all very clever people mind you—Mort Sahl, Jack E. Leonard . . . a few others . . . what would they do at a Saturday matinee at the Palace Theatre, where the audience consisted of Aunt Tilly and the kids?

WILDE: *But in the show business of today, we don't have theatres to entertain the family. And isn't it a question of the times bringing out the kind of—*

JESSEL: Well, a comedian is someone who should be funny. He shouldn't say, "I'm only funny if you've read the *Wall Street Journal* or Earl Wilson's column." And they don't make 'em anymore because, unfortunately, there's no minor leagues for them to start in. George Burns has a very caustic way of saying it: "There's no place to be lousy anymore."

WILDE: *How would you define the word, "comedian"?*

JESSEL: One who . . . I suppose the dictionary would say, "One who comedes" if there's such a word. A comedian is funny . . . is someone who's funny. I think the word—Mr. Carlton would know this . . . is comedy Latin, a derivation of the Latin?

CARLTON: *Comedia.*

JESSEL: *Comedia.* Latin, to be funny, to be humorous. And it's so classified now. For example, I'm going to do a week's engagement with Sophie Tucker and Ted Lewis. Now, yesterday, Miss Tucker, was terribly worried. She said, ". . . because I can't do anything in the theatre that I do in the night club. You see what I mean? It's a different kind of a thing. You can't do what you do in a night club or in the theatre, on the television. So it sort of holds you down.

WILDE: *It creates a tremendous problem for the young comedian.*

JESSEL: Well, of course, it does. He doesn't quite know what to do. It's a terrible problem, terrible problem.

WILDE: *Does the word "comic" mean the same as "comedian"?*

JESSEL: No, I think it's . . . a lesser connotation. You wouldn't say that about Jack Benny or George Burns or Red Skelton or these fellows . . . comic is too small a title. Comic is . . . Morey Amsterdam kind of comic.

CARLTON: A comedian can even play drama.

JESSEL: I think that's it.

CARLTON: A comic can't.

JESSEL: That's right. All of the comedians when I first started were actually fine dramatic actors. They were brought up that way. Sam Bernard, who was what we call a Dutch comedian, but he could play Shylock, he could . . .

WILDE: *Why is that . . .*

JESSEL: Because they started their careers in the theatre, in all kinds of theatre. A burlesque show or stock company. Played like, for example, Potash and Perlmutter comedy— I think they had fifteen companies playing. So a guy that was doing a little "bit" in a burlesque show had a chance to act. And that brought him to somewhere else, and then he went farther than that. *Turn to the Right* had about twenty companies. So somebody saw the fellow in the fifth company in Toledo, brought him in to play in the second company, and then, maybe, in the summer, in the Broadway company in New York. So there was a continuous chance of bettering yourself . . . becoming more expert. Now for example, I met a fellow many, many years ago who was a skate dancer. He used to do a buck dance on skates. He had a million partners. And then he finally got to do a monologue himself, which wasn't very good. And then he did an act with a girl whom he married a short time after. It was a pat, straight routine. If they wanted to change a line, they went out to New Jersey and broke it in for three weeks. That was Burns and Allen. Well, I brought Burns and Allen to New York. And booked them in the Palace with Eddie Cantor and myself. We would meet in the dressing room about ten minutes before . . . "What'll we talk about today?" "Oh, start anything and we'll . . . let's do ten minutes on that," without any rehearsal or talk-over.

WILDE: *Completely ad-lib.*

JESSEL: Just completely impromptu. And that gave Burns the confidence he needed, 'cause offstage, when the show was over, he was so funny. I used to bring everybody of prominence that came to New York, including the Prince of Wales, to hear George Burns in his room at night. Then he developed it by saying, "Well, I'll do a new routine tonight" . . . and he'd try things *that* way. But that's because you had these long bookings. You played on *this* little circuit, *that* little circuit.

WILDE: *A comedian could develop and be trained. . . .*

JESSEL: Oh sure.

WILDE: *And you got a schooling which is obviously not possible today.*

JESSEL: The comedian . . . the comedians unfortunately today would be like the fellow who studies the violin for a little while and goes right into Carnegie Hall. Instead of him going to a little Town Hall in Pittsburgh, another one in Schenectady, and so forth.

WILDE: *Why do they call Danny Kaye, Jimmy Durante, Chevalier, "entertainers" and yet, they do comedy. . . .*

JESSEL: Well, Danny Kaye is not a comedian. Danny Kaye is a very consummate, fine artist and some of the things he does are funny. Some of them are serious. . . . I heard him sing "Molly Malone" one night and make an audience cry. Chevalier is not a comedian. Chevalier is a very fine actor and was a singer of French folk songs. Durante is a thing by itself! A raucous, good-natured fellow with a funny face . . . easy to provoke laughter when picked on at any time . . . and a very warm kind of a guy. They don't have . . . there are some Durantes in Europe . . . fellows like that . . . baggy pants fellows, but . . . he's a thing, Durante's a thing by himself. As is Danny Kaye.

WILDE: *But why are they called "entertainers"?*

JESSEL: Well, that's what they are. I guess Danny Kaye is the best all-around entertainer of our time, without any question.

WILDE: *Did you feel the same way even while Jolson was alive?*

JESSEL: Well, Jolson was the greatest entertainer that ever lived. There isn't anybody around now fit . . . because the Lord God—nature—manifested in Jolson something that he never did in anyone else. There was nobody like him. There's nobody around that compares with him. Jolson did things to audiences that . . . well, for instance, he would say to me one night in his dressing room, "Gee, they're a pipe, never had audiences like 'em, they laugh when they buy their tickets. Show you what I'm gonna do tonight." And he'd tell the *wrong* answers to jokes. They laughed just the same. Nobody else could do it. . . .

WILDE: *His image had the power. . . .*

JESSEL: His authority . . . he had a very small range as

far as singing is concerned. But he was the first fellow to give—I said this when I buried him, I did the eulogy when he died—he gave majesty to the popular song. The last eight bars were as big as *Tosca* . . . he had a God-given thing.

WILDE: *Some years ago, the West Coast Friars Club honored you at a* . . .

JESSEL: At that dinner, I think that's where Jolson got up and said, "Folks, I'll sing all night." And I said, "No, you won't this is *my* dinner. You'll sit right down." I was the only one that had any authority with Jolson the last four or five years. I could walk on the stage when he was on. He wouldn't let anybody near him but me. And that only in the last four or five years.

WILDE: *He had this incredible insecurity.* . . .

JESSEL: I guess it was that too. It's kinder to say it was a continuous insecurity, regardless of how great he was doing.

WILDE: *It's an amazing phenomenon . . . the scales of nature, of life . . . that a man can be given such greatness on one hand and to balance it out—*

JESSEL: I think you're exactly right about that. That's a good thought too! And it's kinder to say it was his insecurity more than his ego that made him act as he did. I'll remember that.

WILDE: *Has comedy changed through the years?*

JESSEL: Well, it's changed because everything is a specialization. It's like being a doctor. You used to go to the average doctor if you had a headache or you had a tummy ache or your nose was bleeding . . . now everything is specialized. I tell a gag, "My son is a doctor." "What does he treat? Eye, ear, nose, and throat?" "No, no, no, just nose. One nostril. The left one." You know. It's a specialized thing now.

WILDE: *With a half dozen or more successful books to your credit* . . .

JESSEL: I haven't had a half dozen. I've had one very successful one. . . .

WILDE: *Well, I enjoyed them.*

JESSEL: Oh, well, they're successful from the standpoint of . . . whoever read them, liked them . . . but not enough read them.

WILDE: *What I wanted to say was you are one of the most literate comedians of our time. Did you have much formal education?*

JESSEL: None. I went to school from the age of eight, and not quite the full year. I think about seven months. And then, as I said, at ten I went away with Gus Edwards.

WILDE: *Then you educated yourself to reach this* . . . *?*

JESSEL: Self-education and . . . a violent desire to read. For example, I have one of the largest collections of religious books of, I guess, anybody anywhere. I have a tremendous library of religioso. But in all fairness, I became literate in a literate age. Every one of the stars, when I first started were men who were qualified, when the curtain fell, at the end of a play, which they used to do, to make a curtain speech. Come down and talk about government, or books, or music. They were . . . these fellows, most of them had played Shakespeare. William Collier, Bernard, Mann, Jefferson DeAngelus, DeWolfe Hopper. Nearly every star wore a fur coat and carried a cane. And on Sunday wore a high hat. Now there's something strange about clothing. I arrange, or try to have, in every place that I speak, and I speak more than two hundred times a year, maybe more, to please see if they'll come with a black tie. It helps manners, it stops people from being raucous. It adds a certain something and makes their wives or their girls or daughters dress. Therefore, everybody's manners are better when they dress for the evening. That's why audiences are so much better in Europe. Much more receptive in Europe than they are in America.

WILDE: *Is there a difference in the reaction you get from groups doing the same material?*

JESSEL: I get much bigger laughter from people not of my religious persuasion. Non-Jewish audiences are much, much better for me than . . . because I'm too close to them. It's like making your family laugh. It's like I'm part of them, you know? Like my daughter said to me once, "Gee, why do you always be so funny? You ought not to be funny."

WILDE: *How does an all-Jewish audience respond in comparison to a non-Jewish crowd to a mixed group?*

JESSEL: A completely non-Jewish audience is much better for me. I make so many speeches for the Catholic Church throughout the country.

WILDE: *How does it happen that so many of the comedians are Jewish?*

JESSEL: Well, I don't think that's prevalent . . . I don't think that's anymore like it was. It used to be *that* way because the Jews who came from Europe, or Russia, or East Asia or wherever they came from had to pick up all sorts of languages and dialects, you know, 'cause they were moved from one part of the world to another. So they became

wonderful mimics and imitators . . . and I think that was
responsible . . . but not in these days. Not in this generation,
I don't think, according to television. Now let's see. All these
fellows that are around now are not of the Jewish faith at
all.

WILDE: *Woody Allen is Jewish, Jackie Mason, Shelley
Berman. These are certainly of the newer generation. On
he other hand, there's Johnny Carson. . . .*

JESSEL: Well, there's Carson, there's Merv Griffin, there's
Mike Douglas, there's, oh, an awful lot of them. Woody
Allen is a very, very literate fellow. He wrote that movie,
What's New, Pussycat? He must be quite a guy.

WILDE: *You've been given the title, "toastmaster general
of the United States. . . ."*

JESSEL: Yeah, by four Presidents.

WILDE: *Because of the great many speeches you give. . . .
But what do you consider yourself? A comedian? An entertainer?*

JESSEL: Well, I consider myself, first a personality. And
then I would say, a scholar on human nature. But I also . . .
I've done some of the lowest comedy things ever done. I
played a thing for years on Broadway called "Professor
Labermacher" . . . with a wig and a moustache and baggy
pants and a torn vest . . . that critics all said was the
funniest monologue on any stage anyplace.

WILDE: *Of all the mediums you've worked in—stage,
movies, clubs, television—which do you prefer?*

JESSEL: I prefer sitting at a desk and creating things to
go on the screen or to go into book form.

WILDE: *How long were you a motion picture producer?*

JESSEL: Eleven years. I made twenty-four pictures for 20th Century-Fox. Trying to make a couple now. And also working, which is very tough, on my own story which is being . . . getting ready, I hope, to be sold to a company. My only problem—we can't get anybody to play me.

WILDE: *Do you still get nervous before a performance?*

JESSEL: The only time I ever get nervous is if I have to go on . . . if I need money, which I do nearly all the time . . . if I have to go on in a night club, I'm terribly tense. I've played in, and I'm going to play again, God willing, a place called the Latin Casino, in Cherry Hill [N. J.]. When I come on, no one is allowed to serve a drink or a glass of water or anything. That's like playing in the theatre. And I'm on the stage. And when you're on a stage, people look up *at* you and up *to* you. There's a presence of superiority in talking *down* to people, instead of being on the level, on the floor. . . .

WILDE: *They might talk back to you.* . . .

JESSEL: Oh, I'm sure it would be murder. I only had that once. I was quite well known at the time and a guy bothered me and I said, "I don't know what to say to you because no one has ever annoyed me before and nearly everybody has too much respect to annoy me like you're doing. I wouldn't know what to say to you."

WILDE: *What have you done to remain a star all these years?*

JESSEL: Well, work . . . and taking advantage of every opportunity.

WILDE: *Weren't you persona non grata on TV for a while*

because of your attitude toward the television ratings system?

JESSEL: Not my attitude. The truth of the matter is I think the amount of television we have is a terrible curse to our country . . . because I see us completely degenerating. It could break your heart when you come from Europe, and go to Detroit, for example, that has a million, five hundred thousand people, almost as large a population as the whole country of Israel . . . and you want to dance in Detroit with your girl or your wife, you've got to take your passport and go over to another country—into Canada. There wasn't a "live" musician when I was there lately. Same thing for Cleveland, Pittsburgh, almost every city. Los Angeles, of course, is like a graveyard. The nation has been sort of intrigued or drugged to stay at home. And the worst impact it has on the country is the loss of newspapers. Now I am responsible, personally—and I think it should be my epitaph —the most important thing I've ever done in my life is to save the domestic economy of Israel. I've kept television out of there. Television would break Israel in about thirty days. That's the most important thing I've ever done as a human being.

WILDE: *Why do you feel it would break . . . ?*

JESSEL: Well, I don't *feel*, I have the actual proof of it. Before Ben-Gurion retired from office, RCA and the Rothschild Foundation were going to bring sets and shows and bring television into the Holy Land. And I was asked by Ben-Gurion to survey what I thought it would do. So, with a big strong camera I took pictures at eight-thirty at night in good weather in ten great cities in the United States. With the exception of these six blocks around Broadway where we are now . . . in ten great cities at eight-thirty on the main streets . . . didn't average thirty people. Then I took pictures of large motion picture theatres with the cashiers asleep at eight-thirty and forty to fifty people inside. Then, again, I pointed out the newspaper situation. Detroit, with one newspaper—and that's shaky. Five and a half million people in Los Angeles county, a newspaper and a half. Now, as against that . . . the city of Tel Aviv has a population of four hundred and forty-four thousand. There are *seventeen* newspapers in Tel Aviv. I don't think we're gonna have even four after the first of the year in New York. Greater New York with fourteen and a half million people! On Saturday night, there will be, almost every night, at least a quarter of a million people on the streets, of all Israel, Arab villages and all. You want to see a movie, you got to call up two weeks in advance. Opera! Theatre! You see groups on the corner discussing . . . "Did you read this editorial in Mirov?" . . . "Did you read this editorial in so-and-so?" Now who discusses an editorial in America? You get one line from Huntley and Brinkley.

WILDE: *Is there something we can do to alleviate that situation in our country?*

JESSEL: Well, I don't know. The government seems to have the right to tell a saloon it's got to close up at certain hours of the night. The government has the right to say you can only have that much morphine if you're in pain. So the government should have the right to say you can't have twenty-four hours a day of television. I find, and I think you'll find, in your time if not mine, that we'll get murdered in the Olympic games. And the only ones that'll win for us will be Americans of the Negro race, because their parents, perhaps, didn't have the money to buy the television. Our children don't play in the streets. As soon as there's any sign of inclement weather, Mama says, "Willie, stay in the house and watch TV." He doesn't become strong and healthy like the other children. I checked on the fact that, oh, about thirty firms who manufacture galoshes, rubber boots, and rubbers have gone into bankruptcy these last couple of years. Nobody plays in the street. Kids stay home. And the terrible insensitivity of most of Madison Avenue. . . . I took this off the air and I had it played for the French government. I've helped curtail television in France and in Italy. In France, they have three hours a day. You can't have it in a hotel or an apartment house. There's eight o'clock in the morning, I think, one; an hour about noon, an hour about seven o'clock. And that's all.

WILDE: *That should be more than enough. . . .*

JESSEL: And the worst impact of all is the TV's image of politics. I also wrote two editorials for the Los Angeles *Times* about how dare anybody bring a television camera into a courtroom. The most innocent person in the world will be tense or shaky, makes him look guilty on the camera.

WILDE: *If professionals get that way . . .*

JESSEL: Of course, they do . . . and politicians . . . now they follow him into the home, as he goes into the john, there's a camera there if he picks his teeth. I was a speaker this last May 8th, at the eighty-first birthday of Harry Truman. I have been speaking at his birthday for many, many years. And when it was over—the luncheon—Jim Farley, Averill Harriman, and I were upstairs and a young fellow was brought in by a Missouri politician. "This is Jim so-and-so" and he said, "Jim, get out of here, I want to talk about you." And he said, "Mr. President," to Truman, "Farley, George, this kid is going to go places. Senator, Congress, governorship. No telling how far he'll go." So Mr. Truman said, "Is he a college man? Lawyer?" "Oh, gosh, he's terribly stupid but he photographs like anything." We elected, and he's a friend of mine, a buck dancer, senator from California . . .

WILDE: *George Murphy. . . .*

JESSEL: And now we have a governor who's never been in a courtroom or anything, Ronnie Reagan. 'Cause he looks good.

WILDE: *What satisfaction do you derive from making people laugh?*

JESSEL: Well, I get a bigger satisfaction out of making them *think* than making them laugh. My best speeches have not been funny ones, by any means.

WILDE: *You've delivered funeral eulogies for some of the greatest stars. . . . Which was the most difficult to perform . . . because of the emotional attachment?*

JESSEL: Jolson's. Not because of an emotional attachment. To have to speak at a man's death and never touch the *man* . . . only his art . . . and his impact on the American scene . . . it was hard to write.

WILDE: *Are all your speeches prepared in advance?*

JESSEL: All my speeches are written. Nearly everything I've written is on paper, otherwise you wouldn't have them in books. They sound like they're possibly being made up but they're not. I read all my speeches. Unless you're an expert you wouldn't know it . . . but it's all there on cards, every word. Not a speech I make, like to sell bonds or to aid the economy of Israel . . . these are *set* speeches and I know them. But every new speech is prepared, and every dinner is prepared. We had a dinner to Jack Warner on the Coast, I was through with that two and a half months before I gave

it. My success as a public speaker, which is practically all
I've done in the last ten years or more, comes from the art
of the budgeting of words. And the budgeting of words is
done particularly by putting speeches on paper. Then you
never say, "Ah, ah, ah, ah, and I'm so glad to be here tonight. Ah, ah, ah . . ." If it's there, you say it. And you can
sum up things . . . this also comes from reading. I've just
finished an album called, "The Legend of Eddie Cantor."
One line describes it, "History on a phonograph record . . .
during this record I want you to laugh because since Eddie
Cantor left no son . . . laughter was his *kaddish*." Now that's
twenty-four words altogether and you just say it that quick.

WILDE: *The friendship you had with Cantor. . . . Were
you closer to him than to Jolson?*

JESSEL: Oh, yes. Cantor and his family. I was his only
full confidant. I had a memorial service up at Grossinger's
last month for fifteen hundred people.

WILDE: *Did you do his eulogy?*

JESSEL: He didn't have any. There were seven people at
his funeral. Three daughters, two grandchildren, his valet,
and myself. He had no services. About a minute and a half.
The daughters said he didn't want anything. And it was all
very secret. No one knew where he was even going to be
buried but me and the family that were in California. But I
think they were wrong. As I told them. I said, ". . . 'cause
he didn't belong to you. Only this which remains is yours to
do with as you may, but he belongs to the world." He was
a very shrewd and great . . . the most resourceful comic
figure that there ever was in America. He was businessman,
lecturer . . . he was the first fellow of his size—from the
standpoint of being a big artist—who looked away from the
mirror of his dressing room to see what was going on in

the alley downstairs. He was the only guy who would come into a town and instead of saying, "Get the notices," would say, "What can I do to help in this town?" Of course, in order to do that, you have to have the authority of success, and a lot of dough . . . but no one else ever did that but Eddie Cantor.

WILDE: *You've probably been associated with, and a friend to, more of the great stars than any other . . . ?*

JESSEL: Yeah, not only the stars. In my time, I knew the Queen of England, Churchill, Somerset Maugham, Charles de Gaulle, Presidents from Wilson on . . . only one I never met was General Eisenhower. But all the rest I had an association with.

WILDE: *There's an affinity comedians seem to have that no other group . . . doctors might get together and they might understand . . . but not like comedians . . .*

JESSEL: That's exactly right. All comedians have the same kinship, I believe, as women in childbirth.

WILDE: *What advice would you give a young comedian starting out today?*

JESSEL: Keep reading and keep trying. Despite the fact that there's so little show business, if you've got it . . . if you've really got it . . . unless you're going to be terribly unlucky, you'll get somewhere.

WILDE: *Thank you very much for talking with me. . . .*

JESSEL: Well, you're about the most sensitive young fellow that I've met to come around in this business in a long time and if there's any justice in the world or if there's anything left of the amusement business, I'm sure you're going to get somewhere. Anybody who can think and talk as sensibly as you do—you may be able to write too.

WILDE: *I am writing* . . .

JESSEL: Well, there you are. That's the thing. Everything dies except the written word. Men that have long since gone, for three thousand years, keep their impact upon life, because of what they have said on paper.

Jerry Lewis

Jerry Lewis was born Joseph Levitch in Newark, New Jersey, on March 16, 1926. His father, Danny, sang nostalgic songs; his mother, Rae, played piano.

In July, 1946, after several years of doing a "single," Jerry teamed up with Dean Martin at the 500 Club in Atlantic City and for the next ten years the duo made show business history.

Working alone since July, 1956, Lewis has proceeded to make his own historical contribution to the entertainment industry as a comedian, singer, actor, screenwriter, producer, and director.

His "Rock-A-Bye Your Baby," released by Decca Records, has sold nearly two million copies—more than Al Jolson's original recording.

Mr. Lewis has appeared in thirty-seven motion pictures, a list, obviously, too long to name.

He is presently the star of his own television program, "The Jerry Lewis Show" for the NBC network.

Jerry is the National Chairman of the Muscular Distrophy Association of America and has raised over $33,000,000 for that charity.

Mr. and Mrs. Lewis (Patti) live in Bel Air, California. They were married on October 3, 1944, and have six sons: Gary, Ronnie, Scott Anthony, Christopher Joseph, Anthony Joseph, and Joseph Christopher.

Jerry Lewis' dressing room at the NBC studios (Burbank) could easily be mistaken for one of the three rings at the Ringling Brothers circus. Technicians, writers, and wardrobe assistants barging in and out, a color television set blaring rehearsal sounds, a twenty-pound tin of freshly boiled crabs perched on the coffee table and Jerry Lewis, sprawled dejectedly on the foam rubber sofa.

He was unhappy over a sketch he was to do the next night on television; and depressed because he couldn't rewrite it in spite of staying up till two the previous morning.

Nonetheless, Jerry welcomed me graciously. He wore a dark blue double-breasted sweater, gray slacks, powder blue sport shirt, white sweat socks, and mahogany loafers—his rehearsal togs.

During the first part of the interview Lewis' "deep funk" thwarted his sincere desire to express his comedic views. Later, a writer came in, they worked out the sketch problem to Jerry's satisfaction, he relaxed, and we developed a good rapport.

He also recorded our talk (as he does all interviews) with a Sennheiser microphone and Nagra tape recorder, considered to be the finest recording devices in the world. He delighted in discussing their reproduction quality, but admitted my Uher 4000-L was "second best."

WILDE: *How old were you when you had your first act?*

LEWIS: Thirteen.

WILDE: *What did it consist of?*

LEWIS: Record act . . . I did Sinatra, I did Igor Gorin, "Largo al Factotum," I did Deanna Durbin's "Il Bacio," I did Grace Moore's "Il Bacio," I did "Poet and Peasant," Wilfred Pelletiere's symphony orchestra . . . oh God . . . Danny Kaye, Groucho . . .

WILDE: *Like Donald O'Connor and Sammy Davis, Jr., you grew up in a show business atmosphere . . .*

LEWIS: Uh, huh.

WILDE: *Is that an advantage, or a short-cut?*

LEWIS: Sure. Absolutely. It's informative, you have more information—you can see all of the things that are right and all of the things that you think are wrong.

WILDE: *Do you feel you got your basic understanding of the profession . . . ?*

LEWIS: Yeah. You absorb.

WILDE: *Like a doctor's son, by the time he's thirteen, he knows the scalpel, knife . . .*

LEWIS: Yeah. I got the basis from my father, without question.

WILDE: *Early in your life were there any comedians who impressed you and thereby influenced your approach to comedy?*

LEWIS: Berle. The master, without question. Berle was a very, very influential character. Very influential. Stan Laurel was a different kind of an influence but at that time in my life, Berle was very effective for me because that was the *bag* I was playing in. Gleason . . . Gleason being the best sketch comic I'd ever seen in my life.

WILDE: *I've heard that you were also impressed with Harry Ritz?*

LEWIS: Oh, of course. I think all comics are. Harry is the same category as Berle. Between Berle and Ritz, I think ninety per cent of your visual comics were born.

WILDE: *How many years did you do the record act before you teamed up with Dean Martin?*

LEWIS: Oh, I was doing that act about five years, I guess.

WILDE: *Where did the material for the Martin and Lewis act come from? Was it strictly ad-lib?*

LEWIS: No. I wrote most of the material. It consisted of a two-way technique that I had learned from my father who had worked with partners all through the years, in burlesque and so on.

WILDE: *When you say, "two-way technique" do you mean the question and answer set-up . . . ?*

LEWIS: Yeah, except that we had a unique device in that we had it planned, and through just the fantastic rapport that Dean and I had we knew when it was happening and what we were aiming for. His doing straight for me, of course, and then my straight for him, because his comic know-how was so intuitive.

WILDE: *Martin and Lewis were considered to be one of the great show biz phenomenons. What was the public appeal of the act?*

LEWIS: Their affection for one another. That's all.

WILDE: *And the audience sensed . . .*

LEWIS: Yeah.

WILDE: *That rapport and the affection?*

LEWIS: Absolutely. Any other two guys could have done the same act and they wouldn't have made a dollar.

WILDE: *When the act started to roll, you did a lot of mad-cap things. I remember in Miami you stopped traffic on Collins Avenue and . . .*

LEWIS: I did it this morning.

WILDE: *Were you expressing your sense of humor or simply trying to call attention to the act?*

LEWIS: Oh, I don't know. I think in the young years, you try everything . . . to call attention . . . but that was my whole attitude of life—which hasn't changed much. It's just slowed down a little because I'm aging rapidly.

WILDE: *When Martin and Lewis broke up, what were the problems you had to overcome doing a single again?*

LEWIS: *Fear.*

WILDE: *How did you do it?*

LEWIS: You fight fear like you do anything. You just don't let it get you.

WILDE: *Was there any specific philosophy you developed, any discipline?*

LEWIS: Yeah. I reminded myself constantly that the seats weren't facing the stage and it wasn't as scary.

WILDE: *If the kind of comedy you do could be given a title or label, what would you call it?*

LEWIS: Human comedy. Provoked and motivated by everything I see . . . and people.

WILDE: *Other than your general comedic talent, why do you think people laugh at you?*

LEWIS: They're laughing at themselves. They won't laugh when they can't identify.

WILDE: *Many people believe the psychological motivation to become a comedian is often based on a great desire to please an audience, to gain their acceptance and love. What do you think drove you to become a comedian?*

LEWIS: Same thing. An audience is nothing more than eight or nine hundred mamas and papas clapping their hands and saying, "Good boy, baby." That's all. You'll find that people who had enough "Good boy, baby," from their actual parents rarely turn to comedy. They are our doctors and lawyers today.

WILDE: *Is it a prerequisite to come from poor and deprived circumstances in order to become a comedian?*

LEWIS: You better. Otherwise you won't know what you're doing.

WILDE: *Why is that important?*

LEWIS: Well, because you have to taste dirt before you can analyze it. You never saw anybody born with a silver spoon in his mouth turn to what we consider good comedy.

WILDE: *There's a fellow around New York who's doing very well. . . .*

LEWIS: London Lee?

WILDE: *Uh-huh.*

LEWIS: Except that he's a marvelous mimic. He's mimicking the best.

WILDE: *He comes from a wealthy family.*

LEWIS: He's using that. You see, London is a monologist. You can come from a wealthy family and be a monologist.

WILDE: *What's the difference between a monologist and a comedian?*

LEWIS: It's the difference between a psychologist and a brain surgeon. And that difference is that a psychiatrist goes and learns what it's all about from the text . . . never has to use his hands. A comedian's got to know what it is to take a pratfall. He's got to know what it is to turn laughter into tears and he's got to do things with his being and his every breath. A monologist just has to learn the words.

WILDE: *Do you think a comedian is born or made?*

LEWIS: A "comedian" is made. A "funnyman" is born. A funnyman is all by himself. There's only been fifteen in the history of humor. Gleason, Stan Laurel, Chaplin, Keaton, Fields, Jack Oakie, Berle. . . .

WILDE: *Then becoming a comedian is something that can be developed?*

LEWIS: Yes.

WILDE: *And can be learned?*

LEWIS: Absolutely. Through a great sense of humor, through a flair for comedy—through a *feel* that they have.

WILDE: *What are the basic requirements to become a comedian?*

LEWIS: Personality, sense of humor, common sense, self-lessness and selfishness . . . you have to care about yourself pretty much to want to do it.

WILDE: *The ego does play a tremendous . . . ?*

LEWIS: [*Long whistle*] Does it ever.

WILDE: *Does intelligence have anything to do with being funny?*

LEWIS: It'll help. It'll really help . . . because then you get into dimensional comedy. Without intelligence you are one-faceted, I think. That's what is known as reaching a crest and then having to go to the inevitable down . . . whereas intelligence helps you to stay on top of things and it helps you broaden your scope and with some degree of intelligence, if not a lot of intelligence, you at least have a shot at expansion.

WILDE: *Most comedians seem to be very aware of people, of human nature, they have a great curiosity. Are these attributes also necessary to become a comedy performer?*

LEWIS: No, I think that those are the things that happen after the fact. Those are part of the extensions of comedy. I think you have to be aware of people, yes, at the beginning . . . because without awareness you are doing comedy in a void, a vacuum. 'Cause what you are really doing is a reflection of them . . . what we said earlier.

WILDE: *Bert Lahr was once quoted as saying that Ed Wynn, Bobby Clark, Chaplin, W. C. Fields, and the like, were serious people. Are all comedians when they are not onstage basically serious?*

LEWIS: I think so. I can't talk for all of them but I would like to bet they are. I don't think you've ever seen a good brain surgeon with the shakes. And I think that whatever that brain surgeon has to do to have a steady hand, I think that's what a comic has to do in his offstage life. To steady his hand, he's got to be a serious man . . . to get up there and make a fool of himself. Ed Wynn, of course, is the prime example.

WILDE: *The nature of show business is very emotional, with many highs and lows, and when a comedian is not working or does not have any prospects for work, he seems to drift into moods of deep depression. Is that a typically human reaction or is it indicative of the comedian's psychological make-up?*

LEWIS: I think it's part of one, part of the other. It has to do a great deal with his psychological make-up but it also has to do with his needs that are being cut off. And I think that that need isn't as devastating a need to him if he were to really believe in his own heart that subsequently he *will* be in front of an audience. But for the most part, most comedians are terribly insecure at what they do, they don't believe that they are going to see another audience . . . so that the depression really falls into a very, very deep gorge, as it were. A lot of people in show business feel that way but I think it's more pronounced with a comedian.

WILDE: *Do loneliness and being a comedian go hand in hand?*

LEWIS: Oh, sure. That's where the expression "in one" came from, except instead of the "in," it was "aw" for alone.

WILDE: *I didn't know that.*

LEWIS: *I just made it up.*

[*Laughter*]

WILDE: *Do you have a formula for fighting depression?*

LEWIS: I'm in one today. I'm in a deep funk. The only way you can fight depression, I think, is just let it take hold and let it get itself over with. I can't laugh or giggle or be pleasant or cute when I'm depressed. Because that's what I'm entitled to be. I don't want to impose it on others so I hide, wait till the depression chews away whatever it has to eat away and get it over with. Sometimes it lasts longer than other times. When you try and figure out what those depressions are, here's where intelligence comes in. You don't begin to try to figure it out—if you're smart—because we pay rent for an awful lot of our living years ago. The rent is only coming due now . . . so depressions could very well be because you were unkind to me yesterday. But it could also be because I was lacking something fifteen years ago. I think it takes that long for some of these depressions to come around.

WILDE: *And you don't feel analyzing it, trying to understand it, is of any value?*

LEWIS: Yes, I think there's a value to it, if you can. But just to make up an analogy doesn't make sense. You're bullshitting yourself. If I can analyze it and find out from where it comes, that would make me a doctor. Since I cannot verify where it comes from—and I believe it comes from someplace—without proof of that I don't know for sure that that's where it comes from.

WILDE: *You've always had great emotional rapport with your audience. Critics talk about the magic that happens between the comedian and the audience. Is it possible to define that intangible quality that makes up that "magic"?*

LEWIS: [*Laughs*] What's magic? When you can define magic, we can get into what you're asking about. You are asking some pretty powerful questions. I think if you were to go to an analyst and say, "What's love," he'll say to you, "What's hate and what's right and what's wrong?" I think that's what you're dealing with. If you want to settle for just an opinion, I think it deals with truth. Sinatra's *magic*. Do you know what that magic is? I think the *truth*. He's an ornery son of a bitch and he makes no bones about it . . . and he walks out on a stage and says, "I'm an ornery son of a bitch."

WILDE: *And they love him for it.*

LEWIS: They love him for it . . . and I got news for you . . . I respect him for it too. I may not like it, but I respect it. He don't bullshit! He's not a hypocrite! He's had some problems and he takes it out on that stage with him and it makes him a hell of a performer. I don't think you can say, "This would be good—I'll be ornery." Because that doesn't make it.

WILDE: *Be yourself?*

LEWIS: Exactly.

WILDE: *What you really are.*

LEWIS: Right.

WILDE: *Why is there such a fine line between laughter and tears?*

LEWIS: 'Cause I think they're one and the same. I call laughter a safety valve. When you're depressed and you're feeling bad and you want to foregt it, you don't say, "Let's go see *Virginia Woolf*." You say, let's go laugh. And the laugh I refer to as a safety valve is a cut-off to the tears. But they are so close you'll notice when you laugh hard enough you're cryin' . . . but you'll notice that you're never, ever depressed and laugh. It doesn't work that way. When you're depressed and your heart is heavy, you can't muster up a laugh. But when you're laughing, you're crying. The tears are rolling, gotta go for the handkerchief. Moreover, I have always had a very, very fine line theory. The fine line I make reference to is—I have been told by some of my constituents at the college that I think in terms of Fromm and Freud . . . because I maintain that laughter is so potent it can kill you. A depression won't kill you . . . you'll just sit in the doldrums.

WILDE: *You believe laughter can kill you?*

LEWIS: It can . . . physically and literally kill you. As a result of the effort, the physical, laughing. Rolling in the aisles came from somewhere. That expression came from somebody that knew when you roll in the aisles that's really laughing. But that's pain when you roll in the aisles. When you can't laugh to a proper standard on the meter seated in the seat, you're into hysteria. You can die from it, if you can't turn that God-damned safety valve off. Example —they use radium to cure cancer. Keep it on too long and you'll kill the whole body. So laughter is the same kind of help when somebody needs it but you better not take too much.

WILDE: *What is the difference between a comedian who acts and an actor who does comedy?*

LEWIS: A comedian who acts has to first act before he can be a comedian. There is no comedian known to our world of humor that's not a good actor. But an actor, just an actor who wants to do comedy, has his work cut out for him. That's why there were five comedies made in Hollywood last year and four thousand dramatic films.

WILDE: *Is it a question of training? Of instinct?*

LEWIS: Well, you've heard this as far back as you can remember: "He's acting like a jerk." He's *what* like a jerk?

WILDE: *Acting.*

LEWIS: Exactly. He *acts* the fool. But you never heard someone say, "He's acting Shakespeare." It's a different term.

WILDE: *Groucho Marx wrote in his autobiography,* Groucho and Me*, "All first-rate comedians who have played dramatic roles are almost unanimous in saying that compared to being funny, dramatic acting is like a two-week vacation in the country." Why is serious acting so much easier for a comedian?*

LEWIS: 'Cause that's what he is—a serious actor. I told you that before. He's got to be an actor before he can be a comedian. The hard job is doing comedy. That's what's rough. A comedian is literally allowing the underlying real thing to come out in front without any guise of comedic tonalities. Acting is a snap but acting for an *actor* is hard work . . . because that's all he does. It *is* like two weeks in the country. Christ, that's a pleasure, and easy . . . that's nowhere near as naked as being a comedian. In the dramatic, you have a mask. You always have a mask . . . and it's Shakespeare's mask that you are wearing—or whoever the dramatic playwright is—but in comedy you're naked. No matter what character you get behind, you're him . . . that's the difference.

WILDE: *Then, in doing the serious role you're hiding behind the character, whatever his behavior is. As the comedian, no matter what the role, you still have to get the laugh.*

* Bernard Geis Associates.

LEWIS: See, when you watch a television show and you see George Segal—you know, George Segal, the actor?

WILDE: *Yes.*

LEWIS: When you see George Segal portraying Tim McCarthy, it's Tim McCarthy beating that woman with the belt. But when Jerry Lewis is playing the silly, nutty professor, they don't turn it off and say, "Did you see what the nutty professor did to the kid?" but, did you see what *Jerry Lewis* did to that kid?" See, you can put anything on Jerry Lewis and it's Jerry Lewis that did it. That's the battle. But George Segal was Tim McCarthy when he hit that woman with the belt. When he gets home at night— George Segal is safe.

WILDE: *The comedian carries the responsibility wherever he goes?*

LEWIS: Whatever his action, yeah.

WILDE: *You once said in a* Look *magazine article that you don't read books because you can learn anything you want without reading.*

LEWIS: From people. True. Anything I've learned, I've learned from people.

WILDE: *By conscious effort?*

LEWIS: Sure. Do you read books?

WILDE: *Yes.*

LEWIS: Would you know what the procedure for brain surgery is from reading books? I could tell you . . . because I watched it. Same thing with an appendectomy, tonsillectomy, . . . amputation, I've seen. You think you could articulate about what makes a submarine go four hundred feet below the surface of the water by reading about it . . . or being in it, like I was? Or jumping. Did you ever jump in a parachute? You can read about it but that ain't gonna tell you anything. I did it. Practical application. I know a lot of guys that have read thousands of books, but I'm still a professor of cinema at the University of Southern California. They can't make it. And I didn't get it because my name is Jerry. I know my racket, and they wanted the one that knew best. A drop-out's a professor! So I must know something about that. Reading books isn't bad—it's just so time-consuming. And I can learn more from sitting with a new acquaintance about what life is all about than I would ever get from a book, cover to cover.

WILDE: *We touched on this a moment ago, but not deeply enough. How much does a man's ego have to do with being a successful comedian?*

LEWIS: Well, I think it has to do with *becoming* a successfull comedian. A big difference. Once he's a successful comedian, ego is only going to instigate a drive that should maintain itself within him. Without an ego, no one's going to know he's alive. 'Cause he's not going to get there.

WILDE: *He's not going to be able to stay alive.*

LEWIS: Right. Ego's very important.

WILDE: *Why is it so many of the top comedians are Jewish?*

LEWIS: Well, we get back to laughter and tears again. Why is it?—better than that question, I answer your question with a question. . . .

WILDE: *'Cause you're Jewish.*

LEWIS: [*Laughing*] Yeah . . . why don't we have a great Mormon comedian, a great white Baptist comedian . . .?

WILDE: *A WASP?*

LEWIS: Uh, huh!

WILDE: *Is it because they've never experienced the prejudice or the persecution or the unhappiness or the hurt that comes from being a member of a minority group?*

LEWIS: I don't think they knew what it was to have to whistle in the bathroom because there was no lock on the door. I don't think they knew what it was to use Sunkist orange wrappers because toilet paper was expensive. And I don't think that they would understand or know how sad and funny that is . . . 'cause that's pretty funny—Sunkist orange. . . .

WILDE: *Not while you're doing it. Later on we can joke about it.*

LEWIS: Yeah, that's pretty funny.

WILDE: *Lenny Bruce said that "Satire was tragedy plus time."*

LEWIS: Uh, huh! It wasn't at the time. After time passed.

WILDE: *Jack E. Leonard is reported to have said, "I really didn't get funny until I had my first fifty thousand in the bank." What advantage is financial security to a comedian?*

LEWIS: None . . . none. It's a detriment.

WILDE: *Why do you say that?*

LEWIS: 'Cause I believe it. Finances cut down on the ego, they cut down on the drive, they cut down on the output.

WILDE: *Berle and Benny and Hope and Danny Kaye have been successful for a long time; they had money twenty-five years ago. Certainly it didn't cut down their drive.*

LEWIS: No, no. You're talking about a handful, name some more . . . we've got four thousand comics, you're talking about six.

WILDE: *I was talking about the successful comedians.*

LEWIS: Well, I think there is a fine line with what I said —in terms of it being a detriment. . . .

WILDE: *You are just as funny today—if not funnier—than when I first saw you in 1949.*

LEWIS: Oh, well, I don't think it has an effect on their humor capacity—I think it has an effect on their desire to go forward and forge ahead and do more and so on. Hope is the exception.

WILDE: *Aren't you doing more than you did twenty years ago?*

LEWIS: I'm an exception to the rule. But read Jack E. Leonard's quote again.

WILDE: *"I really didn't get funny until I had my first fifty thousand in the bank."*

LEWIS: I misunderstood his quote apparently because it sounds different now.

WILDE: *I guess it was a poor first reading.*

LEWIS: No, no, no. I know what I'm thinking about. I understand what he says now. Yeah. Security, of course. I'd like to pass that, because I'd have to get into . . . I agree, yet there's some bite that comes out funny, when it's not really coming from the *gadarum** . . . there's something funny about a man being funny and he knows he hasn't got the rent . . . if you understand what I mean?

WILDE: *To be funny in spite of that?*

LEWIS: *That's* really funny. Then your audience is going to be getting the kind of performance . . . they don't understand why it's that much better. They're not gonna know the reasons. They're not supposed to know. It's like—I have been very, very close with the Menningers and some very, very bright people. I have never been analyzed but I have saved the life of one analyst by treating *him* . . . because he was very, very confident in my intuitiveness, my awareness of him and his problems and so on. I have always been very, very sharp with people. I can smell them a block away and tell you what they're all about. My staff calls me the "Witch Doctor," but I usually know. And I will never forget . . . I was sitting with Carl Menninger years ago. He said, "You know, of course, you could never go into analysis." I said, "Yeah, I figure I couldn't, but why?" He says, "Well, when you can find out the *why* of it you'll find out a lot of marvelous things that will help you." And for months I tried to figure that one out. And finally I called him and I said, "Is it because if I find out everything that's eating me, it's really of no consequence. I won't be funny then." He said, "Exactly. Leave whatever's eating you inside—leave it alone. If we check it out, we may find out it's really bullshit, but you're using it, it's become a tool for you. On the other hand, it might be very, very devastating. It's not going to enhance your comedy, but it can deplete your productivity. If you find out, so what? So don't examine it—leave it alone."

* Jewish word meaning testicles.

WILDE: *What is the difference between a comic and a comedian?*

LEWIS: Well, there's that beautiful list and it's hard to break down. It would need months of careful consideration. You start with funnyman, comedian, monologist, comic, clown, zany, satirist, mimic—they all fall into the category of comedy. I don't really think there is a difference, per se, in those two categories: comic and comedian. Because the comic smacks of funnyman a little bit, the comedian smacks of monologist a little bit—I don't think their titles are solid. A humorist is a man who says things that aren't particularly funny in a funny way. A satirist is teasing, in his own articulate way, about the things that people understand, that they would tease about in a very human way. Satire is dangerous for that reason. Jessel was in here before to see me. I don't know how you title this, but he said, "I ended my show in Vietnam"—and he really sucked me in on this —he said,

> *Now I lay me down to sleep*
> *I pray the Lord my soul to keep*
> *If I should wake before six o'clock*
> *Fuck de Gaulle and Doctor Spock.*

What do you want to title that?

WILDE: *What is meant by a comedian's "delivery"?*

LEWIS: Oh, well, that's punctuation.

WILDE: *How about "attitude"?*

LEWIS: Tonality.

WILDE: *As simple as that?*

LEWIS: Sure. If his tones are ruffled or if his punctuation . . . you do comedy, what happens if you breathe in the wrong spot?

WILDE: *Blows the laugh.*

LEWIS: Sure.

WILDE: *Isn't that "timing"?*

LEWIS: Sure it's timing but it'll get in the way of delivery too. Delivery is—I call it puncutation, because it's a . . . two men will tell the same joke and one will get a helluva thing with it because of his delivery, because of his punctuation of the story. He gives it color. Attitude and tonality are intangibles. But the attitude I think an audience can sense. If his attitude is a complacent one or a passive one and he's marking time, he's gonna blow it. They're gonna know whether he wants to be out there or not, or if he had to do the show or not. I think attitude embraces that.

WILDE: *Professionals often discuss the "quality of the laugh." There's a "cheap" laugh, an "embarrassed" laugh, a "shock" laugh. Would you explain those?*

LEWIS: An embarassed laugh is when you see a comic in a small joint say, "Take the spotlight off the bald man's head—it's shining in my eyes." A cheap laugh: "Lady, did somebody remove your red light?" That's poor. A shock laugh is ending whatever you're doing with a four-letter word.

WILDE: *What kind do you work for?*

LEWIS: Laugh. No titles, just laugh.

WILDE: *But they're warm laughs, they're sympathetic, they're human. . . .*

LEWIS: I hope to God. I don't want a shock laugh, and I

don't want an embarrassed laugh, and I don't want any of those titles. I want them to laugh because I'm going to laugh if they laugh. I'm gonna get pleasant. My oldest son, I wish you could meet.

WILDE: *Gary?*

LEWIS: Well, all of them, but Gary particularly. What a joy to behold! When he watches somebody laugh at something *he* has said, the laugh backs up. They're laughing, and wow, is he having fun at their pleasure.

WILDE: *Isn't that what you do also?*

LEWIS: Sure. But I'm not as stupid as he is. . . .

WILDE: *Why does it take longer for a comedian to become a success than for a singer or a dancer or an actor?*

LEWIS: Because I think that comedy is basically, not resented, but is met with great reluctance. As much as people want it and need it, they're a little reluctant to look in a mirror. Because many of them realize that they are really saying, "There but for the grace of God, go I . . . that's *me!*" Try telling a man about someone slipping on a banana peel with a bunch of bundles in his hands—you try and tell that to a man that's never had it happen to him, and he'll just look at you. "You mean she fell down with a bunch of parcels, slipped on a banana. Was she hurt?" But you tell it to a man that it's happened to, he's so delighted. "Yeah, she slipped and fell? Ho, ho." 'Cause he's been there. That's where the laugh is at. So you'll find that comedy is looked down upon by the masses. Although they love it best, they won't act like they love it best because it's a reflection of them.

WILDE: *Then when a new comedian comes along, it takes people a long time to digest him . . . his point of view. . . .*

LEWIS: Yeah, they're checking him out. What they are really doing is hoping he's a reflection of some people they know. Not them.

WILDE: *Of the total percentage of a comedian's craft, what part is instinct and what part training?*

LEWIS: Jesus, I don't know. [Pause] That's a helluva question. Let me say this: 'Course all of this is off the top of my head . . . I havn't heard some of these . . . It's like saying, "Our baby's two years old now. We'd better put him on a training toilet seat so he knows that's where he goes!" Oh, it's younger than that—nine or ten months. . . .

WILDE: *If you were a father, you would know that.*

LEWIS: [*Chuckling*] That's where he goes and he knows that's the place. . . . When the child is three there's no seat needed any more and there's no diapers needed any more. Instinct takes over. The child won't wet in his pants, he'll go right to where he has to go. If that's the case, then the training is only a minimal amount of time. But the instinct must then take us from that point throughout the rest of our natural lives. . . .

WILDE: *Then until you were thirteen years old you were being trained, and then when you started to do the act your comedic instinct took over and you. . . .*

LEWIS: No, no. It wasn't there for a long while. No, when I was thirteen I had all of the training to take me to that point. But then when I started at thirteen I might very well have still been . . . I might have been involved with training for another ten or fifteen years . . . I don't know when instinct took its hold and projected what it did for me. I don't think training stops with comedy. I think instinct and training work hand in hand.

WILDE: *Is it easier to be funny in a movie or on television then onstage at a personal appearance?*

LEWIS: It's two kinds of funny—motion picture funny and television funny are one and the same . . . and yet they are not. There are three different kinds of funny. Because I can't see what the television audience's reaction is . . . and if I could see it, it wouldn't be telling me anything, because I'm in their home and people are different in their homes. They are safe, they're solid, they're the authority. So that whatever you could see, if you were able to peek in you are not really seeing the same thing you're seeing when they buy a ticket at the theatre or when they go to a night club. But from my point of view, as long as there are three people watching, it's the same kind of fun. You have an opportunity to do much better with film, in design and creation . . . a greater shot at preparation. I have taken up to six months for a joke that flashed on the screen in less than thirty seconds. It's prohibitive in this medium [*television*] . . . so we have to do the best we can with the speed and that's why I'll never like television like I do films. 'Cause film is like giving birth to a baby. You take nine or ten months of your life—you see that all the jokes work. You give them care. Here you grind it out.

WILDE: *You've established an unparalleled record in the movie industry by appearing in over thirty-seven motion pictures that have not lost money. To what do you attribute the success of these pictures?*

LEWIS: Apparently the people are getting what they want. Plus the fact that I know my audience. I've never imposed messages on them. . . . I do all the things visually, they want to laugh at . . . and I don't do Hamlet. They would love to have me do that, only to denounce my turning my back on the comedy.

WILDE: *What elements do you look for in a movie script, before you decide to film it?*

LEWIS: Funny notion. Is it a funny notion. A man and a woman are in an automobile accident and their two kids get killed—that's not a notion for me. Out! Notion: A man wins the sixty-four-thousand-dollar question. They pay him off in brand-new bills. They're so new they stick together. He's so afraid he's going to give them more than one bill when he buys something . . . he don't buy nothing'. "F—it, I'll keep this money for the rest of my life becauce I can't give it away." That's a notion, that would sparkle. That would make me think.

WILDE: *You've done thirty-seven movies. How many scripts did you have to go through before you found one you felt you could do something with?*

LEWIS: I wrote sixteen of them. Is that telling you something?

WILDE: *I didn't know that.*

LEWIS: Sure, because you can't find them. Billy Wilder wanted me to do *Some Like it Hot.* I won't get in drag. That's not my idea of funny. I'll get in drag if it's funny and if you just do it and get it over with. But an elongated drag . . . it was a great film, I'm sorry I didn't do it.

But I'm still glad that I didn't, because I know how unhappy I'd have been doing it.

WILDE: *By directing your films do you feel you can best capture your own comedic spirit?*

LEWIS: Oh, sure. The director is in complete control. Then you're not dealing with someone else's tastes.

WILDE: *Or someone else's opinion about what's funny.*

LEWIS: Right. And until they eat dirt, I'm not going to let them analyze it.

WILDE: *Do you find all your years as a performer helpful in the field of producing and directing?*

LEWIS: Oh, sure. Very important. You're dealing with people. A good director is a man who can deal with people. And I have the greatest rapport in the world with actors and actresses because of my being on the same side of the stage they are. The communication's better. You get performances you want and it's great fun.

WILDE: *In your present movies, do you aim your comedy at a specific age group, or a particular segment of the American public?*

LEWIS: No, not really. But they say so. When they say, "You do pictures for kids!" I say, "Yep," because I maintain —*who* takes the kids? Some grandmother. But if they prefer not to let us know that they—as adults—laugh at this kind of nonsense, let them hide . . . slink down in the seats and look around before they laugh . . . which they do!

WILDE: *In England and France you are acclaimed a great clown, as well as a fine motion picture director, and yet the American critics have been extremely harsh on you. What is the reason for that?*

LEWIS: Well, first of all, we don't have American critics.

We have American denouncers. They like to denounce things, 'cause if they didn't denounce then they'd be part of the masses that like it. And they are not about to be like the masses. Now, if the masses were to denounce what I do, all the American critics—as you call them—would think I'm marvelous. When the masses loved Laurel and Hardy, nobody ever proclaimed them of any worth. Fields, too. When the masses chose to grow and get on to other things to love, the critics silently . . . at night . . . snuck in and discovered what the masses had already abandoned. I sent a critic a note once. I said, "I would appreciate your writing me in the return mail, what you are going to say after I croak. I'd like to enjoy it now. 'Cause I've read everything you had to say while I'm alive, I'd like to know what you're going to say when I'm gone."

WILDE: *Why do people who have no training or experience in comedy feel qualified to judge or criticize a comedian?*

LEWIS: Well, he's up for grabs. Like the village idiot. Because it's looked down upon—we get back to that. But that's the payment you make for the plus factor. And the plus factor of that is: Two woman walking in Beverly Hills and they see Clark Gable, rest his soul—let's say, Robert Taylor. And they go, "Oh, there's Robert Taylor." They do it *sotto voce*. But when they say, "There's Red Skelton!" They don't whisper and their faces open up. Big difference. So for that kind of payment and that kind of pleasure, they got the right to do it.

WILDE: *The comedian still has to stand the greatest criticism.*

LEWIS: Sure. Absolutely. Court jester.

WILDE: *There's always been much talk about the spon-*
sors, networks, and ad agencies interfering and stifling the
creativity of comedians. Do you find their restrictions in-
hibit you?

LEWIS: No. No, you can get around them. 'Cause they're
the funniest.

WILDE: *How do you overcome them?*

LEWIS: You join them but you don't let them know you're
joining *them*. You let them think you're disonant but you
use them as material.

WILDE: *Could you give an example?*

LEWIS: I do executives all the time. Anytime I'm *klutz**,
I'm an executive. See, the executive is not the authority. The
masses are the authority.

WILDE: *After all is said and done.*

LEWIS: That's right. *They* dictate. It's like back to the
court jester. The king is sitting there, and the court jester
is not allowed in . . . in this meeting that involves land
grants, war, fiscal processes etcetera. The minute the mi-
graine develops in the king because of the over-burden of
all this crap upon him . . . that's when he comes in. And if
he had any brains he'd have had him in on the meeting, it
would have lightened it a little . . . and he wouldn't have
had a headache. (He was always a *schmuck*!**)

WILDE: *Each week you appear in a different one-hour TV*
program which takes an enormous amount of effort and
planning. Would you describe the step-by-step process in
putting the show together?

* Jewish word for poor soul.
** Jewish word for idiot, imbecile.

LEWIS: No. You haven't got enough tape.

WILDE: *The meetings with the writers, for example, isn't that how it really starts?*

LEWIS: Well, sure, we decide on a theme. But we're writing four shows in advance all the time. It's rough. Step by step would take all the tape you've got. I find that what I believe pleasurable is usually what people find pleasurable. But it's really such a burden . . . it's such a dirge . . . it wouldn't be of any interest. Very honestly.

WILDE: *Why is that?*

LEWIS: Because it's such . . . there's no pleasure in it. It's hard, God-damned hard work. And I can't imagine anyone reading it in your book and saying, "Isn't that fun or interesting. It's really a pain in the ass. Whereas film . . . the six months of preparation are love moments, every one of them. Point: This show is on tomorrow night and it's over. Negative is forever . . . so you can give it the kind of love and care. My films are always there. . . .

WILDE: *And you put your heart, your soul, your emotions . . .*

LEWIS: Twenty-hour day. Never leave the set, never have lunch. That's why I really dislike this medium—it makes me feel dirty. I hate this medium because I'd like it to be better to itself. But it's the authority that's doing it . . . the masses.

WILDE: *Do you have a particular joke or story that represents the epitome of or sums up your sense of humor?*

LEWIS: Not that you could print.

WILDE: *Can you offer any council or consolation to the young comedian on his way up?*

LEWIS: Well, for a young comedian on his way up, I don't really believe he's entitled to condolences. I think he's entitled to congratulations. He doesn't need consolation . . . from me. Rather than consolation, I give him a bravo. Keep coming! That's all I can tell him. It's important to think in terms of *keep* coming because there's gonna be an awful lot of people on the ladder kicking at him. Avoid lying. 'Cause it'll kick you . . . it'll chase you right up an alley and kick you right in the balls.

WILDE: *Honesty?*

LEWIS: Yeah. But that's not something a young comedian is going to pay any heed to now. He's gonna have to be fortyish. And if I can quote from a very, very bright man, I believe it was Aristotle—I remember who's band he was with—but he's supposed to have said: "The most exciting part about being forty is the ecstacy of the thought that you are not twenty any more."

WILDE: *Thank you for taking time out to talk to me. Sorry I caught you in a mood.*

LEWIS: It made me feel better. That's all it takes when I'm depressed, if I just talk. You don't necessarily have to talk about what you are depressed about—just talk.

Danny Thomas

Danny Thomas was born Amos Muzyad Jacobs in Deer-field, Michigan, on January 6, 1914. His first professional job in show business was with a Detroit radio station.

He worked at a Chicago night club for three years where Abe Lastfogel of the William Morris agency discovered him. Lastfogel booked him into the La Martinique in New York and from that point Thomas' career skyrocketed.

In radio, Danny Thomas appeared as a regular on the Fanny Brice "Baby Snooks" program and then with Don Ameche and Frances Langford in their "Bickersons" series.

Mr. Thomas entered television in its early days and starred in the "All-Star Revue" and "The Danny Thomas Show." His "Make Room for Daddy" series, based on Danny's own life, is one of the longest running comedy series on television. It received the Sylvania Television Award as the best comedy program of the year and later was presented an Emmy for the best new program—the first of five statuettes the program earned.

Danny Thomas' movie credits include: *The Unfinished*

Dance, The Big City, Call Me Mister, I'll See You in My Dreams, and *The Jazz Singer.*

He has recorded songs from *The Jazz Singer* on the RCA Victor label and a singing comedy album called "An Evening with Danny Thomas" for MGM Records.

Mr. Thomas' lifetime charity work is the St. Jude Children's Hospital in Memphis, Tennessee, which he raised funds to build and continues to support.

Danny and his wife, Rosemarie, have three children: Marlo, Theresa, and Charles Anthony.

A Danny Thomas story *

If you can picture, please, a middle-aged gentleman on the wealthy side of the financial ledger, walking in the business district of his hometown on a balmy summer's evening, happens to be passing a pet store. It's a warm night, and through the pet store door, out into the night air, there comes to the ears of this man a most familiar strain of music . . . and he pauses and he listens, and he hears [*sings a few bars of "Kol Nidrei"*]. This man stands in his tracks, motionless—this is the music of his faith. . . . And the chanting continued, and he walked into that little pet store as though hypnotized, and he got inside the store and stood in complete awe and amazement at what he saw and what he heard . . . [*sings a few more bars of "Kol Nidrei"*] coming from a parrot! Now this is incredible. You have every right to disbelieve it . . . but there it was, my friends. . . . This little parrot, sitting on its perch, chanting the sacred and semi-sacred Hebraic hymns. . . . And a costly bird it was, but no matter what its cost, this man had to make the purchase—and buy it he did.

* Reprinted with permission from George Jessel's *You Too Can Make a Speech* (Grayson Publishing Corp., New York).

He took it home, and every night he'd sit on the back porch rocking to and fro, and the parrot would chant to him simple little Sabbath hymns like . . . [*sings a little Jewish song*]. The man was so happy with life, he could hardly wait for the high holidays to come. Finally, the week of *Rosh Hashanah* rolled around—*Rosh Hashanah*, taken from the Arabic, *Rosaseenee*, which means the head of the year—the New Year—a very happy holy day. . . . And the old man dashes down to the tailor shop, and has a *tallith* made up for the parrot—that's an old prayer shawl —also a *yarmulke*, a little black hat. . . . And he had the same outfit made for himself. They walk out of the tailor shop, father and parrot. . . .

Now, the day of *Rosh Hashanah* came, and they walked down to the synagogue, the old man sprightly, running up the steps, with the parrot following closely behind. . . . They get to the front door and there's a fellow called the *shames* takes care of the synagogue, also takes the tickets on high holidays. It gets very crowded, and the *shames* says: "Vait —! Vere you going with a boid . . .? Vat you think we're havin' here—a zoo?" The old man says: "Don't be zo smart —dat bird could pray better than you, the Cantor, the Rabbi, and me put together. . . ." Naturally, the inevitable cliche arose . . . : "Put the money where the mouth is. . . ." So, they make a slight wager, and while they're betting, the other members of the congregation come up the steps—and before you know it, they are all in the argument, they are all betting, and there is a forty-eight-hundred-dollar bet— on a handshake, of course, they don't carry money on this day (you don't know what research I went through with this story!). Now there is forty-eight hundred dollars bet, and the old man says: "Vait till you hear that boid make you lose all this money. . . . Okay, sweetheart—make a little a chant. . . . Darlink, ve're vaiting . . . go ahead . . . make a chant. . . . I think it can be something simple . . . like . . . [*sings a few bars*]. Nothing comes out of the bird—not a peep—not even "Polly-wants-some-matzo." Nothing. One hour—begging, pleading, crowding, pushing—nothing comes out of the bird—and he blows the bet. He loses forty-eight hundred bucks. Now he forgets the services—everything. He's incensed and demoralized and embarrassed. He grabs the bird by the throat; he takes him home and throws him on the floor; and he goes into the kitchen and begins to cry for what he is going to do. He takes the biggest butcher knife he can find and starts to sharpen it—kratch-kratch-kratch. In comes the parrot. . . . The parrot looks up at the old man and says: "Nu—what are you doing?" And the old man says: "You got a tongue now? You're talking . . .? Got your voice back . . .? Cost me forty-eight hundred dollars. You wouldn't make one chant. . . . I'm going to take that knife and cut off your head. . . ."

The parrot says, "Vait—vait—don't be such a *shlob*! Vait—vait for *Yom Kippur*—we'll get bigger odds. . . ."

THIS INTERVIEW was tape-recorded at the Thomas dining room table in his sumptuous Beverly Hills home. Mr. Thomas greeted me courteously, and after watching gleefully as I energetically prepared the Uher 4000-L he remarked, "Ah, the enthusiasm and ambition of youth—it's wonderful!"

Mr. Thomas, dressed for a golf date, wore chartreuse slacks and a light green and avocado crew-neck shirt. He carried four cigars in his left hand, and he held an unlit stogie, as we talked, in his right.

WILDE: *There has been considerable conjecture about the number of years it took you to break through into the "big time"—that is, having to play the small clubs and struggling to earn a living. Would you set the record straight once and for all?*

THOMAS: Yes. It's a good question . . . because the record has been kinda bolexed up. In the early 1930's there were a bunch of young people on the program in Detroit called the "Happy Hour Club," and if my memory serves me correctly, it was shortly after repeal of the Volstead Act, in the first year of the Roosevelt Administration, that beer gardens opened . . . and this "Happy Hour Club" on WNBC, in Detroit, took talent out for one dollar a performance. That was late '33, early '34. And from that point in Detroit through June of 1940. Then the 5100 Club in Chicago—August 12, 1940, through July 4, 1943—ten years.

WILDE: *During the three years at the 5100 Club you were getting a good salary?*

THOMAS: Yes, I started there at fifty dollars a week but I got fifty dollars as a salary only once. I got a ten-dollar raise every week. Actually, those were, I think the happiest days of my career. . . . Those were the ambitious days . . . the days of being rewarded without asking. Every week you got a ten-dollar raise and business just kept getting better and better. They were the secure years.

WILDE: *Did your long stay there help you to develop your style and to find yourself?*

THOMAS: It did. It was really a postgraduate course in your chosen field. Everything before it was a real good education, preparatory education . . . but the 5100 Club was really where the act—my style of entertaining—was truly formulated. I had a chance to be bad. I had a chance to fail and be forgiven . . . because I certainly couldn't be in top form every night, three shows a night, for three years in a row. And I would try things, because I was amongst friends.

WILDE: *What were some of the obstacles you had to overcome before you achieved universal acclaim?*

THOMAS: I never set out to achieve universal acclaim, by the way. As a matter of fact, I never set out to make good in show business, after Detroit. It's a very strange phenomenon, but I made good when I wasn't trying. It was pure accident. . . .

WILDE: *How do you account for that?*

THOMAS: I don't know, I just don't know. I just wasn't trying. Everybody came to the 5100 Club and wanted to sign me up for something in New York. I turned down *Oklahoma*—the Persian Rug Peddler. I just didn't want to leave. I turned down every night club engagement I was offered in New York. I turned down the Chez Paree in Chicago for the following season.

WILDE: *Was it insecurity?*

THOMAS: No, it was security, actually. I was very happy where I was and I didn't want to go anywhere. I felt I had given everybody a chance to see this young entertainer in Detroit—several years of it. I was very popular in Detroit under my real name—Amos Jacobs . . . and how many times do you have to get knocked to the canvas to find out you're not the champ? So, I skipped it. I went to Chicago to be a radio actor, take advantage of the dialects that I did in comedy, be a character actor. Matter of fact, even when I came out here to Hollywood, my only goal away from my status as an entertainer—and I had no worries about that once New York had accepted me—out here, I was just going to be a character actor. So, actually, a bit of advice: You shouldn't aim high. You shouldn't have ambition to be universally or nationally acclaimed. You should be the best of whatever you are, wherever you are . . . and aim for no more than within you. It's like golf. You swing within yourself—don't try to swing like Arnold Palmer. Swing like you. And sooner or later, somebody is gonna like *you,* and say, "I want that particular face, that particular physiognomy, that particular voice to work for me!" And from there everything rolls. No one is really the *best.* There is no one best. There is no one so all-consummate in any field. There's no perfection in life. So, these are bad adjectives: the "greatest," the "best." You're the best of whatever you are.

WILDE: *As you look back now during the period you were struggling to gain recognition—*

THOMAS: You keep saying . . . I never struggled to gain recognition. . . .

WILDE: *Let me rephrase the quest—*

THOMAS: Never did. And it's a bad thing, and I don't know who wrote it. Let me say this: After Detroit, yes, we struggled to gain recognition in Detroit, and then decided to quit . . . that it was over . . . now we would work without recognition. And incidently, that to me is the most enviable place you can be in show business. To be wanted, highly desired, without recognition. Now that's strange. It doesn't apply in the entertainment field, because you have to sell tickets, if they've got your name out on the marquee. But you could be a supporting act—a very highly desired supporting act. No, it does apply, by golly. It's like the character actor in the movies. There's no tremendous recognition . . . but you know when you see his face, you say, "Hey, this is gonna be a good picture." Walter Huston told me that years ago, rest his soul. He advised me, he said, "Don't let 'em make you a star, boy." 'Cause he saw me in the first movie I was in and he liked me. I didn't know from nothing about the movies . . . I'm there, reading my lines . . . playing an older man, Pinarus the Greek in *Unfinished Dance* with Margaret O'Brien. . . . And he said, "Don't let it be your name on that marquee that's gotta sell those tickets, but you be the best at what you are, boy, you be the most sought after character actor and have one price—three days, three weeks, or three months—one price!" He was wonderful!

WILDE: *But you didn't take his advice.*

THOMAS: I accidently didn't take his advice. . . . You think I'm such a big movie star or something? I'm a television comic.

WILDE: *Back in the 5100 Club, where did you get the material you used?*

THOMAS: In the early days I traded parodies with visiting acts . . . acts that were going through. They'd come and see you, and you'd have a parody or two that they didn't have. In those days, everybody had the same act. The material was pretty much the same. You were playing to the cosmopolite, the merchant, the buyers and sellers. They were the ones who were out night-clubbing, in the main. But as time went on, the neighborhood people, ordinary family, *haimasha** people came along . . . and then you had your high school and college proms. Now you just couldn't play to metropolitan type people. Now you had to play to everybody.

WILDE: *What about the jokes? Were they basically stock stories that you. . . ?*

THOMAS: That you embellished, yeah. We had fellows write material for us, in those days . . . like, Jerry Seelin. Well, there were other Jerry Seelins around then . . . for ten dollars you got a parody written or . . .

WILDE: *Was that what the act basically consisted of?*

THOMAS: Yeah. The comedy came out of the parodies in the early days—but then the truth came forth. You came out. Like, "The Ode to the Wailing Lebanese." That happened purely because of my sincere emotional plea to the boss to let me off one performance to see the All-Star Football game in Chicago. Arch Ward from the *Tribune*, who instituted it, rest his soul, had sent me two tickets . . . I did a benefit for some organization he was with . . . and the boss wouldn't let me off and I began lamenting the fate and destiny of a man who works seven nights week, never a night off . . . and I likened it unto the fate and destiny of

* Jewish word meaning warm and homey.

the poor Lebanese minstrel who was hanged by the Turkish government for singing propaganda against that government and it was the truth. . . .

WILDE: *The tirade against the bosses routine.* . . .

THOMAS: It was originally the "Ode to the Wailing Syrian." When all of Lebanon became a republic in '46 . . . my father was such a stickler for being Lebanese, you know, proud, nationalistic heritage thing . . . so we changed it to the "Ode To The Wailing Lebanese." And in truth it was a man from Lebanon—a true story—who was hanged for chanting this propaganda. He was a street singer but this was a tirade against the bosses. The "Flat Tire— No Jack" story came out of a rewrite of the Irishman who went to borrow a sleigh in the winter to haul coal. Then it was later modernized to an Irishman who wanted to borrow a lawnmower. It was once told as a musician going to get his trombone out of hock and knowing full well that the pawnbroker would not give him the trombone without the redeeming five dollars so he could play the date, get the five dollars and pay him off . . . and on the way his own mind does the slow burn that the pawnbroker will not give him the trombone without paying. . . .

WILDES: *You switched it to the fellow—*

THOMAS: Charlie Carlisle, who was at the Bowery at the time—you know Charlie—he was the one who suggested it to me. I was with a bunch of guys—Danny Rogers and his partner, who now is a social director at one of the Miami hotels, good singer—and we all used to go to a cafeteria— Buddy Lester, Harry Jarkey, Harvey Stone—we used to hang out together. And we were talking and they said, "Jake,"—that's my nickname—"is the best one to tell that story because his Yiddish dialect is better than any of ours."

It was like a bunch of guys saying, "Here's a great story, who should tell it?" So they decided, in that particular story, *I* should be the one. The first time I told it, I think I told it in a minute and a half. You know, blarump! Each night . . .

WILDE: *You started to find . . .*

THOMAS: Find things . . . while you were working. It was never written, it was never set down on paper. Neither was the "Ode" . . . "Toledo" was never on paper. We're strong for "Toledo."

WILDE: *Suppose you found a joke you wanted to use. How many times did you try it in front of an audience to see if it worked before you decided to take it out? Could you know immediately?*

THOMAS: No, it would be unfair. Because your own delivery might have gotten in its way, something you tried with it. No, I'd give a routine, on a regular basis, about a week—twice a night.

WILDE: *In developing a piece of material, let's say, there were thirty jokes in the routine. What was the criteria you used for taking out a gag?*

THOMAS: Not necessarily the audience's reaction to it so much as my own comfort in doing it. It didn't always have to be funny. It could be informative. It could be a statement of fact which has been my mode of operation in story telling. Story tellers and true monologists are not out to get a scream every time they open their mouths. As a matter of fact it would be bad to. If you were the most hysterically funny man in the world, it would be bad for the audience to sit through your performance without any relief. There should be quiet moments . . . which some of your fast monologists call "lulls"; I call it "reverent applause." It's pacing . . . it's like conducting a symphony orchestra, or sometimes it's been likened unto fighting the bulls—the passes. There are times when you taunt him, there are times you leave him alone for the moment, and then you start him up again. I used to purposely dump an audience, just to see if I could get it back again and—

WILDE: *What do you mean "dump"?*

THOMAS: To just let it go, get a whole big lull, a real lull. . . .

WILDE: *For a minute or two?*

THOMAS: Yeah, sure, just like nothing. Turn your back on them and talk to the orchestra leader for a minute and then come back and see if you could get them again. Just to train your mind. . . . I wouldn't do it now. It's a waste of time. That's another thing. When you combine a lot of stuff in a story, it can go on ad nauseum . . . and I committed that sin, too. I used to do an hour and twenty minutes. And then one year the bulb lighted up and I thought, "This is ridiculous. I'm garbaging up. This is really being a mad egoist. To make those poor people sit that long when you could get the same effect in a lot less time." So I boiled an hour-and-twenty-minute act down to fifty-two minutes.

WILDE: *Is it possible to develop one's instinct to know what's funny and what an audience will laugh at, or are you born with that ability?*

THOMAS: No, trial and error, for gosh sakes. I don't think anybody is born with the ability to make people laugh unless he's got a funny rubber face or something . . . got a squeaky voice or he walks funny . . . something like that. I think it's a desire, actually, it's a calling, You know, this may sound ridiculous to you, but to me the entertainment of people is a calling just like the ministry. You have to *want* to entertain people. Oh, extroversion comes into it—a man is an extrovert, he wants to be *on*—but I think there's so many of us that don't particularly want to be on. I now avoid many so-called opportunities to perform.

WILDE: *Isn't that because you've reached the pinnacle of success? You've been given every humanitarian award; you have the respect and admiration of your fellow performers; you have the love and adulation of the American public. . . .*

THOMAS: Yeah, sure. Of course, the appetite is . . . I mean the hunger has been satisfied but it'll never be satisfied to the extent you won't eat. You gotta perform to stay alive. A couple of years ago, in a magazine article or something, I said that "It must be obvious to people [and I named a few performers] we don't do this anymore to make a living. We do it to stay alive." Like, I say, it's the calling. I want to make people happy, of course. I have an opportunity to perform nonprofessionally, so to speak, every year when I go on tour for St. Jude's Children's Research Hospital. And that's another thing. You have to give. . . . If you are thinking only of yourself and how much you can take out of this business from a monetary standpoint, I don't think you'll last long. I don't think you'll live through it. It's like the evil eye of the camera, you just can't escape it. People will judge you for what you have given, and not because you're charitable do they come and applaud you. . . .

WILDE: *Then it is possible to develop the instinct to know what's funny? It's not something you're born with?*

THOMAS: No, I think strictly experience—trial and error.

The wonderful thing about the early days was that we had a place to be bad. Today, you guys have to come on television and be good, now, this second!

WILDE: *We don't have the places to work they had in your time.*

THOMAS: Except locally. You see, if you can win the friendship of the audience . . . my advice, and I think it is sound, to all young performers is to stay home and try to develop into being the big fish in that small pond.

WILDE: *When you were working mostly night clubs, what were the technical steps in developing a piece of material? For instance, how did "We're Strong For Toledo" come about?*

THOMAS: Well, "Toledo," of course was born on the floor . . . it was in defense of outhouse humor. It happened at the 5100 Club. (Here we go again with necessity being the mother of invention. All the clichés apply in our business, all the old wheezes.) One night, a man yelled out, "Do the outhouse routine!" Now, in the audience was Ashton Stevens, the famous critic. In order to apologize to Mr. Stevens and Ben Bernie, who was my greatest benefactor in those days, I began defending the small town, the so-called antiprogress people—the people who like the gentility of life, the horse and buggy days, and so on—and all to get to the jokes about the outhouse. But I had to set it up so that Ashton Stevens wouldn't think I was kind of a foul comedian—who was this guy talking about the little house back of the big house?—and, by golly, I made that comedy material acceptable. That was a great lesson for me. I began doing that, with anything that was mildly off-color—like "Chloe." "Chloe" had as dirty a line in it as—if you wanted to weigh it and measure it—as had ever been said on the stage. But the way I set it up . . . I would say to the people: "There is a story in song I would like perform for you, except for one line. And but for this one line, this story in song could be performed at a Girl Scout meeting. It's a very interesting story, about a woman who has lost track of her husband at Miami Beach. I want to do it for you, and I apologize now for the one line." Then I would say, "Picture if you will . . . so and so and so and so," and I would set up the whole thing. And then the last line of the song was the line and when I read it, they screamed, and I waited until the laugh began to dissolve, and as it did, I said, "That's the line." It was bigger than the punch line and it was most acceptable, and every night people said, " 'Chloe,' do 'Chloe'!" The whole routine cost ten dollars. But it served in the clubs for years. I don't do it anymore. As a matter of fact, I haven't said *hell* or *damn* on the stage since 1950.

WILDE: *It's amazing what—*

THOMAS: You see, the only interesting part of my career were the so-called struggling years, the years when you didn't have too much to eat . . . when you used to chip in . . . a bunch of the guys and gals and go to different flats each night and eat together and laugh. We laughed—we were the happiest people in the world. Broke but happy, but ambitious—wanting to go, wanting to make it in this business. But not to the degree we talked about . . . we wanted to be accepted, that's all.

WILDE: *Were there any comedians you studied or were—?*

THOMAS: The greatest influence I had was Abe Reynolds, the Yiddish comedian of burlesque. I was a boy in the burlesque theatre for several years as a candy butcher, selling refreshments. I watched all the burlesque shows that came and Abe Reynolds was really my idol. Which was why, when

I went into show business I thought being a Yiddish comedian was the best. So, I was a Yiddish comic for years and years, even in the 5100 Club, ninety per cent of my material was Yiddish. I had to lose the dialect, which was my daily speech, when I came here to Hollwood. My manager, Mr. Lastfogel, said, "It's very critical. There's something we have to do about it." "Well, what can we do?" "You're just going to have to lose it." I said, "But that's the way I talk. What do you want from me?" So he said, "Well, it's certainly not your heritage, for heaven's sake." I said, "Well I lived with it. *Shabbos Goy** on Canton Avenue in Toledo with the orthodox Jews. So I began talking with a western drawl, and I taaaked lak thaat for six months. And I talked to everybody that way. It was kinda southern—it was a south western drawl. I'd say, "Well, set down and let's have some dinnah!" Then when it came time for me to perform before an audience who knew me, they would expect me to say, "Well, good evenin' y'all." So now for the first time I went out and I said, "Good evening!" I didn't say, "Good eveeenin!" I was more startled than anybody. . . .

WILDE: *So you lost—*

THOMAS: I grew up in Toledo, right in the middle of the country, middle America. Middle America speaks English the way it's written.

WILDE: *General American.*

THOMAS: General American. General English; actually better than the English by far. We do not say, "Nevah." We say never. We don't leave out a syllable, we don't leave out

---

* Literally, Sabbath Gentile. Usually a boy hired by the sexton to put out the lights in the synagogue when services were completed on the Sabbath.

a vowel sound . . . It's neve*r*. It's "si*r*." Si*r*, boy that "r"— you can hear it all over the place.

WILDE: *Did you consciously figure out what your comedic image and point of view were going to be?*

THOMAS: I was always aware of the injustices to my fellow man . . . to ethnic groups. I always was a champion of helping those who could not help themselves. I guess because when I was a boy *we* were helped a lot, we were on state relief a couple of times. I always had a love for the police departments of cities because the police of Toledo were very friendly with the underprivileged children— which was why when I went to New York and found a Police Athletic League, P.A.L. . . . oh I wanted to help there . . . and I said these things on the beer garden and night club floors of Detroit and was bawled out for it by the agents and the managements, too. I was told several times, "What do you care who loves who? What is this crap you're doing? Get out there and do a couple of them off-color parodies and songs and introduce the acts and get off. A guy brings a broad and he's on the make—what are you doing, making him think about God and his family. You're lousing up everything." I used to sober people up. And I was bawled out for it and told not to do it. . . . Then I strayed from it for a time, but I could only stray away for a time. I came back to the basic, *me*. I'm a preacher, I guess, a minister, a priest, a rabbi. Walter Winchell dubbed me "The Preacher" in New York.

WILDE: *So it was never premeditated?*

THOMAS: No, I didn't plan it. See, I'm Lebanese. Now, we are descendants of the Phoenicians. We go as far back as things ever got written on paper. Our people were born to the alphabet . . . the first word uttered by man was recorded by our people. If you ever read *The Prophet* by Gibran, it would give you a better insight into the thinking of my family. Kahlil Gibran is a member of my mother's family. This is the way we think, we're philosophical people, herding sheep on the hills of Lebanon just below the Cedars ... people who are very, very rich in thought. ... They have little of the monetary things of life, but they somehow don't need them.

WILDE: *You've often talked about the period of indecision concerning plastic surgery on your nose. What made you decide not to have it fixed?*

THOMAS: Well, I guess, I must have been chicken to go through the operation, number one. That could be the most important reason. The decision not to do it was based on ... no assurance in my own mind that I could really make it in the movies. On the other hand, my face was at that time more than acceptable in night clubs—it was highly desirable. I was working the best clubs in the country and somehow had a marquee value. Don't ask me why, but people came. And every time I worked New York—I worked Fort Lee, New Jersey [the Riviera]—jambo, it was jammed ... and the nose was important to the act it seemed, sticking out over the microphone. ... They wanted me to have it fixed but I wouldn't do it. I would say, "If you're gonna have a nose, *have one*. I swear, I don't see how some of you people can breathe. Look, at some of those perforated warts, here!" And I'd point to some young lady with a little tiny nose. And they'd scream.

WILDE: *You do a great deal of comedy and yet you are often referred to as an "entertainer." What is the difference between an entertainer and a comedian?*

THOMAS: Well, an entertainer covers more bases. An

entertainer generally sings, he's a story teller . . . if he can dance, that's nice and fine too. Like Sammy Davis, Jr., he's an entertainer . . . Danny Kaye . . .

WILDE: *As compared to a comedian?*

THOMAS: Well, Milton Berle who's one of the great monologists of all time. Bob Hope is purely a monologist. I'm a story teller. My singing seems highly acceptable in cafes. It is in TV when it's dramatic, when it's sentimental. I never did consider myself a singer, but people expect me to sing. . . . But my songs come out of the philosophy of the story. So I sing and I tell stories and I do monologues, too. . . . I found something out years ago. People believe me. Which is why I've used very little fantasy in all the successful years. The only fantasy routine I ever did that was really successful was "South Pacific." And it was pure fantasy. . . .

WILDE: *"Sure gave me a lousy corner, didn't they?"*

THOMAS: Yeah, isn't that a funny joke? That was Jerry Seelin . . . he was very important to that routine. In fact, he did most of it. I built it up to where it was going to be a television special. When I first got it, I said I got the movie rights . . . it generated interest in the routine. That's the only fantasy I've talked about doing a television show. But in the main, people believe me. I speak of the foibles of the common man, I talk about a man in trouble. Show me a man in trouble, I'll show you a funny man. I talk about my own impoverished years and they're funny . . . they're funny to look back at now. I talk about my own ugliness, so to speak. I'm not really ugly. I'm an un-handsome man, I'm an un-pretty man, but far from so horrible. Like once they told me in Detroit that I was too ugly for night clubs, for supper clubs, that I shouldn't stand there and entertain people while they were eating. *Grotesque* I'm not!

WILDE: *Beauty of soul and kindness of the heart are more enviable qualities than being physically attractive.*

THOMAS: I never seriously considered having my nose fixed for the sake of vanity . . . so that I would look that much better. There's a little bump here and I would sure like to have removed 'cause I breathe better when it's out of the way. [*Lifting tip up*] It's a double deviated septum and this is a muscle that has grown here. I've even been wary of having it removed for fear it might change my face . . . but the doctors have told me it wouldn't change the shape of the nose. I never want to lose the hook. The hook is part of my . . .

WILDE: *What are the requirements necessary to become a comedian?*

THOMAS: I honestly cannot answer that question. I don't think anybody can. The only real requirement—I say I can't answer the question and then I proceed to answer . . . that's what you get for talking off the top of your head— would be the honest desire to make people laugh. If that is uppermost in your mind, you're a cinch to make it. But if anything else gets in the way—such as: by making people laugh, I will make X number of dollars and then I will invest the X number of dollars in something else and then I will become a tycoon and then I'll have seventeen houses and fourteen dogs and thirty-eight horses and three tennis courts and then a yacht— if any one of these things interferes with your *sincere desire* to make people laugh, you won't make it. It has to be a way of life, the calling. I go back to the ministry. Making people laugh is so important. The morale of the nation, the morale of the world, depends upon the people who make them laugh—to forget their troubles. I don't care what the politics of the man, I don't care if he kicks babies and dogs and steals from blind people —if he has a real ability to make people laugh and to forget their troubles, I say he was worthwhile . . . he's had a good reason to be born.

WILDE: *After listening to you over the years one realizes you have quite a large vocabulary and are extremely articulate. How did you acquire this skill?*

THOMAS: "Acquire" is the right word. I've had one year of high-school education. I speak by ear. I learned by ear. I generally talk up a dead end street; I get myself blocked in because I don't have as large a vocabulary as my speech would indicate. Yet, I've never been a . . . what's the word?

WILDE: *Lexicographer?*

THOMAS: Yeah, something like that. . . . He saves up words, he gets the word out of the newspaper every day and he looks it up in the dictionary and he knows its meaning and he uses it three times and now it belongs to him. There are many people who speak . . . who use words that people do not understand . . . and they feel this makes them something. I've always tried to speak to my audience and make myself understood and I feel that if I understand it, they'll understand it. I've never gotten a diploma in English.

WILDE: *You said earlier that your voice was highly acceptable. It's really a fine voice. Did you study singing?*

THOMAS: No, no. I was a choir boy in the old St. Francis Assail's Cathedral and I also sang in the Jewish choir in our local synagogue. . . . The only studying I ever did was to be a cantor in the movies. I didn't study voice so much as the lyrics to the Hebrew songs.

WILDE: *There was a great line from a song you did in* The Jazz Singer—*"Living the Life I Love."*

THOMAS: Yeah. Jerry Seelin and Sammy Fain and I wrote that. There's a line in the middle that I used on a night club floor, because people would be sitting there, frowning, trying to drown their sorrows or lose their thoughts, not paying much attention to you, and I'd say, "I don't know why you're not smiling. You got up this morning, didn't you? . . . That's something to be thankful for, isn't it? . . . You got up, you're sitting here." That's how we got the bridge of that song. . . .

> *Just let me earn my daily keep*
> *I don't need a bank full*
> *And when I lay me down to sleep*
> *If I just wake up in the morning, I'm thankful.**

WILDE: *We touched on this briefly before . . . is it necessary for a comedian to resort to dirty material in personal appearances?*

THOMAS: Only if his audience insists on it. That's the only time. A lot of young comedians I've seen . . . I've said, "Gee, you got a couple of pieces there that are awful dirty. Why don't you throw them away?" "Yeah, but Mr. Thomas, they get screams." I would say, "Well, let me give you a few lines that I used to do!" And I would tell them, "Boy, it broke my heart to lose those screams." But as time went on I had twelve-year-old girls with their parents sitting in the audience at the dinner show and I didn't want to have two standards. My midnight show is exactly the same as my dinner show – in a given engagement – 'cause we do not

* Copyright MCMLIII by Harms, Inc.

change material. We used to in the old days, you know, you did two different performances a night.

WILDE: *The people from the first show stayed over. . . .*

THOMAS: They stayed on. . . . But in your cafés today, there's a complete turnover . . . especially resort clubs, gambling casinos. But it's really up to the audience. If they will not laugh heartily at anything but dirt, then that's what you do for them. But *I* don't do it. That's what the people that play those places have to do. I would not do it.

WILDE: *There is a theory among comedians that the more financial security and public acceptance they get, the funnier they become.*

THOMAS: True.

WILDE: *What is the reason for that?*

THOMAS: Acceptance. It's much easier to make them laugh if they're smiling as you walk out. "And here he is now, Bob Hope." Well, he proved it to me years ago in Detroit . . . and I've given this example to a lot of people. You see, acceptance is everything. When I say something today and they laugh at it, some innocuous thing that I've thought of just at the spur of the moment . . . my mind goes back to that incident in Detroit when I saw it happen with Bob Hope . . . and then my heart moves with compassion for the younger people coming up whom I know would bomb with the same line. As you are climbing, its *what* you say and *how* you say it that gets you to where you become a *who*. And when you become a *who*, your material doesn't have to be as good. Now, you just can't say, "Oh, I'm Mr. Big and I will now go in there and do them a big favor by showing up." You have to be diligent in your search for new material and good material but every now and again you will say something that for all intents and purposes isn't nearly as funny as the audience tells you it is, and it's only because it's you. They like you.

WILDE: *It's like after doing thirty-five great minutes that the audience has loved and then you ad-lib a line that isn't as funny but you get a big laugh.*

THOMAS: That right. Once they've accepted you . . . I remember when Bob Hope got on my night club floor in Detroit—I was making eighty, eighty-five dollars for that engagement by then; he was doing the Pepsodent radio show —and he was there in Detroit with a revue at the Michigan Theatre. As I remember . . . Betty Hutton was in his party. The original Lone Ranger was there, Jerry Colona . . . I have a picture of it some place in the scrapbook . . . they insisted we get him up. He was a little reluctant but he got up. It was spring and he had on gray slacks and a blue blazer and there were some mud spots on his slacks . . . splashed by an automobile, no doubt. I was on for an hour and I thought got good response, 'cause I threw the book at them. I wanted this man Bob Hope to know that us young entertainers in Detroit are pretty good too . . . with the four-piece band behind you. Here's a guy got twenty-six musicians, right?

WILDE: *Right.*

THOMAS: Which is what I have today. I used to have a three-, four-piece orchestra, only the piano had a sheet of music and that was the lead sheet and the rest of the guys are trying to follow. Anyway, this great star, Bob Hope of the "Pepsodent Hour" . . . highly accepted man . . . this is 1940 . . . he taught me something . . . he just opened my eyes. After one hour of real struggle, ambition, and

trying to please that audience . . . he got up on the floor
and after tumultuous applause died down, he looked down
at his trousers and said, "And I want to tell you, those
Detroit cab drivers come awful close!" . . . and looked at
the audience and down came the ceiling, the plaster shook.
I stood back there and learned a lesson. In other words,
there's a champion out here, boy, pay attention. This is boss
man talking now, Mr. Bob Hope . . . my name was Amos
Jacobs at the time . . . and I learned, I stood there and
watched the king say these pearls, "Those Detroit cab
drivers come awful close." And I remembered it.

WILDE: *During the Civil War, Abraham Lincoln was
criticized for habitually telling jokes, and his explanation
was, "I laugh because I must not cry." Why is there such
a close relationship between humor and pathos?*

THOMAS: Well, Gibran, in *The Prophet,* said it very suc-
cinctly: "What is your sorrow but your joy unmasked?"
You have the two masks, that's a human being. Your joy is
your sorrow unmasked. And vice versa. The consummate,
the complete human being laughs and cries. He has happy
days and he has sad days. That's really the basis of my
humor. I do what is called "about-face" humor. I will lead
you down the path of drama or sadness, compassion, sympathy, and just about the time I figure the tears ought to
be gushing, I just flip it over and "naw, naw" I was only
kidding.

WILDE: *Was that technique something you discovered . . . ?*

THOMAS: I discovered that, yes . . . just found it. Pure
accident. Like in the "Ode to the Wailing Lebanese," when
I spoke of this man who was about to extemporize this song
and he was to be hanged, I said, "The song was recorded on

the spot . . . and the record was later given to his widow . . . and she in turn had over a million copies printed and sold—and that's how Decca was born!" Well, I accidently said it because it was so quiet in the joint that you had to relieve them. See, just as you relieve them of the pain of laughter—and there is pain to laughter—you then must also relieve them of the drama of the moment, too. Phil Foster has always said, "You bum, you ain't funny. They're just relieved to know you don't mean it." But the secret is to get them to listen. Like Mike Todd. The greatest compliment I ever had paid to me in my whole life was when Mike Todd lifted a cup of coffee and got caught in the middle of the dramatic moment of the "Ode to the Wailing Lebanese." Later he said, "I didn't dare sip it, and I couldn't set it down, 'cause I couldn't set it on the saucer quietly enough. You dirty bum, you hung me up with holding a cup of coffee suspended in mid-air for three minutes . . . and you don't do that to Todd, you bum, you do it to those yokels." And that was his way of paying me a compliment.

WILDE: *One last question. In an* American *magazine article you said, "For me the luckiest breaks have come from being discouraged, unrecognized and broke. The only real security I know is a store of resourcefulness acquired by looking misfortune squarely in the eye." Does that philosophy sum up your advice to the young comedian?*

THOMAS: Of course. It is to take a liability and make it an asset. I have never lamented too long, any misfortune in this business, any part that I didn't get because I used to operate on the theory that every step backwards was four giant steps forward.

Ed Wynn

Ed Wynn was born November 9, 1888, in Philadelphia, Pennsylvania. He made his first professional stage appearance on August 8, 1902, in Norwich, Connecticut. Twelve years later he starred in the *Ziegfeld Follies of 1914* and has been a star ever since.

Wynn, known as the "Fire Chief" to millions of radio listeners beginning in 1932, is credited with *audience* reaction coming over the air from studios. Radio audiences had to keep quiet. They sat in front of huge glass curtains and heard the broadcast over microphones; the curtains prevented any audience sounds going over the air. Ed Wynn refused to go on radio unless he could hear the people laugh as he was used to in the theatre. They lifted the ban as an experiment for his first appearance. It was an instantaneous success. They did away with glass curtains, and audiences then laughed as they wished and eventually took part in the programs.

Wynn also has the rare distinction of being one of the few comedians to write his own show material. He authored (book, music, lyrics) as well as produced *The Ed Wynn*

Carnival, The Perfect Fool, and *The Grab Bag*—making him a manager-producer-owner-actor-composer-author-lyricist.

As one of the pioneers of early television Wynn won a number of Emmys for his own comedy show and for Best Comedian of the Season. Later, he also received awards for acting in such dramatic shows as *Requiem for a Heavyweight, On Borrowed Time,* and *The Man in the Funny Suit.*

Movie-goers will remember him best from *The Great Man, Marjorie Morningstar, The Greatest Story Ever Told,* and the *Diary of Ann Frank,* for which he was nominated for an Oscar for the best supporting actor.

Ed Wynn comedy routine

Lou Derman, for many years one of Mr. Wynn's key comedy writers, was kind enough to furnish the following sketch from a 1944 radio show. Ed Wynn plays the part of Uncle Bubbles.

BEULAH: Uncle Bubbles, Uncle Bubbles . . .

BUBBLES: Beulah, aren't you asleep yet?

BEULAH: But Uncle Bubbles, I want to hear my bedtime story.

BUBBLES: I've got a lovely story tonight . . . it starts in an art gallery. . . . Our hero is looking at the paintings. He has what they call an odd and ends shape . . . people consider it very odd where it ends. He looks like a typical wolf . . . all the girls call him parcel post . . . because he's a fourth-class male. . . . Now in the same art gallery there's a girl looking at the paintings . . . she is very ethereal . . . her figure reminds you of a zephyr . . . a Lincoln Zephyr . . . she is so stout she always dresses to fascinate.

BEULAH: Uncle Bubbles, I don't understand you at all. What do you mean fascinate?

BUBBLES: Well she has ten hooks on her dress but she's so fat she can only fasten eight. . . . Anyhow, the hero sees the girl looking at a picture and talks to her. He says, if you had your choice would you take home a Van Gogh or a Van Dyke . . . and she says, if I had my choice I'd take home Van Johnson. . . . He asks her if he can see her home . . . and she says she'll send him a picture of it. . . . This makes them sweethearts. She takes him to her home. . . . It's eight o'clock . . . at ten o'clock she says, do you really love me dear . . . ? and he says, what do you think I've been doing for the past two years . . . shadow boxing? The girl's mother says to her husband, I think that fellow is going to propose to our daughter . . . don't you go into the room without whistling first. And the husband says, why not? . . . no one whistled to warn me. . . . The girl introduces her sweetheart to his future mother-in-law. . . .

BEULAH: Uncle Bubbles, what is a mother-in-law?

BUBBLES: A mother-in-law . . . for heaven's sake, everyone knows what a mother-in-law is . . . a mother-in-law is gangbusters in a two-way stretch. . . . He looks at his future mother-in-law and decides to marry his girl anyhow because he's in love. . . .

BEULAH: I have to interrupt you again, Uncle Bubbles. Love sounds so mysterious.

BUBBLES: Love is not a mystery. . . . Here's how love works: you meet an eyeful . . . who makes an armful . . . so you give her an earful . . . then you're hopeful . . . you feel awful till the preacher makes it lawful . . . in a few years you have your hands full because you've a roomful. . . . One day while the couple's eating popcorn he pops the question . . . she questions her pop and they pop out and get married. . . . One night after they are married, while she's washing the dishes, the husband says to her, I can't bear to stand here watching you spoil your hands washing those dishes . . . so I'm going out on the back porch. . . . Five years after they are married he finds the girl is still in love . . . but her husband has no idea who the fellow is. When he finds out, he runs away to Egypt to look for the Nile River. He searches for weeks but he can't find it, finally he does—he hits the Nile right on the head. He lands there in a B-twenty-nine and cracks up. . . . He tries to make a native girl understand him. He says, me . . . B-twenty-nine in crack-up. . . . The native girl says, me B-seventeen in October. . . . This is too much for him and he rushes back home to try to make up with his wife. Whether she will take him back or not is the issue and at the finish of the story, Beulah, we hear the husband singing to his wife . . . the issue song. Is you is or is you ain't my baby. . . .

JOSEPH VIGGIANI, of the Ashley Famous Agency, (Wynn's agents) arranged this meeting at the Plaza Hotel in New York. Mr. Wynn answered the questions while we had breakfast. (It was 9:30 in the morning.) He wore gray flannel trousers, blue blazer, an off-white shirt, and a blue polka-dot tie, knotted like a string bow tie.

Midway through the interview we were interrupted by four members of the Executive Committee for Parkinson's Disease. (Wynn was honorary chairman.) A photographer snapped publicity pictures while Wynn joked and jested with the committee women.

Wynn took great pride in his long list of theatrical credits. Unusually serious but extremely outgoing, he was delighted to express his comedic views, often interrupting the question before it could be framed.

At no time during our discussion did he attempt to be funny except to illustrate a point, but in the car driving to Kennedy Airport he related a joke Red Skelton had told him.

WYNN: [*Gazing out window at Central Park*] Many years ago [Enrico] Caruso and I would walk around the reservoir each morning . . . he liked me. I was a kid, of course. . . . Every morning he would get me up and say, "Come along to the reservoir!" And then later, it got to be a habit.

WILDE: *Has comedy—what makes people laugh—changed much since those days?*

WYNN: Definitely, except you can still make them laugh with what they call "corny" things. I put on a funny costume

369

last night*, walked out, and the audience screamed on my entrance. That kind of comedy we did in those days was not topical comedy. It wasn't, "Did you hear what happened at the World's Fair . . .?" No, the style of comedy has changed like the style of music or the style of clothes.

WILDE: *You say you did not use "topical material"?*

WYNN: Well, we did. I would go to Cleveland, I'd have three or four jokes about Cleveland as an opener.

WILDE: *Did you always want to be a comedian?*

WYNN: Yes, starting at about nine years of age. That is what my family told me. I was thrown out of school more than anybody in the world.

WILDE: *For being funny?*

WYNN: I wanted to be funny. We were from Philadelphia and my family used to go to Atlantic City for the summer. We had a crowd like all the kids do . . . and I used to be the biggest attraction on that beach in the morning. I will never forget it. At Virginia Avenue where the Steel Pier is, they would hang on the boardwalk and go on to the pier and watch us. That I know for a fact because those were my first press notices. I was twelve, thirteen, fourteen years of age. I had a sense of the ridiculous when I was a child. A great sense of fun. I could have made you laugh at a thing which my good taste could not permit me to try to be funny about now: death. I don't see anything funny in death anymore. If I have learned anything with maturity it is that I have a dignity now . . . I must limit myself to certain subjects for fun. I musn't make fun of deformity or do jokes about blind people. I had a very fertile mind when

* With Carol Burnett, on her television show.

I was younger. I could write. I can write very well now;
but I could create unbelievably then. I can say this because it is not coming from me . . . Jack Benny has already
made the statement. George Burns, Red Skelton, men like
that. They say I was the greatest comedian of the first half
century. They claim they all came to study me when I was
in the theatre. I was not a singer. I was not a dancer. So
I became a student of comedy . . . how to make an audience
laugh. I found that costumes were part of it. I found that
props were part of it. I had some of the greatest props made
you ever saw. I played a couple of musical instruments. I'd
take out a violin right in the middle of the show and start
playing "Listen To The Mocking Bird," and then press a
button and a little bird would come out of the violin . . .
crazy things like this . . . what you would call a "clown"
today.

WILDE: *Is that the kind of comedian you would describe
yourself as being?*

WYNN: I belong to a school you probably never heard of.
I was what you called an "Algus" clown. This means—as
far as I have been able to find out—there was a great Ger-
man clown, I believe his name was Algus, and he used to
wear funny costumes and originated that sort of thing.
Life magazine, in 1950, gave me a front page and about
four pages inside on the Algus clown thing. I would write
a show like *The Ed Wynn Carnival,* or *The Grab Bag,* or
Evening's Entertainment, or *The Perfect Fool,*—the music,
the lyrics, the book, everything; and my comedy was more
or less a monologue all the way through the show. I never
did situation comedy. I brought out comedy in jokes.

WILDE: *How did you start?*

WYNN: I ran away from home and went with a repertory

company . . . ten, twenty, thirty cents to get in. I got twelve dollars and fifty cents a week. After nineteen weeks the thing folded. Stranded in Bangor, Maine. Nobody could get out of town and the state of Maine was always a dry state. I played the piano—only sixteen years of age—in a whore-house, practically, to get the money to leave. The next time I left home I had written an act for vaudeville—in those days they didn't have night clubs. My whole family was manufacturers of ladies hats . . . I never got any theatrical ability or encouragement from anyone in my family. I have had people say I was the funniest guy in school you ever saw. No, I did not get it from a nice little cultivated Jewish family, as I think my father and mother were.

WILDE: *That brings up a fascinating point. Why do you think so many comedians are Jewish?*

WYNN: I can only answer that in a superficial way. It is just an opinion. They have been the most persecuted race throughout the ages; for centuries, a Jew couldn't do this, a Jew couldn't do that. The minute there was an opening— to what we today call freedom—I think these people branched out and all these suppressed things happened. . . .

WILDE: *Living in a democracy and having the opportunity to express their frustration and—*

WYNN: The Jews are the only mass of people who love to hear jokes about themselves . . . who can laugh at them-selves. Though I never experienced any persecution. I think so many comedians being Jewish . . . is an outlet. Something that never happened with generations gone. There is a young fellow who was going to be a rabbi—Jackie Mason. He is funny as hell. He will never be the kind of comedian we have had . . . he will be a great monologist.

WILDE: *When you were getting started did you have a comedian you particularly admired?*

WYNN: Yes, Raymond Hitchcock.* I thought he was the finest English-speaking person—for diction and so forth. He was a student of the English language. And I had another one I admired. I watched their timing, how they turned ... but I never wanted to imitate ... I never wanted to imitate either of them. I wanted to create right from the beginning.

WILDE: *Did you feel it was important for a comedian to speak good English?*

WYNN: I did. I had a definite reason. I used to wear funny clothes and it seemed to me, the contrast—which I think is all theatre—the contrast was important. I am not an authoritative person, you see, but the other comedians of the old school say that I was a teacher. I remember the great Laurel and Hardy when they were starting. I walked into the commissary in 1933 out there [*Hollywood*] to make a picture for MGM and one of them jumped up and said, "Here's the master." I looked at him as though he was nuts because I thought *they* were the greatest.

WILDE: *Today the young comedian is faced with the difficult period of "finding himself." How did you do it?*

WYNN: There are certainly many methods. . . . I was born in a school . . . we didn't have any teachers. We were thrown into vaudeville and you had to follow an elephant act and you had to make good.

WILDE: *Is there such a thing as a "natural" comedian?*

* A well-known comedian in the heyday of vaudeville.

WYNN: I should think so. I don't know. That has never been asked me.

WILDE: *A comedian must have timing, delivery, good taste in material—these are abilities that can be learned. Yet, often people say, "He's a natural comedian."*

WYNN: I think a fellow who can speak English can go out and buy a monologue and get by . . . but he'll never be a Jimmy Durante; he'll never be what they say I was; she'll never be a Martha Raye or a Lucy Ball. These people have a certain something that never was taught to them. I played with a girl last night [*Carol Burnett*] . . . she has a sense of comedy, there is no question about it. I think to be an eccentric comedian—to be like Red Skelton—I would say that it is born in him; you might cultivate it to a point.

WILDE: *Today the young comedians have to analyze comedy and discuss theory, whereas in the vaudeville days you all had a chance to go out and perform it.*

WYNN: I will go along with that. I think we do have methods. Jack Benny has a method where he lets the other people get the laughs. He does "reaction" comedy. Now you get another fellow, like Jack Lemmon—he does "situation" comedy. I could tell jokes with funny make-up and a funny costume and along would come Cary Grant and open the wrong door and you see two nude women and they would laugh just as much at that—as they would at me. I think that in school, if you want to be a comedian, you could learn to be a Jack Lemmon but I don't think you can learn to be an Ed Wynn or an Eddie Cantor.

WILDE: *On the Academy Awards show, in which Jack Lemmon was the Master of Ceremonies . . . now this is not deprecating Mr. Lemmon's talent. . . .*

WYNN: No, of course not . . . he wasn't humorous. . . .

WILDE: *He couldn't hold the show together . . .*

WYNN: Of course not!

WILDE: *Like Bob Hope . . .*

WYNN: Of course not!

WILDE: *And yet Mr. Lemmon is one of the funniest light comedians around. Why is it a variety comedian can go into a legit show or into motion pictures and take to it easily but it's extremely difficult for a movie star or stage actor to do a night club or vaudeville act?*

WYNN: If you see Hugh O'Brien do a TV show, they write something about guns. There is no creation here. In the days of radio, if they engaged W. C. Fields, they would talk about booze. If they engaged Adolph Menjou they would talk about clothes. But when they engaged me or someone in that category, they had to write funny stuff. In my case, I wrote all my own material.

WILDE: *Can all performers who do comedy be called comedians?*

WYNN: Well, there are several categories of comedians—there is the *light* comedian, the *eccentric* comedian, the *low* comedian. The fella that was able to marry the girl—like Bob Hope and Jack Lemmon—he would be called the *light* comedian. Now the *eccentric* or *highly styled* comedian—the Jimmy Durantes or the Ed Wynns—we can never marry anybody. We could never get the girl . . . we were way out. Today most comedians are *monologists.*

Let us say you see a comedian and you laugh hysterically and you are a shoe salesman. You have no histrionic ability at all. You go home and you make your family laugh as much as that guy made you laugh. That man was a *gag* comedian. Now, say, you see Ed Wynn and you laugh hysterically . . . and your family asks you if you enjoyed the comedian and you say, "Sure, I never laughed so hard in my life." And they say, "What happened?" And you say, "You really have to see it yourself, I can't tell you." That comedian is a *true* comedian. He, in my opinion, has a method of telling his jokes, and his humor is fun—wit.

WILDE: *Your definition of "comedian" has often been quoted.*

WYNN: I coined an expression which is now twenty-two years old. All the comedians have used it but they give me credit for it—even Berle, who would steal anything. I am very proud of this: *A comedian is not a man who says FUNNY THINGS. A comedian is a man who says THINGS FUNNY.* A comedian is not a man who opens a funny door. He opens a door funny. It's a *funny* door when Fibber Mc-Gee opens it and everything falls out and they laugh. It doesn't make him funny. Now Lucille Ball—she does things funny. Most comedians—you wait to hear the line; when you hear the line you laugh. It even goes for my dear friend and the number one guy today—Bob Hope.

WILDE: *What are the requirements to be a comedian?*

WYNN: That would be impossible to define. You have to have a sense of the ridiculous . . . you have to see something funny in everything. A man said to me, "Did you see Lou Holtz? He just had a baby and he's seventy-one." I said, "That's why I'm so tired, I'm the father of Lou Holtz's baby." You see, it's the sense of the ridiculous. You see a coffin go by and you say, "That's a mean piece of furniture." This is where the English comes in. There is not a thing you cannot make a joke about.

WILDE: *What is the difference between "wit" and "humor"?*

WYNN: I have not been able to find—even in Webster's Dictionary—a satisfactory explanation of the difference between wit and humor. I made up my own explanation of it. I say that humor is the *truth* and wit is the exaggeration of the truth. Humor means laughter or fun. Mark Twain was a humorist. He told a true story about the kids—but he told it in a humorous way. If I tell you a joke—which is an exaggerated joke—that to me, is wit not humor. I'm no authority on this, believe me.

WILDE: *Is there ever such a thing as a "bad audience?"*

WYNN: I think audiences vary in their enthusiasm. In the real old days of vaudeville there were about twelve first-class vaudeville theatres. You could stay in New York for three months and play two shows a day. You could play a theater on a Hundred Twenty-First Street and be a riot and then go to the Colonial on Sixty-First Street and Broadway and be a flop with the same act.

WILDE: *What was the reason for that?*

WYNN: Well, either I, as an actor, did not do right or the variation of the audience. You can't blame it on anyone; that was just a week you didn't do good.

WILDE: *Could it have been because of the social level or educational factor? One group was a better class. . .?*

WYNN: If you were an oral comedian, I would say so. But not with pantomime—I think that is general. If you are depending on word of mouth I think the educational factor would have a great bearing on it. I can make up a joke, like I did the other day. I said, "In the valley, the

front of your door is all full of water down there . . . and
that is because the Jolly Green Giant peas in the valley!"
You see, I wanted to make a little dirty funny thing to make
the writers laugh, and they did—they screamed. Now, there
actually are audiences who would scream and yell at that,
and then there are people who would be terribly offended—
and rightfully so. I am making a very broad analogy
here.

Jack Benny wrote an article about comedians about four
years ago . . . and he spoke about all of them and in the
last paragraph he wrote that "undoubtedly the greatest
comedian and the man who taught all of us something was
Ed Wynn." Well, Jack Benny said this, I didn't. The other
day I went down to help the Hollywood Palace celebrate its
first birthday. In the dressing room, I think it was Bing
Crosby said, "There is a guy who was the funniest guy of
any of them." And he pointed to me. And George Burns
said, "I will tell you why. . . ." I didn't argue with them. I
sat there like an ass, you know, they were talking about
me. ". . . this fella had a method of talking that everybody
tried to copy. . . ."

WILDE: *You have been a star longer than—*

WYNN: Not because of talent, though. Because of health!
I have lived longer.

WILDE: *What are the problems in remaining a star? What
do you have to do to stay on top?*

WYNN: In 1934, at their tenth reunion, the Yale class of
1924 made me an honorary member. I am the only honorary
member of any Yale class since its inception. And being of
Jewish extraction—and that college having a reputation of
not wanting Jews, all this makes it a terrific honor. I left
something up there they still use. It is called ED WYNN'S LAD-

DER OF SUCCESS. [*See below*] People like Jolson, Cantor, Skelton, Marx, Wynn . . . we went up there one rung at a time . . . we had a hell of a time to get to the top. The thing is to stay there—which is difficult because of the changing times. Now, along comes a guy and he goes from there to there [*pointing from bottom of ladder to top*] and he is up

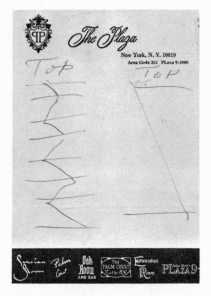

there where we worked like hell to get. But what happens when they fade out a little? And it happened to me, it happened to Jolson, it happened to Cohan—we went back to there [*pointing to rung next to the top*]. We had a foundation. This person is going there. . . .

WILDE: *The same place he came from—the bottom.*

WYNN: The Beatles you will see go boom. There is no set format for success. I have tried to devise one because I make a lot of speeches at art schools like Santa Monica College. I have two words that can possibly be a format for success. I think an actor should make a "goal." The other word is "persistence." I do not care who teaches you—who tells you—that is the only way. Now the road to success is, say, up there [*pointing to top of ladder*], but what happens along the road? You fall in love . . . you go off the road; your mother dies . . . there are a million things to distract you from going to your goal. But persistence pushes you back into the lane. You make a goal and you go after it. As what's his name said, "you gotta be true to yourself. . . ."

WILDE: *Young comedians often become discouraged. . . .*

WYNN: I was in vaudeville for eleven years before Ziegfeld discovered me . . . from 1903 till 1914 when I went into the Follies. I could not get in unless he wanted me. I was a terrific hit and he held me over another year . . . with all the great comedians of those days.

WILDE: *What advice would you give a comedian just starting out?*

WYNN: Work as hard as you can . . . don't be embarrassed by your friends. They will say, "What are you doing?" You will say, "I played at little Jewish wedding on Third Avenue." That doesn't mean a thing. Your friends won't do a bloody thing for you. Please believe me. I have done more for people than the average man does; they don't come back. Someone wrote a brilliant line. It is the most ripping, caustic line I have ever heard: "Always remember that a kindness will never go unpunished." It's cruel but it's true! I will tell you another thing to push around in your mind: I think our own evaluation of ourselves, like if you say, "Well, I'm a bum comedian," . . . you will be taken for a bum comedian.

You would think that the way the younger generation treats me that I would be a great authority on it. You know my advice to young actors? Save your money! That is the only advice I know. I can't tell you how to be comical because when I was on Broadway being comical, it was different. I'm not opposed to the present way—but it was different.

WILDE: *When you say "Save your money," do you mean don't be extravagant . . . because there are certain expenses a comedian must incur?*

WYNN: All I mean is that you do not have to end up in the Actor's Home. That's all. I am on the committee of the East and West homes. And you would be astonished to see the actors who were sensational coming into the homes.

WILDE: *Why is that?*

WYNN: They spend their money.

WILDE: *Unnecessarily.*

WYNN: Well, an actor makes a big salary. The government takes a hell of a chunk out of it. But the average actor thinks that this is his capital—that is the big mistake. An actor earns, say one thousand a week and he thinks that is his income. It is not at all. It is only about four hundred . . . in adapting some of my so-called philosophy—I love philosophy—you can be a failure twenty times and still be a tremendous success. The only time you can actually be a failure is when you blame it on somebody else. That is my piece of philosophy. When you say, "If it were not for that guy, I would have gotten the part," for example. The minute you say that you are a failure.

WILDE: *How many years have you now been in show business?*

WYNN: Sixty-three years . . . yes, it's amazing. I have the record of being the longest standing star of any actor who ever lived in America. The longest star formerly was Fred Stone. Forty-one years he was a star. But you see how my talk is unabashed. . . . I am not ashamed to tell you that I am still a big star. I must be . . . they pay me big money.

VIGGIANI: The last time you did the *Entertainers* within a radius of four blocks you had your name on four marquees at the same time.

WYNN: *You, Bridget, Mary Poppins, The Greatest Story Ever Told,* and the *Entertainers.*

WILDE: *You have been in every phase of show business. . .*

WYNN: Everything to burlesque and opera.

WILDE: *Which medium do you like the—?*

WYNN: The stage. I was asked last night to return to it. I was offered two plays. One, a comedy; one a drama. But I don't want to go back on the stage. I think the stage was the most exciting. Live TV was exciting. . . . But at my age I would like to take things a little slower. Pictures have been a God-send to me. But I am still persistent . . . still ambitious.

[Mr. Wynn died on June 19, 1966, several months after this interview.]